Encountering Buddhism

SUNY series in Transpersonal and Humanistic Psychology
Richard D. Mann, editor

Encountering Buddhism

Western Psychology and Buddhist Teachings

Edited by
Seth Robert Segall

State University of New York Press

Published by

State University of New York Press, Albany

© 2003 State University of New York

For information, address State University of New York Press,
90 State Street, Suite 700, Albany, NY 12207

Production by Judith Block
Marketing by Fran Keneston

Library of Congress Control Number
Encountering Buddhism : Western psychology and Buddhist teachings / edited by Seth
Robert Segall.
       p. cm. — (SUNY series in transpersonal and humanistic psychology)
       ISBN 0-7914-5735-4 (alk. paper) — ISBN 0-7914-5736-2 (pbk. : alk. paper)
       1. Buddhism and psychoanalysis. 2. Psychotherapy—Religious aspects—
Buddhism. 3. Spiritual life—Buddhism. 4. Buddhism—United States—History—
20th century. I. Segall, Seth Robert. II. Series.

BQ4570.P755 E62 2003
294.3'375—dc21

                                                                    2002029179
                             10 9 8 7 6 5 4 3 2 1

To our families . . .

To our teachers in Buddhism and in Psychology . . .

George Atwood

Ruth Denison

The Ven. Dr. K. S. Sri Dhammananda

Joseph Goldstein

Lama Anagarika Govinda

Jon Kabat-Zinn

David Kantor

Jack Kornfield

Joel Kramer

Toni Packer

Larry Rosenberg

Joshua Sasaki Roshi

Alan Senauke

Maylie Scott

Jack Roy Strange

Frederick J. Streng

Christopher Titmus

Ferris Urbanowski

Sojun Mel Weitsman

Janice Dean Willis

And to the awakening and liberation of all beings . . .

May all beings be safe.
May all beings have mental happiness.
May all beings have physical happiness.
May all beings live with ease.

The Tao that can be spoken is not the Tao.
—Lao Tzu, *Tao Tê Ching*

Whereof one cannot speak, thereof one must be silent.
—Ludwig Wittgenstein,
Tractatus Logico-Philosophicus

Samuel Beckett once said:
"Every word is like an unnecessary stain on silence
and nothingness." On the other hand, he said it.
—Art Spiegelman, *Maus II*

Contents

Acknowledgments

The editor would like to thank:

The Perseus Book Publishers, a member of Perseus Books, L.L.C., for permission to quote from *The Leaf and the Cloud* by Mary Oliver, copyright © 2000 by Mary Oliver.

Kōsen Nishiyama Roshi for permission to quote from his translation of the Shōbōgenzō. (Dōgen [1983]. *A Complete English Translation of Dōgen Zenji's Shōbōgenzō [The Eye and Treasury of the True Law]* [K. Nishiyama, Trans.] [vol. 3]. Tokyo: Nakayama Shobō. [Overseas Distributor: Japan Publications Trading Company. San Francisco, CA, Elmsford, NY, and Tokyo].)

Windbell Publications for permission to quote from G. W. Nishijima Roshi and C. Cross's translation of the Shōbōgenzō. (Dōgen, E. [1994]. *Shōbōgenzō, The Eye and Treasury of the True Law* [G. W. Nishijima & C. Cross, Trans.]. London: Windbell Publications.)

Introduction

A half-century ago psychoanalysts Erich Fromm and Karen Horney began a fruit-ful dialogue with Zen interpreter D. T. Suzuki (Suzuki, Fromm, & De Martino 1963; Fields, 1992; Morvay, 1999), marking a significant milestone in the emerg-ing romance between American Psychology and Buddhism. In doing so, they were following in the footsteps of Carl Jung (1935/1960) who had already opened a similar dialogue in Europe. In the decades since then, thousands of Western psychologists have subsequently had their own personal encounters with the Bud-dha's teachings. Some of those psychologists have had little use for Buddhism, no doubt viewing it as exotic and impenetrable nonsense. Others, like Richard Alpert (Ram Dass, 1971) of Harvard University and Larry Rosenberg (Rosenberg, 1999) of Brandeis University, were so moved by their encounters with the East that they transcended their roles as psychologists to become renowned spiritual teachers. Most psychologists encountering Buddhism, however, have fallen between these two extremes in their response to the *Dharma*; they have struggled to integrate Buddhist teachings with their scientifically derived understanding of human na-ture, and have simultaneously maintained an awareness of the tensions that ex-isted between them. They also often observed significant, and at times dramatic, shifts in their personal lives and professional practices as a consequence of this in-tegrative struggle. The essays in this book offer the reader an opportunity to "lis-ten in" as this third group of psychologists explores the personal, intellectual, and professional ramifications of these encounters.

In the half-century that has passed since the initial dialogue between Psycho-analysis and Zen, both Western Psychology and the Western understanding of Bud-dhism have undergone radical transformations. Western Psychology has undergone successive and simultaneous revolutions in cognitive psychology, systems theory, neuropsychology, evolutionary psychobiology, artificial intelligence, biological psy-chiatry, attachment theory, object relations theory, self psychology, traumatology, humanistic psychology, and transpersonal psychology. Western Buddhism has, at the same time, been transformed by the arrival of successive waves of Buddhist teachers from within the Japanese, Korean, and Vietnamese Zen traditions, the Burmese lay meditation and Thai forest monastery traditions, and from the Tibetan Diaspora. In addition, the West has seen the arrival of a significant number of Asian immigrants who have brought other practice forms (e.g., Pure Land and *Nichiren* Buddhism) along with them. This has, in turn, brought about a degree of dialectical tension between the North American Buddhist practice community, with its membership of primarily European-descent converts, and ethnic Asian immigrant religious communities whose memberships are following the traditional practices of their (or their parents') birth religion and homeland.

All of these transformations have had consequences for the Western understanding of Buddhism. These consequences have included:

1. *An increasing appreciation of the multifaceted nature of Asian Buddhism.* While initial Western practitioners seemed more aware of Buddhism as a philosophy, or as a methodology for the direct apprehension of reality, more recent practitioners have become also aware of the role of faith, devotional practice, and other-power practices in various Buddhist communities, as well as the seeming surface contradictions (and perhaps deeper contradictions) between different philosophical strands of Buddhism.

2. *A growing number of Western practitioners who have studied within more than one Buddhist tradition.* It is no longer uncommon to see Western Buddhist teachers who have studied and practiced extensively in more than one Buddhist practice community. In recent historical times, Buddhist interdenominational cross-dialogue had become exceedingly rare. There is now the possibility for extensive interdenominational dialogue in the West, with a consequent possibility for the development of new syncretic practice forms.

3. *A developing awareness of the parallels that exist between the Buddhist conception of the nature of mind and the understanding that is emerging through advances in Western neuropsychology, cognitive psychology, and artificial intelligence.* There is a dramatic parallel between the models of mind being developed by contemporary Western theorists who are studying the nature of higher mental processes and the Buddhist core doctrine of *anatta*, or "nonself."

4. *A deeper appreciation of the similarities that exist between the Buddhist and existential/phenomenological approaches to the understanding of Being.* Buddhist understandings of the self/other and mind/body dichotomies echo existential themes of being-in-the-world (Heidegger, 1947/1973) and the lived body (Merleau-Ponty, 1963). In addition, some types of Buddhist meditative practice seem to be strikingly phenomenological in their approach to apprehending reality.

The fact that Buddhist teachings simultaneously parallel both contemporary scientific and existential/phenomenological approaches to psychology can be of enormous value to the West; Buddhism's insistence on finding "middle-way" solutions offers an opportunity to heal the rift between these disparate realms. In my own graduate training in the 1970s, for example, I was exposed to several scientifically oriented cognitive-behavioral therapies, which emphasized the value of self-monitoring one's ideational process and addressing dysfunctional beliefs. I was also exposed to a number of experiential approaches that devalued attention to ideation, and instead emphasized the monitoring of affective and somatic aspects of experience. As a practicing psychotherapist, I found myself vacillating between these approaches for decades in a kind of muddle-headed eclecticism. This sense of muddle-headedness cleared, however, when I read the Satipatthāna Sutta (1995), the discourse of the Buddha on "The Foundations of Mindfulness," which views the monitoring of ideational, affective, and somatic experiencing as a single integrated process. My new understanding allowed me to deploy both cognitive-behavioral and experiential techniques from within a unified theoretical approach. Similar Buddhist "middle-way" approaches to issues of subjectivity and objectivity, determinism and free will, and the nature of the Self may eventually prove to be equally helpful to Western psychology. Above all else, Buddhism represents a distinctive and compassionate response to the human dilemma that resonates with modernity.

The authors of the essays within this volume represent a range of Western Psychological approaches (Psychoanalytic, Existential/Humanistic, Cognitive-Behavioral, and Transpersonal), a range of experience within Buddhism (especially Theravāda and Mahāyāna), and a range of responses to Buddhism (from committed adherence to cautious skepticism). Each of these authors has attempted to tell the story of his or her encounter in his or her own unique voice.

In the first chapter, Andrew Olendzki, Ph.D., a Pāli language scholar, formerly executive director of the Insight Meditation Society, and currently executive director of the Barre Center for Buddhist Studies, has written a primer on the psychology of early Buddhism as it is portrayed in the Pāli *Nikāyas*. These Pāli texts comprise (along with the *Vinaya*, or code of conduct for monks, and the *Abhidhamma*, or doctrinal exegeses) the *Tipitaka*, or core scriptures of Theravāda Buddhism. (They also have a status, in their Sanskrit, Chinese, and Tibetan translations, as a kind of "Old Testament" to the "New Testament" of the Mahāyāna *Sūtras*.) Dr. Olendzki has taught the Buddhism and Psychology course at the Barre Center for many years, and serves as a great resource for those interested in what the Pāli texts actually mean and how they relate to contemporary psychology.

Dr. Olendzki's chapter is followed by a series of chapters by Jeffrey Rubin, Ph.D., Belinda Siew Luan Khong, Ph.D., Jean Kristeller, Ph.D., and myself. These chapters share common ground on a number of points. The authors, like Dr. Olendzki, are primarily steeped in the Buddhism of the Pāli canon and the corresponding Theravāda meditation practices. In addition, all four authors struggle with the question of what stance Western Psychology in general, and they themselves in particular, should take vis-à-vis Buddhism. One of their primary questions is whether to identify themselves as Buddhists or not.

Dr. Rubin, a psychoanalytic psychologist with two decades of experience with *vipassanā* (insight) meditation, reviews the history of Western Psychology's responses to Buddhism in chapter 2. These responses have included (1) an early historical response in which Western psychology related to Buddhism from a position of superiority, and (2) a later response in which Buddhism assumed the superior position. Dr. Rubin calls these two positions "Eurocentrism" and "Orientocentrism," and argues that neither position is in itself sufficient. Arguing on behalf of a "middle-way," solution, Dr. Rubin suggests that Western Psychology and Buddhism must engage in dialogue as equals, for each has something distinctively unique to offer to the other. Dr. Rubin then goes into detail about how the methods of each system determine and limit its findings and how these methods and findings can complement and balance each other.

Dr. Khong, an ethnic overseas Chinese psychologist who grew up in Malaysia and now lives in Australia, looks at Buddhist teachings in chapter 3 and declares that the Buddha teaches an attitude, not an affiliation. She is very much interested in Buddhist themes, how they dovetail with Phenomenology and Existentialism, and how they can be employed in psychotherapy, but she does not think that this means she must adopt a Buddhist identity. Dr. Khong grew up as a nominal "Sunday School" Buddhist in Malaysia, but only came to understand the Dharma as an adult after having first addressed her personal issues from within the framework of Western Existentialism. In a way, she only became a Buddhist after she stopped being a Buddhist—a deliciously Buddhist paradox.

I also struggle with the issue of identity in chapter 4 and decide that "being a Buddhist" is an oxymoron. This chapter deals with my struggle to assimilate Buddhist teachings and my experiences as a meditator to my own Western psychological viewpoint, one that is marked by a fair amount of distrust, wariness, and skepticism. The chapter explores the Buddhist concepts of mindfulness, nonself, and interbeing, and the consequences of these concepts for an understanding of ethical behavior within the vocabulary of Western biology, physics, psychology, and philosophy. It also explores the development of Western Buddhism as it emerges through a dialogue with the Judeo-Christian tradition, the Existential-Phenomenological tradition, and the Western Enlightenment.

In chapter 5, research psychologist Jean Kristeller, Ph.D. provides an auto-biographical account of her gradual involvement with Buddhism through her experiences in Japan, and subsequently at Swarthmore, Yale, the University of Massachusetts Medical Center, and Indiana State University. Her life has been greatly affected by her encounters with meditation and Buddhism, but she has also retained strong ties to both her Judeo-Christian upbringing and to the philosophy of logical positivism. Her unique familial connection with the Japanese aesthetic and her personal meditation experiences, however, have caused a shift in the kinds of scientific questions she chooses to address in her research. These have included scientific studies of meditation and its effects on the mind-body process, and the role of meditative awareness in the development of self-control strategies.

Theravāda texts and practices are only the beginning of Buddhism, however. Over the next two millennia bodies of literature emerged in which a new set of authors discovered their own authentic voices within the Buddhist tradition. This occurred as new cultures of awakening developed throughout Asia, both as the consequence of reform and renewal movements within early Buddhism itself, and as different ethnic communities assimilated early Buddhism to the needs and requirements of their own unique cultures. One thinks immediately here of Indian Mahāyāna writers like Nāgārjuna (2nd century C.E.) and Śantideva (7th century C.E.), and of writers from China, Tibet, and Japan, such as Huang Po, Milarepa, and Dōgen. The next two chapters explore the writings of two of these later authors, Nāgārjuna, associated with the earliest flowering of Mahāyāna Buddhism in second-century India, and Dōgen, associated with the renewal of the Zen Mahāyāna tradition in thirteenth-century Japan.

In chapter 6, Kaisa Puhakka, Ph.D., a transpersonal psychologist with over three decades of meditation practice, describes the impact the writings of Nāgārjuna have had on her philosophical and spiritual development. Along the way, she explores the usefulness of Nāgārjuna's dialectic in understanding the dilemma of postmodern intellectual thought. Last of all, she applies the dialectic to her own experiences at a Zen *sesshin* in a way that will ring immediately true to anyone who has ever been on an extended meditation retreat. The intimate examination of what seems uniquely personal often uncovers and clarifies universal truths, and this seems especially so of Dr. Puhakka's discussion of her sesshin experience.

In chapter 7, "Reflections on Mirroring," Robert Rosenbaum, Ph.D., explores Dōgen's 13th-century fascicle, *The Eternal Mirror,* and the light it reflects on the 20th-century Kohutian concept of mirroring. Dr. Rosenbaum is a humanistic psychologist with over two decades of experience as a Zen practitioner. Rosenbaum's playful and paradoxical style draws heavily on a Zen tradition which uses language to point to phenomena that cannot be directly expressed through words. Rosenbaum's chapter makes use of Nāgārjuna's dialectic which Kaisa Puhakka introduced for us in chapter 6, and also more fully introduces the concept of "emptiness" that plays such a major role in Mahāyāna thought. The nonduality of absolute and relative truth, another key Mahāyāna insight, is also explored through Rosenbaum's insightful clinical vignettes, which show how an appreciation of absolute reality can be brought to bear in dealing with the relative reality of psychological problems. Rosenbaum, like Rubin in chapter 2, suggests that the truths of Buddhism and Psychoanalysis can easily become one-sided. The absolute truth of Zen and the relative truths of psychoanalysis are both reflections of a larger truth that cannot be expressed in language, but which can be experienced in a moment of enlightenment. I suggest something very similar from a Theravāda perspective in chapter 4, when I explore the absolute truth of nonself and the relative truth of our experience of self. Buddhism always seeks to find a middle way, pointing to the one-sidedness of clinging to any specific pole of the dialectic.

In chapter 8, I examine the same realm of copresence and emptiness in psychotherapy that Rosenbaum explored from a Mahāyāna perspective, but from my own (mostly) Theravāda vantage point. The chapter, entitled "Psychotherapy Practice as Buddhist Practice," is a meditation on what it means to practice psychotherapy from within a Buddhist container. The emphasis of this chapter is not on technique, for example, how a Buddhist practitioner heals clients differently than non-Buddhist therapists, but on how the feel of being a therapist is different for the therapist when he or she is practicing as an expression of his or her Buddhist commitment. While Rosenbaum stresses the differences between *dokusan* and psychotherapy, I focus more on the parallels between interpersonal meeting in both traditions, and in spiritual life in general. As Martin Buber (1958) wrote, "All real living is meeting." Rosenbaum and I both end up saying very similar things about empathy using very different vocabularies. This parallelism demonstrates how the different vehicles of Theravāda and Mahāyāna Buddhism can be seen as expressions of one Dharma (Goldstein, 2002), refracted through different cultural and historical lenses, but pointing to the same underlying reality.

In chapter 9, Eugene Taylor, Ph.D., who wears multiple hats as a historian of psychology, a meditation researcher, and an Asian scholar, recounts his own personal historical narrative as he discloses the details of an academic life devoted to exploring the interface between Western Psychology, and the psychologies implicit in Buddhism, Vedānta, *Sāmkhya*, and Yoga. As a psychologist whose life has at various times intersected with the major figures in modern Western humanistic and transpersonal psychology, Dr. Taylor is uniquely qualified to explore the interstices of the current historical dialogue between Eastern and Western psychologies. Dr. Taylor is concerned that much of this dialogue is being dominated by Western clinicians whose understanding of Buddhism is at times superficial, and at other times, simply erroneous. Nevertheless, he is optimistic that historical factors have us poised at the dawn of a more profound intercultural dialogue, which may yet transform the narrow boundaries of Western psychology and introduce a new epistemological frame for the understanding and transformation of human consciousness.

I hope the reader of this book will be able to experience vicariously some of the excitement, wonder, and gratitude that we authors have experienced as we have explored the Buddhist path. The truths to be found within Buddhism, however, are neither confined in nor limited to Buddhism: the Dharma is the property of all wisdom traditions and all seekers who are interested in the development of wisdom and compassion. They are also the property of the Human Sciences. They lie waiting to be rediscovered again and again from generation to generation. They require no identification as a Buddhist, only an open mind and a willing heart.

Seth Robert Segall
April 26, 2002

REFERENCES

Buber, M. (1958). I and thou (2nd ed.). (R. G. Smith, Trans.). New York: Charles Scribner's.

Fields, R. (1992). How the swans came to the lake: A Narrative history of Buddhism in America (3rd ed.), (revised and updated). Boston: Shambhala.

Goldstein, J. (2002). One dharma: The emerging western Buddhism. San Francisco: HarperSanFrancisco.

Heidegger, M. (1973). Letter on humanism (E. Lohner, Trans.). In R. Zaner & D. Ihde (Eds.), Phenomenology and existentialism (pp. 147–181). New York: Capricorn Books. Original work published in 1947.

Jung, C. G. (1960). Psychological commentary (R. F. C. Hull, Trans.). In W. Y. Evans-Wentz (compiler and ed.), The Tibetan book of the dead or the after-death experiences on the bardo plane, according to Lāma Kazi Dawa-Samdup's English Rendering (3rd ed.), (pp. xxxv–lii). London: Oxford University Press. Original work published in 1935.

Merleau-Ponty, M. (1963). The structure of behavior (A. L. Fisher, Trans.). Boston: Beacon.

Morvay, Z. (1999). Horney, Zen, and the real self: Theoretical and historical connections. American Journal of Psychoanalysis, 59, 25–35.

Ram Dass (1971). Be here now. San Cristobal, NM: Lama Foundation.

Rosenberg, L. (1998). Breath by breath. Boston: Shambhala.

Satipatthāna Sutta. (1995). In B. Ñānamoli & B. Bodhi (Trans.), *The middle length discourses of the Buddha: A new translation of the Majjhima Nikāya* (pp.145-155). Boston: Wisdom Publications.

Suzuki, D. T., Fromm, E., & Martino, R. (1963). *Zen Buddhism and psychoanalysis.* New York: Grove Press.

CHAPTER 1

Buddhist Psychology

Andrew Olendzki

THEORY AND PRACTICE

Since the subject of Buddhist psychology is largely an artificial construction, mixing as it does a product of ancient India with a Western movement hardly a century and a half old, it might be helpful to say how these terms are being used here. If we were to take the term *psychology* literally as referring to "the study of the psyche," and if "psyche" is understood in its earliest sense of "soul," then it would seem strange indeed to unite this enterprise with a tradition that is perhaps best known for its challenge to the very notion of a soul. But most dictionaries offer a parallel definition of psychology, "the science of mind and behavior," and this is a subject to which Buddhist thought can make a significant contribution. It is, after all, a universal subject, and I think many of the methods employed by the introspective traditions of ancient India for the investigation of mind and behavior would qualify as scientific. So my intention in using the label Buddhist Psychology is to bring some of the insights, observations, and experience from the Buddhist tradition to bear on the human body, mind, emotions, and behavior patterns as we tend to view them today. In doing so we are going to find a fair amount of convergence with modern psychology, but also some intriguing diversity.

The Buddhist tradition itself, of course, is vast and has many layers to it. Although there are some doctrines that can be considered universal to all Buddhist schools,[1] there are such significant shifts in the use of language and in background assumptions that it is usually helpful to speak from one particular perspective at a time. In all that follows here, therefore, it needs to be understood that we are drawing on the earliest strata of the Buddhist tradition, that is, on the Pāli literature that was composed in India somewhere between the sixth and third centuries B.C.E. It was during this era that the "core curriculum" of the Buddhist tradition was formed, and this is the body of surviving material that is chrono-logically closest to the time of the historical Buddha, Siddhārtha Gautama Śākya-muni. Little of what was composed during this time was disputed by later traditions (insofar as it is included in the later Canons), but this earlier material lacks the myriad innovations and refinements—many incorporating profound and useful psychological insights, many responding to local and emerging issues—that came to be articulated in later centuries.

It was a very interesting period of time, intellectually vital and religiously experimental. There was a whole movement surrounding the Buddha, often re-ferred to as the *Śramana* movement, characterized by the investigation of the human condition using various experiential methods. Many of these methods were certainly psychological, and we might even call some of them scientific. Re-belling against an orthodox intelligentsia that relied on revealed scriptural au-thority to guide a ritual communication with external deities, the *Śramanas*, or Wanderers, were more apt to use yoga, asceticism, and meditation to access an internal landscape and gain personal insights into the nature of their own minds and bodies. Their methods of inquiry constituted a body of shared praxis, and the experiences accessed and insights gained were largely repeatable and verifiable. Thus the tradition went beyond the contributions of a few indi-viduals, and built up profundity and authority over many generations. The Buddha was both an heir to this psychologically investigative tradition and one of its greatest contributors.

The fruits of these ancient Indian investigations of the human condition, just as the modern field of psychology, can be usefully summarized under two headings: the theoretical and the practical. Theoretical psychology attempts to ar-ticulate models of the human mind and of experience which are based on both general principles and on detailed explanations of phenomena and their dynam-ics. Practical or therapeutic psychology seeks to heal human suffering or to rectify abnormal behavior through various methods of intervention and transformation. A similar distinction was current during the time of the Buddha, when all the re-ligious and philosophical systems were said to be comprised of both a *dharma*, or theoretical teaching, and a *vinaya* or mode of living. In ancient India the term "dharma-vinaya" was a compound, suggesting that theory and practice were indi-visible, and were viewed as two facets of the same continuum. "Whose dharma-vinaya do you follow?" was a common inquiry between passing wanderers. As is still the case today, the viewpoint one has of the nature of one's situation is cen-tral to shaping how one goes about living life; and one's lifestyle, how one behaves and chooses to live, will naturally reflect one's broad understanding of what it means to be human. The dharma or theory has to do with what we know or believe, while the vinaya or practice has to do with how we act and what we do. The two will always mutually define and inform one another.

A MIDDLE WAY

The broad outline of early Buddhist theoretical psychology was remarkably similar to how we might frame the issue today: an organism, comprised of both physical and mental factors and processes, lives in a dynamic equilibrium with its environment, both shaping and being shaped by that environment as a response to various internal and external sets of conditions. The psychophysical organism has the ability to perceive or "know" its environment to various levels of accuracy, through mediating systems of sensory representation, as well as the capacity to respond and act with varying amounts of autonomy. The deeper questions, both then and now, have to do with the nature of this organism, the quality of its experience, and the extent to which it is capable of knowing itself and transforming itself in ways it finds meaningful. The theoretical issues have to do with explaining how it all works, while the practical matter is usually more about achieving and sustaining a state of well-being.

The Buddhists of ancient India faced an interesting dilemma in approaching these questions, one that is very familiar to us today. The existing explanations for the nature of the self (i.e., the organism) and its capacity for transformation ranged between two sorts of account, neither one of which seemed adequate. On the one hand is the theory that we can best view the individual organism as consisting of a mysterious essence, a soul or self, with a divine origin and destiny. By its very nature this self is ineffable, and is something difficult or even impossible to experience directly. In India the soul, called ātman or jīva, was thought to be something that preceded birth and survived death, and was reborn many times in different circumstances, some more exalted and others more challenged than the environments currently inhabited. It was also thought that this self could achieve a sort of apotheosis, and could eventually be healed of all of its suffering by absorption into a larger cosmic or divine reality. On the other hand, there were a number of theories that tended toward a materialist reduction. According to this view, the unique pattern of activity we call an individual emerges from a complex mix of impersonal factors and processes: substances, elements, aggregates, spheres of sense activity, patterns of organization, and so forth. These coalesce in stable systems for a period of time according to the conditioning influence of various causal forces, undergo all sorts of transformation and change as these factors are rearranged, and then pass away through disintegration to their constituent elements. From this perspective a person is born, survives for a time, and then passes away, with no hope for further meaningful development or for reconciliation of existential tensions outside the limits of this life span.[2]

The Western civilization of the past few centuries, which has shaped the modern psychological tradition, has offered essentially the same range of options for understanding the human condition. On the one hand, religious explanations have revolved around a notion of the soul as something outside the measurable material world, and I think it is appropriate to include here the theorizing about consciousness begun by Descartes. Scientific explanations of the human mind, body, and behavior, on the other hand, have inclined toward a reductionist model that seeks to explain these phenomena entirely in terms of physical structures and processes. But a significant explanatory gap still remains between the distinct phenomenology of lived human experience and the physical processes that give rise to them. And without the convenient notion of a soul (however ill-defined), there is an additional burden of having to define and account for the issue of personal identity in a constantly changing environment, a matter of particular interest to psychologists.

What concerned the ancient Buddhists about these two alternatives is that one seemed to make too much of human beings while the other regarded too little. Like the modern theoretical psychologist, they could find no credible empirical evidence for many of the claims of the soul theorists, and unlike the modern psychologist they saw the human condition in a larger light and needed a model that could account for the continuity of personality traits over several lifetimes. This is of course a major point of departure between the ancient and modern approaches to the problem: the literature of early Buddhism indicates that although the techniques of mental concentration and introspection did not yield evidence of the ineffable soul, it did reveal that the continuity of individual personhood carried over many lifetimes. The problem with the ancient materialist reduction was that it did not provide an explanation of how this could occur. Although the modern reductionist is not faced with this problem, there is still the need for explaining how the wet brain can yield subjective experience that is textured and nuanced in just the way it is.

The theoretical psychology of Buddhism resolved the tension between the ineffable and the merely material, the eternal soul and the annihilated life, using a model that attempted to thread a line—a middle way—between these two explanations. The Buddhists were saying that we are indeed composed of impersonal material elements that are combined in special ways that account for the complexity, tone, and content of human experience. It is also the case that the patterns of coherent and stable organization we call individuality do not entirely dissipate at the end of this lifetime; there are ways continuity proceeds after our apparent physical death. But this need not be explained in terms of a nonphysical essence that evacuates the body, bringing various individual characteristics with it, and then reenters another body at the moment of conception. One of the memorable ways of expressing the paradox of the more subtle Buddhist view is the phrase "Rebirth occurs, but nobody is reborn." This sums up not only the process of rebirth between lifetimes, but also of the nature of personal identity from one moment to another, as we will see later.

The objection might be raised that we are rapidly getting in to fringe material here, and that the contemporary psychologist rightly has no interest in attempting to account for life beyond the threshold of death. But the point is that the theoretical models developed by the Buddhists to account for this transition, which I repeat was a matter of empirical observation to them, required a unique and effective new approach: process thinking. They developed sophisticated ways of analyzing the human experience into a set of processes, functions or events, called *dharmas* (alas, not the same word as *dharma* used above), and of understanding how these arising and passing episodes of meaningfully interdependent occurrences are synthesized into dynamic, unfolding patterns of coherence. The world of human experience, in short, is constructed, and it is possible to understand—and to directly witness! —the manner in which this happens.

The process of constructed experience cannot be adequately expressed using the notion of a soul or of nonmaterial consciousness, for this would violate the laws of conditionality that account for the creation and dissolution of all discernable phenomena. On the one hand, if the soul is not constructed then it stands outside the causal order, which is unacceptable. Divine creation or intervention is not adequate to escape this difficulty, since according to the early Buddhists the divine orders of being are part of the causal system rather than exempt from it. On the other hand if the soul is constructed, then it can no longer be properly considered a soul, but is rather a changing complex of phenomena like everything else. Nor can constructed experience be explained as nothing more than the workings of materiality, since considerable nonmaterial dimensions of the unfolding reality can be directly known and understood by cultivating techniques of introspection. These nonmaterial dimensions of experience extend in time beyond personal death, but also in space to other spheres of sensation, and in the present moment to subtler levels of consciousness and human experience. There is also a qualitative argument to consider: since consciousness is the very tool that constructs meaningful human experience, such experience can never be adequately accounted for without inclusion of the nonmaterial qualia of consciousness. In other words, we cannot reduce to materiality a process of which the material is only one of several components, the others all being nonmaterial.

SUBJECTIVE EXPERIENCE

So what are some of the main features of this process-based model of the human mind and body? Perhaps the most unique and important principle of the Buddha's approach to the mind is the insight that the mysteries of the human condition are best explored in the dynamics of subjective experience as it unfolds in the present moment. Buddhist theoretical psychology is a science of experience, in which the stream of consciousness itself, as it is presented to the attentive and carefully trained observer, is the field of investigation. The entire Śramana movement was skeptical of the revealed sources of knowledge on which the orthodoxy was established—ancient myths, inspired hymns passed down over many generations, detailed sacred protocols for all aspects of the religious life—and appealed instead to the direct experience of each practitioner. Neither had they much use for schemes that relied heavily on logic, reasoning, and theoretical conceptual knowledge. Śramana adepts would go off into the forest alone, cross their legs, shut their eyes, and look very closely at what was going on. They would observe the various effects of fasting, breathing exercises, and other yogic disciplines on their experience, and they organized their observations and insights in formal teachings and systems of great subtlety and complexity.[3] It was a remarkably scientific endeavor in many ways, in which the human body and mind served as the laboratory for investigation. As such, the entire tradition is more of a descriptive phenomenology than a theory of mind. The Buddha was not saying, "This is what I theorize human experience to be." Rather, his message (paraphrased) was, "This is what I've seen in my personal experience." And further, "Don't take my word for it; examine it for yourself, and you too can see exactly what I'm talking about."[4] Much of what he points to does not require years in the wilderness to access, but is available to all of us in this very moment.

The first thing this introspective approach highlights is the centrality of consciousness. Our experience is ordered around and consists of moments of "knowing" strung together over time, much like William James's stream of consciousness. *Consciousness* is a multivalent word in English, and can mean many different things in various contexts. It is used here simply as a moment of awareness, a moment of knowing some aspect or quality of the subjective present moment. It might be a sensation, a thought, a perception—anything we are capable of noticing. What gives us the ability to have such experience is as much a mystery to us today as it has ever been. But as a tool consciousness yields the simple ability to be aware of something, and this is the heart of the Buddhist science of experience. As a phenomenological pursuit it was not necessary to explain consciousness or to account for how it does what it does. It is enough simply to explore its texture, its range, its dynamics as moments of knowing are followed by other moments of knowing in the stream of consciousness. This is why Buddhists are so interested in the practice of meditation. Meditation involves bringing attention to the present moment of experience and observing what is happening there. The entire Buddhist theory of reality is built around the investigation of that moment of knowing, which is always present and accessible to all of us at any time.

By means of patient observation and, most important, the resolute reapplication of attention whenever it wanders (which it is sure to do), patterns in the flow of consciousness will become apparent. The second basic insight to emerge from this direct observation of the mind and body is that all human experience manifests through one or another of six sense systems. That is to say, all human experience consists of seeing, hearing, smelling, tasting, touching, and thinking (in its broadest possible sense). A three-way interaction takes place between (1) particular organs of perception that are features of the evolved psychophysical body, (2) particular packets of data from the environment to which each of these perceptive organs is uniquely receptive, and (3) the process of cognizing or knowing these objects of perception by means of a corresponding episode of consciousness. The Buddhists call these "sense doors," since information enters experience through these gateways as travelers would enter a walled city or as a person would access a house.

For example, the eye is an organ of perception that has evolved to be sensitive to a certain range and quality of reflected photons, and along with its retina, optic nerve, and corresponding areas of the visual cortex of the brain it is part of an entire psychophysical system capable of translating "objective" features of the environment into "subjective" units of visual knowing. The light to which this optical system is receptive, as reflected by the various surfaces extended throughout our environment, constitute objects of visual perception. According to this way of understanding, the organs of perception and the objects of perception are in symbiosis; neither is primary to the other, and neither is meaningful without the other. From a systemic perspective, the organs and objects of perception cocreate one another, and thus experientially the categories of objective and subjective lose their meaning. But these two are not sufficient in themselves to yield human experience, for the crucial factor of consciousness needs also to be factored in. Buddhist thought understands consciousness to emerge from the interaction of sense organ and sense object, to constitute that very interaction, and also to itself consist of the information carried by the interaction of the two. In other words, visual consciousness arises from the interaction of the eye and visible forms, and the coming together of these three factors constitutes what we call visual experience.[5]

The other systems of sensory perception construct experience in a similar manner: the ear, the nose, the tongue and the body interact with sounds, smells, tastes, and "touches," giving rise to the knowing of sounds, the knowing of smells, the knowing of tastes, and the knowing of physical sensations. The sixth system of perception, patterned after these five, consists of the mind interacting with mental objects to yield the knowing or cognizing of mental objects; the interaction of these three result in mental experience. The mental objects mentioned here include anything and everything in our inner life that cannot be construed as the immediate product of the functioning of the other five systems—thoughts, concepts, ideas, images, memories, intuitions, and so on—as well as any perception served up by the other five perceptual systems. When we add up all these components—six sense organs, six sense objects, and six modes of consciousness—we come to a list of eighteen basic categories of experience, which the Buddhists sometimes refer to as the eighteen elements.[6]

THE CONSTRUCTION OF REALITY

And that, from the phenomenological perspective, is all there is. Which leads us to the third great insight of Buddhist theoretical psychology: all of our experience is constructed. According to this analysis, the "world" of human experience is woven together in our minds from these eighteen constituents, in six groups of three factors each. There are only moments of "knowing" manifesting in the six different modes we call seeing, hearing, smelling, tasting, feeling, and thinking. This matrix of eighteen elements is the universal framework on which all of our experience is built, and we are incapable of experiencing anything that does not pass through one of these doors. This is not, at least from the perspective of early Buddhism, an idealist philosophical position that reduces material phenomena to the mental. Neither is it in itself denying that there is a great world out there including mountains and oceans and stars. It is merely concentrating its attention on a description of what one observes when one regards the details of lived experience. Because this is all that really matters. Buddhist psychology is built on a study of "that which appears," and considers metaphysical and ontological questions to be largely irrelevant. The *content* of the data coming into the system from the outside world through the senses is not nearly as important as understanding the *process* by which this data is handled by the system. Since we are translating certain features of the environment (e.g., photons, wave patterns, molecules) into an internal language of consciousness (e.g., sights, sounds, smells, tastes), the "text" written in that language becomes far more significant than the raw material from which it was compiled. The transformation process from the outer to the inner life is so profound as we create a cognizable reality that any attempt at "objective" assessment of the preconstructed world is doomed from the outset to be nothing more than another construction. The world of our experience is structured in such a way that it becomes fundamentally impossible to work in any realm other than that of the derived subjective construction. The only world we can explore is the inner world, which is really just a virtual world.

So the study of reality becomes the study of the human construction of experience, and this is why early Buddhism is so thoroughly psychological in nature. Each of us is constructing our own reality, and understanding how we do this becomes crucial to our ability to experience happiness and meaning in our lives. Some of the principles we must follow in the process are universal, and the Buddhist tradition has much to say about these. Other aspects of the construction process are personal and arise out of unique conditions for each of us, and understanding these forms the basis for personal spiritual development and self-understanding.

One of the things that is so interesting about our construction of ourselves and our experience is that at times it is not very refined. There is a way in which we are "cobbling together" the moment as best we can. How we construct any moment's experience, how we see and hear and think and react to anything in the environment, is going to be conditioned by a very complex network of causal influences. Some of these conditions are going to come from the past: how we were raised, what language we have learned, what mistakes we have made, and so forth. All of those details are combining to influence who we are in the present moment. Some of the conditioning factors are going to be embedded in present circumstances: the mood we are in, the temperature of the room, the arising of a certain object of experience rather than another. Every situation is unique, and so much of what makes up the fabric of our lives consists of responses to changing circumstances in the environment. And much of how we construct a reality is also going to have some influence on the future: the attitudes and assumptions we bring to this moment effect the unfolding of phenomena for ourselves and others in the next moment, and the decisions and actions we take influence the causal chain of events leading to how the future will unfold for us. Not only will each successive moment of the mind be influenced by the immediately preceding moments, but sometimes apparently minor elements of present experience can plant seeds that come to fruition a long time from now. So the construction process

that is happening at any given moment has causal influences from the past, from
the present, and it influences the future as well.

DISTORTING THE TRUTH

A fourth important insight of Buddhist psychology is the observation that our experience is constantly changing. We experience ourselves and our world as a parade of phenomena arising and passing away, one after another, in a seemingly
perpetual flow. However much our senses may be taking in and processing information in parallel—and it is a prodigious amount of information—still constructed
conscious human experience can only unfold in series, one moment after another.
There are two consequences of this. One is that we can never, strictly speaking, be
aware of two things in the same moment. When it appears that we are dong this,
say the Buddhists, we are actually cycling between two or more modes of consciousness very rapidly. Another more significant consequence is that we can
never have precisely the same experience twice. Since by definition each experience is constructed from elements unique to each moment, the phenomenology
of the present moment will always reveal change and permutation. Even if we
seem to be looking at the same object over time, we may actually be seeing it from
slightly different angles each time, the lighting of the room can be changing in-
crementally, or the internal changes of our mood, assumptions, expectations, and
so on are influencing what we see. When we recall a memory or conjure an image
in our minds, it will always be constructed in somewhat different internal circumstances. Though we may be oblivious to much of this detail much of the time,
the closer we look at the nuances of our experience, as meditation practice invites
us to do, the more fluctuation and change we are capable of discerning.

The extent of the changeability of all that surrounds us and all we consist of
is hidden from our view to an astonishing degree. This is partly due to the fact
that the brain has evolved to distort the environment in a manner that helps us
survive. The barrage of information that comes into the mind through the various sense doors is so vast and urgent that the mind has had to develop strategies
to simplify and organize this data into manageable units. The Buddhist psychologists identify a number of distortions of perception, distortions of thought, and
distortions of view that work on different levels of scale to contribute greatly to
the flaws of human understanding.[7] One of these is the tendency to construct stability in a milieu that is profoundly unstable. The mind creates fixed images,
ideas, and attitudes from the swirl of input, like snapshots of the flux, and then
processes these as symbols of reality. Rather than opening up to the full range of
sensory diversity at every moment, which would be tiresome if not overwhelming,
the human mind, more often than not, is working from a vastly simplified copy

that has been generated by the mind itself. On the perceptual level this can be an icon or image stored in short-term memory against which the incoming data is checked from time to time for variations. For example, a cursory phenomenological examination of the blind spot caused by the exit of the optical nerve from the retina will reveal how a vast segment of our visual field is "filled in" by simple cutting and pasting. On the cognitive level, we develop a number of learned ideas that interact with one another in various sorts of processing activities. The idea itself becomes a sort of symbol that can be manipulated in the language of mental processing, but as a symbol it is taking its meaning not from careful attention to subtly changing circumstances each moment, but from a fixed or stabilized notion that has been constructed and then relegated to memory. And the same is true on the third level, the level of our attitudes or beliefs. We get in the habit of thinking of ourselves as a particular person with particular views, and we become accustomed to regarding the world in certain ways that have been learned and remembered. All our subsequent experience then unfolds within an often very narrow habitual range that has been defined by these views or beliefs.

Buddhist psychology recognizes that the products of these distortions of the mind are "mere" conceptual constructions. That is not to say that they are all false, since many provide useful, even crucial advantages in how we relate to the environment. In fact, their truth or falsity is not even a major issue, since they are virtual tools used for working in a virtual world. The important point is that they are only maps we create of a terrain, and all sorts of difficulties result in our taking the maps to be anything more than the conceptual constructions they are. In addition to the distortion of mind that stabilizes the impermanent world into quasi-permanent images, the Buddhists identify three others. We also create "things" and "persons" out of the flux of phenomena by creating certain artificial and arbitrary boundaries between "this" and "that" and between "self" and "other." That is to say, we construct the idea of the self from a milieu that is inherently without self. From the phenomenological perspective the world, along with our experience of the world, consists of a seamless unfolding of experience. Our patterning of this flow of both the objective and subjective worlds into definable units is another example of the mind projecting its meaning onto the world, and the objects and subjects that derive from this process of projection have no more than the provisional validity of conceptual constructions.

The two other distortions of the mind have to do, respectively, with the projection of "satisfaction" and "beauty" onto a flow of experience that intrinsically contains neither. Happiness or suffering is rightly defined entirely in terms of human desires that are either fulfilled or frustrated. Similarly, something is deemed attractive or repulsive according to the degree of projection of human likes and dislikes. In both cases the distortions of mind are yielding qualia that have everything to do with the response of the organism to its own internal constructions, and very little to do with the nature of the environment itself. All this results in the insight that our view of the world and of our selves is something distilled from changing moment-to-moment experience into a set of ideas and conceptions that help interpret things for us. Useful inquiry into the nature of it all, therefore, will come not from the further manipulation of these derived symbols (which by this analysis consists of little more than a rearranging of deck chairs), but from deep examination of how the construction process itself takes place in the very moments of awareness that comprise our experience. The question is not What is the nature of the world out there? but rather, How does the mind go about constructing stability, identity, satisfaction, and beauty from an environment that itself lacks these qualities, and What are the consequences of these distortions for the subject who constructs them?

A COLLECTION OF AGGREGATES

A final component of the theoretical Buddhist psychology worth mentioning in this broad overview is the observation that the mind and body are manifest and reveal themselves in experience through five interdependent categories of phenomena called aggregates.[8] The aggregates are: a physical or *material* dimension to all experience that supports, nourishes, and molds the mental dimensions; the episode of awareness or *consciousness* through which each moment's experience manifests and knowing takes place; a *perception* or cognitive content by means of which we discern the qualities and features of any experiential object; a *feeling* or affect tone that is either pleasant, unpleasant, or neutral; and a more complex function the Buddhists call *formations*, which have to do with the manifestation of various conative patterns in the construction process: patterns of intention and of action, and of the dispositions that are shaped by these over time. These five aggregates all arise and fall together as a unit, moment after moment, and neither one of them can be considered primary or more essential than the others.

We have already discussed the extent to which the early Buddhists recognized consciousness as an essential factor in the construction of experience, constituting at once the agent, the instrument, and the activity of experience. Consciousness is that which cognizes an object, the instrument by means of which the organ of perception is capable of knowing its immediate object, and is also itself nothing other than this process of knowing. But unlike idealists or soul-theorists both ancient and modern, this consciousness was understood by the early Buddhists as thoroughly interdependent with materiality. All attempts to reduce one to the other were shunned, and in a manner that can be taken as strikingly modern in its scientific mood, consciousness and materiality were construed as cocreating one another. This stance not only embodies the mind firmly in materiality, but also allows for a significant degree of mental influence on the bodily processes. The four great elements themselves constituting materiality—earth, air, fire and water—can be construed in two ways. Physically, they manifest in various combinations to form the "stuff" we can trip over in the night; psychologically they manifest as the subjective bodily experience of resistance, movement, and heat (respectively; the cohesive role played by water is said by the meditative tradition to be experientially indiscernible). Consciousness itself, as we have seen, can take purely mental objects, as in the case of internal mental experience. But consciousness also stands as the sole means of manifesting the material world, since it is only through being cognized as a sense object that the vast range of physicality can manifest in our experience. We can perhaps begin to glimpse the profundity of the Buddhist insight that "the entire world is manifest within the fathom-long carcass"[9] of the human psychophysical organism.

The analysis of experience into five aggregates further recognizes that mind involves more than just consciousness, and emphasizes the functioning also of cognitive, affective, and conative aspects of the mind. The aggregate of perception, present in any moment of experience, supplies information about "what" it is we are sensing or thinking. We have learned through a lifetime of training how to make sense of the data entering our senses, and various systems and subsystems of the brain assemble these data into discernable categories of perception: blue, green, long, short, table, chair. These categories are to some extent built into the hard-wiring of our sensory apparatus, are greatly influenced by shared social conventions such as language, symbolic structures and culture, and are also shaped by a host of personal and idiosyncratic experiences throughout our learning process. While consciousness allows for the basic cognizing of an object to occur, it is perception that shapes our cognizing it as a particular object. The aggregate of feeling involves those functions of the limbic system that identify each experience as pleasant, painful, or neither pleasant nor painful. According to this model every single experience involves an affect tone: we either like it, dislike it, or "feel" neutral about it. How any given sense object affects us will also be determined by a range of influences, some of them built into the structure of the various nerve receptors, some conditioned by social or cultural factors, and some based entirely on unique personal history. This feeling tone has a huge impact on the dynamics of our minds and bodies, and understanding the influence of the pleasure/pain response on human behavior is a major part of the Buddhist analysis of experience. The aggregate of formations has to do with the conative loop created by the choices we make, the actions we perform, and the changes of disposition these choices and actions then have on the psychophysical organism. The volitional choices we make in any instance will be heavily influenced by the dispositions remaining from previous actions, and will further mold our dispositions for the future. A process model of human personality and behavior emerges that allows for both a level of free will and a level of determinism, and which construes identity as a constantly changing pattern of activities and strategies rather than as a substantive entity. The Buddhist aggregate of formations also reveals a sophisticated understanding of unconscious processes in a model discovered entirely from the close attention to the working of the conscious mind.

A FRAMEWORK FOR HEALING

How does such a theoretical understanding of the human condition contribute to the practical and therapeutic goal of alleviating suffering and bringing about a deep sense of peace and happiness? In a number of ways. To begin with, the first step in any healing process is overcoming denial and recognizing that there are identifiable symptoms that need to be addressed. Because of the ways the mind tends to distort or mask some of the basic features of our experience with illusion, as described above, it is no small accomplishment to expose some of the ways this happens. The first step in the Buddhist process of healing, called in the tradition the first noble truth, points to the unsatisfactoriness of the human situation, and to the fact that suffering manifests in many ways we are not accustomed to acknowledging. The pursuit of pleasure, the avoidance of pain, the denial of change, the illusion of identity, the projection of beauty, the ignoring of death—these are all aspects of a daily coping strategy that is inherently limited in its ability to provide any lasting sense of safety, meaning, or fulfillment. The first thing the Buddha, as the Great Physician, does for us is to throw back the sheets and reveal the true nature of the mind and body. There is nothing evil or disgusting or inherently flawed about the psychophysical organism, it is just that it is suffering from an affliction and is in need of healing.

The second step to the healing process is to identify the causes of the illness, which is done in the second noble truth of the ancient medical formula employed by the Buddha. The problem turns out to be relatively simple: a thorn is embedded deep in our hearts, the thorn of craving or desire, and the agitation of its presence is driving us mad.[10] Like the injured lion made ferocious by the thorn in its paw, so also the human mind and body are driven by desire to act and respond in very unwholesome or unhealthy ways. The desire for relief from suffering only fuels behaviors which embed the thorn deeper and lead to further suffering. The desire that lies so deeply implanted in the human psyche can be quite naturally accounted for, and manifests in two related but opposite ways. First we have the positive expression of desire, the desire to get, to have, to possess, to accumulate. This arises, in humans as in all other animals, in response to the experience of pleasure. We want more of what gives us pleasure, we want the pleasure to continue and to grow, and we want to organize our lives around the pursuit and preservation of pleasure. The negative expression of desire is the desire for pain to go away—the avoidance or denial of, the resistance to, the aversion or aggression toward what we do not like. Whatever does not give us pleasure, and especially whatever we identify with the experience of pain, is something we want to stay away from or destroy if we can. This too is rooted in primitive instincts of survival. Practical Buddhist psychology has mapped out the terrain of desire in great detail. Careful and honest introspection can reveal the dramatic effects these positive and negative expressions of desire can have on how all experience is constructed. In particular, we can see how often both forms of desire serve to motivate a dysfunctional response that the Buddhists call clinging or grasping. Pleasure and pain are both natural affective aspects of all experience, but because of the underlying tendencies of craving and aversion—the thorn embedded in the heart—they can trigger the pathological response of attachment. It is this attachment itself, according to the Buddha's analysis, that is responsible for the full range of phenomena we experience as suffering.

Why is it that we all seem to have this underlying tendency toward wanting pleasure to continue and pain to cease, and why do we so often act in ways that have just the opposite effect? It turns out that to the two aspects of desire we need to add a further basic cause of suffering: ignorance. The three factors are usually listed together—greed, hatred, and delusion—but these terms are just a shorthand for a list of dozens of afflictive mind states that grow out of these three roots. The notion of ignorance or delusion is used in a precise manner by the Buddhists. It is not a lack of intelligence or lack of capability, but rather the effect of the distortions of mind referred to earlier. Delusion is seeing what is impermanent as stable, seeing what is without self as possessing a self, seeing what is unsatisfactory as satisfying, and so forth. Desire is only present in the mind because of our lack of understanding around these fundamental aspects of experience. If we truly accepted that all things change, we would not expect pleasure to continue or pain to be effectively avoided; if we truly understood nonself, we would not become attached to people and things as if they were entities on which our happiness depends; if we could see clearly that there is something unsatisfactory, even in situations where we can cover its trail by pleasure, we might be able to open to what is painful and avoid the double injury of resisting or denying the inevitable. Desire and ignorance are interdependent, and each reinforces the other. So the second noble truth of Buddhism identifies greed, hatred, and delusion as the root causes of suffering—whenever these are present in a moment's constructed experience, suffering is also being created.

The solution to the problem, then, expressed in the third noble truth, is the cessation of suffering by means of the cessation of desire and ignorance. The great discovery of the Buddha was that the pathological psychophysical dynamic causing suffering can be healed, and he demonstrated this by his own "awakening" under the Bodhi tree at Gaya. Notice that this is a practical, not a theoretical, accomplishment. The theory revealed the nature of the problem and pointed in the direction of the solution, but the culmination of the entire Buddhist program is in the radical transformation of persons. The Buddha went on to live for forty-five years as an Awakened One, a Buddha. During this time his experience was still ordered around the five aggregates—he had a body, was conscious, perceived, felt pleasure and pain, and made choices. But all this was ostensibly done without manifesting even a moment of greed, hatred, or delusion. The traditional way of expressing what happened to the Buddha that night is that the fires of greed, hatred, and delusion became extinguished (nirvāna). Knowing that everything was merely impermanent, conditioned, selfless phenomena, there was no motivation to cling to what was liked or push away what was disliked. Without the distorting projections of desires on to experience, he was said to be able to see phenomena clearly. Perhaps most important, the Buddha said that anyone can accomplish the same transformation, and spent his life teaching a very precise but flexible method to help others experience the same alleviation of suffering.[11]

The fourth and final of the noble truths is the path leading to the cessation of suffering. While the first three truths analyze and articulate the theoretical underpinnings of the human condition, the fourth truth has more to do with the practical task of purification and transformation. How to bring about the radically healing transformation of awakening is a matter of great diversity in the Buddhist tradition. All schools more or less agree on the first three noble truths, but thousands of years of tradition have elaborated greatly on the methods and strategies that can be used to get free of attachments and illusions.

PRACTICAL BUDDHIST PSYCHOLOGY

The first and foremost item on the Buddhist agenda for healing—not necessarily in its textual formulation but certainly in its practical application—is mindfulness. Since the entirety of our virtual world is being constructed in the present moment, it is crucial to learn to pay attention to this moment. Paying attention sounds simple; one might think we do it all the time, but we actually pay attention very little to what is going on in our present experience. The human mind is constantly swinging into the future and the past, and like a pendulum it passes through the present moment barely enough for us to keep our bearings. There is nothing inherently wrong with the complexity and richness of the inner life that involves remembering and planning, imagining the future and honoring the past. The Buddhists are not saying that we should cut off our sensitivity to the full range of experience and live ordinary life in some sort of eternal present. But in order to get beyond some of the embedded habits of the mind, in order to get free of some of the distortions and confusions to which we are subject, we need to train ourselves to attend very carefully and very deliberately to the process by which we construct past and future experience in the present moment. And this is largely what mindfulness practice is all about. It is accessing the present moment, and it involves cultivating the intention to attend to what is happening right now. Left to its own inclinations, the mind would much rather weave its way through some thought pattern that makes us feel good about ourselves, and lead us away from any kind of insight that might threaten ours ideas about ourselves. It is, as we have seen, the predilection of our latent tendencies to pursue pleasure and avoid pain, and this is as true in our subtle mental world as it is in the coarser sensory realm. It is not that the mind has to be beaten into submission (a not very successful strategy, on the whole), but it needs to be carefully and gently encouraged through constant practice to look carefully and deeply at what is unfolding in the immediately present moment. One can do this while driving a car, during a meditation retreat, or it can be done sitting here in this very moment: by simply attending carefully to what arises and passes away in experience.

The second endeavor that helps to further the practical process of seeing more clearly is noticing various aspects of behavior. We can use the interest and capabilities cultivated by mindfulness to notice what we are actually doing when we act, moment to moment. This too seems to be stating the obvious, but modern psychology reveals in ever-greater detail the extent to which so much of our behavior is unconsciously motivated and unconsciously executed. By noticing the texture of the mind in the midst of behavior—the taste of desire, the feeling of aversion, the inclination toward or away from some object of experience—quite a lot of unconscious patterning can be revealed. Attending to the details of behavior is a way of developing clarity about what is happening. Mindfulness involves taking activities and behavior that had been perhaps unconsciously conditioned and bringing them to conscious awareness. This awareness can itself be profoundly transformative. The Buddhist emphasis on ethics in behavior is not a prescription for right behavior as opposed to wrong behavior, but rather an invitation to notice the details and the nuances of one's own behavior. The act of witnessing what we do will gradually and naturally effect changes in the quality of our actions. One of the ways this process is represented in the Buddhist tradition is through the use of the paired terms *wholesome* and *unwholesome* applied to the full range of mental, verbal, and physical actions. Because of a convenient play on words in the Pāli language, the words for wholesome and unwholesome, *kusala* and *akusala*, can also be taken to mean "skillful" and "unskillful." This places the whole field of ethical behavior in the realm of gaining understanding and capability rather than conformity to normative law. Thus the skills gained through mindful awareness of experience naturally flow into the skillful execution of behavior. Well-being itself, it turns out, is a skill that can be learned.

Another important tool for helping us get more clear in the practical psychology of Buddhism is learning to calm the mind. The delusions we are wrapped up in, according to the Buddhist analysis, are primarily fueled by restlessness; both inattentiveness and unskillfulness always arise in conjunction with an agitation of mind. Moreover, this restlessness or agitation is not intrinsic to the working of the mind, but is a mode of operation learned through culture and reinforced by conditioning. The mind is capable of attaining states of tremendous serenity and calm, but we seldom allow it the opportunity to settle in to these deeper states of consciousness because of our demands for constant information processing. As the mind gets quieter, it does get less capable of the far-ranging but shallow processing to which we accustom it, but rather than dulling the mind this deepening process greatly strengthens it. There are many metaphors in the Buddhist tradition that talk about increasing the power of the mind through the development of concentration.[12] One such metaphor likens the flow of consciousness to a mountain stream. If, on the one hand, there are many outlets to that stream, the force of the water at the bottom is going to be very small, since its hydraulic energy will be dissipated. If, on the other hand, one stops up those outlets to the stream, the flow of water at the bottom is going to be much more powerful. In the same way, the ability of the mind to be aware in the moment is dissipated by the complexity of our sensory lives, perhaps even more so now than was the case in ancient India. What has come to be called multitasking, the tendency to process information and respond along multiple parallel tracks, can be likened to the opening of the channels in the waterway. The mind's energy flows out through multiple channels, and perhaps even accomplishes a number of tasks, but each outlet is relatively weak and each task is attended with little mindful awareness. Calming the mind with meditation has the effect of closing off these sensory outlets so the quality of awareness strengthens and deepens. Then when the mind attends to something, it does so with the full weight of its capabilities. As when the point of a sharp blade of grass is carefully directed, the mind can in this mode penetrate the illusions woven by the construction of experience in a way impossible to the uncultivated or undeveloped mind. It is important to recognize, of course, that as the mind becomes more calm, it also becomes more, rather than less, alert. The tranquillity that comes from concentration is not a sluggishness or drowsiness; the inherent function of the mind—awareness—is enhanced by its stillness, not impeded. Although to an outside observer the meditator may seem to be asleep or in a trance, the inner experience of the concentrated mind is quite active in its own way. So the practice of meditation, which is so central to most forms of Buddhism, involves the cultivation of a state of mind that is both tranquil and alert. That such a state is possible may seem unlikely due to our verbal tendency to define things using opposites, but it can be easily verified by personal experience with a little bit of training, a lot of patience, and some diligent application.

As the mind calms down and interest in the investigation of experience increases, a whole inner life opens up in great detail and texture.[13] This becomes the ground for the final step in the practical Buddhist program of transformation, the gradual, but sometimes dramatic, development of wisdom. Wisdom is not the same as knowledge, although the latter is helpful to its development. Wisdom involves the gradual and often very subtle growth of understanding—of the world, of experience, and of oneself. It is the antidote to the distortions and illusions mentioned above, and as such, wisdom holds the key to the cessation of suffering. Understanding impermanence, through clearly seeing the ways that the illusion of continuity is constructed, draws back one of the three principle veils obscuring our relationship to the objects of our experience. Understanding the unsatisfactoriness and the ultimately disappointing nature of whatever is impermanent illuminates how we are habitually driven by attachment to what is pleasing and aversion to what is displeasing. And understanding the extent to which substances and self-identity are manufactured and then projected onto all experience removes the final obstacle to what the Buddhists call "seeing things as they really are." The progress of insight into these three characteristics is termed *wisdom,* and as it develops it considerably changes the way we construct ourselves and the way we respond to unfolding events. It turns out that the Buddhist notion of the cessation of suffering has to do with a major transformation of how we construe ourselves and our world. The change is from habitually and unconsciously responding to things with attachment and aversion, to gradually increasing the ability to manifest equilibrium in the midst of experience. This state of equanimity culminating the path is often confused with detachment or disengagement, but most Buddhists would argue that just the opposite is the case. When the various egoistic illusions and projections are withdrawn, one is capable of a much greater intimacy and a fuller involvement with every aspect of experience.

The final awakening (*sambodhi*) or cessation of suffering (nirvāna) to which both the theoretical and the practical elements of Buddhist psychology progress, has been the subject of much puzzlement and confusion. In the earliest literature of the tradition, it seems to be defined primarily as the absence of the three basic roots of all unwholesome and unskillful states: attachment, aversion, and misunderstanding (i.e., greed, hatred, and delusion). All of human suffering can be seen to emerge from these three fundamental human psychological reflexes. But through the systematic practice of training in awareness, behavior, concentration, and wisdom just outlined, it is possible for humans to radically transform and even eliminate these unconscious tendencies of the mind, and it is the result of this process that the Buddhists are calling awakening. Although the notion of nirvāna inevitably took on religious and mystical connotations, and quite rightly functions as a symbol of an ultimate apotheosis in the Buddhist tradition, from the practical perspective of the early teachings the term is embedded in a psychological context. The awakening of the mind from the slumber of its delusions is something that happens to a person in this lifetime, as it did to the Buddha under the Bodhi tree, and the concept does not make much sense other than as a transformation that occurs to a person. More specifically, the transformation involves the extinguishing (lit. nirvāna) of the three unwholesome roots, which are latent tendencies of the human mind, and thus the liberation of a person from all forms of suffering. It need not be considered anything more than this, but more significantly, neither is it anything less.

Properly understood, this teaching left by the Buddha, along with his own example of its fulfillment, is a remarkable legacy that can challenge and inspire people of all generations throughout the world, both past and future. We are entering an age when the understanding of the human mind, the last great frontier of scientific knowledge, is beginning to advance dramatically, and if we allow it, a tremendous contribution can be made by the study of this ancient but universal science of the mind. As we bring modern knowledge into contact with ancient wisdom, something unique and dramatic may very well unfold. The dialogue is just beginning.

NOTES

1. For an intriguing new look at this issue, see Goldstein, J. (2002).

2. For a fascinating ancient account of some of these differing theories, see the Samaññaphala Sutta (1987).

3. The Samaññaphala Sutta (1987) is also an excellent place to see the description of a comprehensive and systematic program of developing these practices of observation

and analysis. See also the Mahāsatipatthāna Sutta, or "The Greater Discourse on the Foundations of Mindfulness" (1987).

4. This sentiment is expressed by the adjective *"ehipassika"* applied to the teaching of the Buddha, a word meaning literally "come and see." We also find this attitude in the Kālāma Sutta (1999) and in many other places in the early literature.

5. An excellent, if dense, presentation of this model of perception can be found in the Chachakka Sutta (1995).

6. For a brief discussion of the elements, see the Bahudhātuka Sutta (1995).

7. The classical reference for these distortions (*vipallāsa* in Pāli) can be found at Anguttara Nikāya 4:49 (1999). My alternative translation, with commentary, can be seen in Distortions of the mind: Angutarra Nikāya 4:49 (2001).

8. These aggregates (*khandha* in Pāli, *skandha* in Sanskrit) are discussed in many places throughout Buddhist literature. Some basic explanations are accessible in the Mahāpunnama Sutta (1995), the Mahāhatthipadopama Sutta (1995), and Alagaddūpama Sutta (1995), as well as the entire Khandhasamyutta (2000).

9. Anguttara Nikāya, 4:45, and so on.

10. This compelling image is described in a poem found in the Attadanda Sutta (1985). See also my translation with commentary in "The thorn in your heart: Selections from the Attadanda Sutta of the Sutta Nipāta" (1999).

11. The story of the Buddha's struggle for awakening and accomplishment of the task is well told in the Bhayabherava Sutta (1995), the Ariyapariyesanā Sutta (1995), the Mahāsaccaka Sutta (1995), and the Mahāsīhanāda Sutta (1995).

12. See for example the Samaññaphala Sutta (1987). Other useful similes can be found in Anguttara Nikāya (1973) 5:23, 5:51, and 5:193.

13. It is said of one of the Buddha's greatest disciples Sāriputta, for example, that he had "insight into states one by one as they occurred" (Anupada Sutta, 1995).

REFERENCES

Alagaddūpama Sutta (1995). In B. Ñānamoli and B. Bodhi (Trans.), *The middle length discourses of the Buddha: A new translation of the Majjhima Nikāya* (pp.224-236). Boston: Wisdom.

Anguttara Nikāya 4:45. In N. Thera & B. Bodhi (Trans.), *The numerical discourses of the Buddha* (p. 90). Walnut Creek, CA: AltaMira Press.

Anguttara Nikāya 5:23 (1973). In E. M. Hare (Trans.), *The Book of Gradual Sayings* (Vol. 3), (p. 11). London: Pali Text Society.

Anguttara Nikāya 5:51 (1973). In E. M. Hare (Trans.), *The Book of Gradual Sayings* (Vol. 3), (p. 52). London: Pali Text Society.

Anguttara Nikāya 5:193 (1973). In E. M. Hare (Trans.), *The Book of Gradual Sayings* (Vol. 3), (pp. 167-171). London: Pali Text Society.

Anguttara Nikāya 4:49 (1999). In N. Thera & B. Bodhi (Trans.), *The numerical discourses of the Buddha* (pp. 91-92). Walnut Creek, CA: AltaMira Press.

Ariyapariyesanā Sutta (1995). In B. Ñānamoli and B. Bodhi (Trans.), *The middle length discourses of the Buddha: A new translation of the Majjhima Nikāya* (pp. 253-269). Boston: Wisdom.

Attadanda Sutta (1985). In H. Saddhatissa (Trans.), *The Sutta-Nipāta* (pp. 109–110). London: Curzon Press.

Bahudhātuka Sutta (1995). In B. Ñāṇamoli and B. Bodhi (Trans.), *The middle length discourses of the Buddha: A new translation of the Majjhima Nikāya* (pp. 925–930). Boston: Wisdom.

Bhayabherava Sutta (1995). In B. Ñāṇamoli and B. Bodhi (Trans.), *The middle length discourses of the Buddha: A new translation of the Majjhima Nikāya* (pp. 102-107). Boston: Wisdom.

Chachakka Sutta (1995). In B. Ñāṇamoli and B. Bodhi (Trans.), *The middle length discourses of the Buddha: A new translation of the Majjhima Nikāya* (pp. 1129-1136). Boston: Wisdom.

Goldstein, J. (2002). *One dharma: The emerging Western Buddhism.* San Francisco: HarperSanFrancisco.

Kālāma Sutta (1999). In N. Thera and B. Bodhi (Trans.), *The numerical discourses of the Buddha* (pp. 64-67). Walnut Creek, CA: AltaMira Press.

Khandhasamyutta (2000). In B. Bodhi (Trans.), *The connected discourses of the Buddha: A new translation of the Samuytta Nikāya* (pp. 853-954). Boston: Wisdom.

Mahāhatthhipadopama Sutta (1995). In B. Ñāṇamoli and B. Bodhi (Trans.), *The middle length discourses of the Buddha: A new translation of the Majjhima Nikāya* (pp. 278-285). Boston: Wisdom.

Mahāpunnama Sutta (1995). In B. Ñāṇamoli and B. Bodhi (Trans.), *The middle length discourses of the Buddha: A new translation of the Majjhima Nikāya* (pp. 887-891). Boston: Wisdom.

Mahāsaccaka Sutta (1995). In B. Ñāṇamoli and B. Bodhi (Trans.), *The middle length discourses of the Buddha: A new translation of the Majjhima Nikāya* (pp. 332-343). Boston: Wisdom.

Mahāsatipatthāna Sutta (1987). In M. Walshe (Trans.), *The long discourses of the Buddha: A translation of the Dīgha Nikāya* (pp. 335-350). Boston: Wisdom.

Mahāsīhanāda Sutta (1995). In B. Ñāṇamoli and B. Bodhi (Trans.), *The middle length discourses of the Buddha: A new translation of the Majjhima Nikāya* (pp. 164-179). Boston: Wisdom.

Samaññaphala Sutta (1987). In M. Walshe (Trans.), *The long discourses of the Buddha: A translation of the Dīgha Nikāya* (pp. 93-97). Boston: Wisdom.

The distortions of the mind: Anguttara Nikāya 4:49 (A. Olendzki, Trans.). (2001). *Insight,* Spring/Summer, p. 37.

The thorn in your heart: Selections from the Attadanda Sutta of the Sutta Nipāta. (A. Olendzki, Trans.) (1999). *Insight,* Fall, p. 38.

CHAPTER 2

Close Encounters of a New Kind
Toward an Integration of Psychoanalysis and Buddhism

Jeffrey B. Rubin

The relationship between psychoanalysis and Eastern meditative disciplines has intrigued me for many years. I have immersed myself in both traditions since the late 1970s in the hope of ascertaining what light they might shed on the art of living. Judiciously integrating them can open up new vistas that might ultimately enrich our lives and the lives of the people in pain with whom we work.

Imagine the following scenario: A person is in a room with a minimum of sensory stimulations and distractions. She is still, alert, and relaxed. Her eyes are closed. She pays careful attention to whatever she experiences moment-after-moment . . . I could be describing an analysand in psychoanalytic treatment. In this particular instance I am actually depicting a person meditating. What I hope to do in this chapter is interest you in the possibility that one's experience on the meditative cushion might enrich one's experience in the psychoanalytic consulting room and one's experience in the psychoanalytic consulting room might aid one's experience on the meditative cushion.

An increasing number of people that I know both in and outside of therapy complain of being too burdened and distracted. They feel oversaturated with e-mails, faxes, and pagers. They frenetically juggle multiple conflicting roles and responsibilities—parent, therapist, spouse, lover, friend. They often feel a hollowness in their lives. Those of you who feel more grounded and less depleted may still long for a life of greater inner peace and equanimity.

Imagine that you could find a sanctuary in your daily experience from the cognitive overstimulation and the frenetic pace that all too often consumes us. Imagine that within this safe haven you might quiet the inner maelstrom and gain a measure of clarity and focus about what you feel and who you are. Imagine further that you could see and work through restrictive psychological identifications and conditioning. You could then have a less insulated and egocentric view of self and reality. There might be a profound sense of connectedness with yourself and other people. Imagine even further that if this happens then something *sacred* will be revealed. Your daily life might be infused with greater meaning and purpose. You might then live with greater compassion and wisdom . . . This is part of the promise of Buddhism.

WHOSE BUDDHISM IS IT ANYWAY?

Buddhism, like psychoanalysis, is not one thing. Meaning, as the Russian thinker Bahktin (1986) knew, is the product of an interaction or dialogue between reader and text, rather than a singular essence waiting-to-be-revealed in a neutral, fixed, manuscript. There is thus no singular, settled, or definitive Buddhism (or psychoanalysis). "Buddhism" and "psychoanalysis" are heterogeneous and evolving; a plenitude of beliefs, theories, and practices, cocreated and transformed by readers and seekers from different historical, psychological, sociocultural, and gendered perspectives (Rubin, 1996, p. 3). There is thus no such thing as "Buddhism." Given the diversity in theories and practices within Buddhism it is more accurate to speak of Buddhisms rather than Buddhism (Rubin, 1996).

There have been several major schools of Buddhist thought (e.g., Theravāda, Zen, Ch'an, Tibetan, and Korean) that have developed in different historical ages and cultures and that have adopted different theories and practices. To cite two examples among many possible ones: anyone familiar with classical Buddhist texts knows that the Buddha was not averse to profound philosophical exploration. After all, he offered profound examinations of the nature of mind, self, suffering, and the path to inner peace. But in answer to cosmological and metaphysical questions—the existence of a divinity, divine realms, afterlife, and so on—he is said to have likened the questioner to a man who was shot by an arrow and would not pull the arrow out of his body until he had been told where the arrow was made, what it was made of, and who shot it. The man, that is, was suffering; and his time could best be spent, asserted the Buddha, in the pragmatic and therapeutic task of pulling out the arrow and relieving his suffering rather than engaging in endless intellectual speculation about the nature of the universe. And yet, despite the avowedly pragmatic and nonmetaphysical orientation of the Buddha, subsequent schools of Buddhist thought such as Tibetan Buddhism posit the existence of various deities and adopt a cosmology with magical dimensions that seems quite foreign to the nontheistic worldview of classical Buddhism (as well as the contemporary West).

The methods, no less than the worldviews, of schools of Buddhism can also differ greatly. Classical Buddhism placed great emphasis on individual practitioners awakening to their own asleepness through concentrated meditative practice focused on a clear and direct apprehension of reality and living a life based on Buddhist ethical principles of nonviolence and nonharming and attention to compassionate action, livelihood, and speech. As he was dying, the Buddha was reported to have said to his attendant, Ānanda: "Be a lamp unto thyself; pursue your deliverance with diligence" (Burtt, 1955, p. 49). No one was selected to teach or govern the Buddhist community that outlived him. The Dharma, that is, the teachings of Buddhism, not a person or an institution, would be the teacher (Kornfield, 1977). In Tibetan Buddhism, however, surrender to the guru as well as various imaginal and visualization practices are an essential facet of the path to awakening. In Pure Land Buddhism from China, faith is absolutely central to one's salvation.

In the face of these and other differences in worldview and practices, Buddhists offer an interesting spin to the culture wars that conservatives and multiculturalists engage in in academia in the United States. Members of every school of Buddhist thought universally idealize the Buddha as the founder and most enlightened exemplar of Buddhism, even as they then proceed to present their particular brand of Buddhism as the best and most enlightened version. But to have assimilated the crucial currents in the social sciences and humanities in recent years is to be profoundly skeptical about any such claims to objectivity or truth. We are now infinitely more attuned to the way that such claims are illusory and are based, as Foucault repeatedly asserted, on power and a will to dominate. The interesting question then becomes not Whose Buddhism is the correct one? but rather, What becomes evaded and suppressed by such claims to cultural hegemony?

The implications of Foucault's reflections on knowledge and power for my own discourse are at least twofold: (1) there is no single or superior Buddhism; and (2) the Buddhism one chooses to practice or utilize in a study such as this one needs to be justified in terms of its usefulness or pragmatic yield rather than spurious claims to some putative objectivity or authority.

In this chapter I will focus on classical Theravāda Buddhism arising in India in the sixth century B.C. My reflections will also be informed, sometimes only implicitly, by the iconoclastic spirit of Zen Buddhism of China and Japan, with its eschewing of metaphysical speculation and its attention to the truth of one's experience, rather than conventional or received knowledge. Let me give one example of how the spirit of Zen has shaped my conception of Buddhism. Buddhism is conventionally treated as a world religion with sacred doctrines, ancestor worship, a community of believers, "houses of worship," religious icons, ritualistic practices, and so forth. Believing in Buddhist doctrines such as rebirth and reincarnation, from this perspective, would seem to be central to being a Buddhist. But the answer to the Zen kōan "Where did Nansen go after death?," for example, is "Excuse me, I've got to make dinner" (Hoffman, 1975, p. 129–132). An answer such as this raises provocative questions about this conception of Buddhism. Immersion in the antimetaphysical world of Zen—with its emphasis on actuality as opposed to religious doctrines or theories about human beings and the cosmos—can widen our view of it. Might Buddhism be more fertile than the traditional conception implies?

What is most radical and interesting about Buddhism from my perspective (which I realize may be a minority one outside Zen Buddhism), are the meditative methods of self-investigation (by which I mean the operationalizable techniques for studying human thought and emotions) and the Buddhist ethics, not its conventional religious features. I see no evidence that a Buddhism without rebirth or reincarnation, which from my perspective are experience-distant constructs, far removed from the actual experience of many if not most practitioners, would lose its emancipatory possibilities. In the spirit of Zen, I shall focus on meditative methods of self-investigation and Buddhist ethics, rather than Buddhist doctrines and speculations such as reincarnation and rebirth.

From the perspective I shall be taking, Buddhism can be considered an ethical psychology with a highly developed method for self-investigation. Buddhism is most potentially liberatory and transformative, according to this vision, when it is shorn of some of its doctrinal elements such as reincarnation, magical cosmologies, and so on. When its experience-near method and its ethics are juxtaposed with psychoanalytic methods of self-inquiry and psychoanalytic perspectives on human development, the dynamics of interpersonal relationship, and the process of change, new and evocative insights and approaches to human being-in-the-world emerge.

My choice of focusing on one tradition, namely, Theravāda Buddhism and occasionally on Zen, is not meant to cast aspersions on other Buddhist schools of thought such as Tibetan Buddhism or the Pure Land sects of Buddhism in China. Different schools of thought are different vehicles. I have chosen Theravāda Buddhism because in my experience it offers a highly sophisticated phenomenology of mind, a nontheistic worldview, and an ethics grounded in various facets of everyday life, and is thus very amenable to dialogue and integration with Western psychological thought. The Buddha's reflections bear repeating.

> Would he be a clever man if out of gratitude for the raft that has carried him across the stream to the other shore, he should cling to it, take it on his back, and walk about with the weight of it? Would not the clever man be the one who left the raft (of no use to him any longer) to the current stream, and walked ahead without turning back to look at it? Is it simply a tool to be cast away and forsaken once it has served the purpose for which it was made? In the same way the vehicle of the doc-

trine is to be cast away and forsaken once the shore of enlightenment has been attained. (Smith, 1996, pp. 209–210)

Before presenting a brief overview of Theravāda Buddhist thought so as to contextualize my subsequent discussion, let me delineate the perspective I shall adopt in this study. Broadly speaking there have been three stages in the drama of psychoanalysis and Buddhism. The work of psychoanalyst Franz Alexander (1931) represents the first stage of the encounter of psychoanalysis and Buddhism. Alexander (1931) falsely equates meditation with regression and pathology. In his blanket dismissal of Buddhism as a training in an artificial catatonia, Alexander (1931) illustrates the Eurocentrism that has plagued psychoanalysis. Eurocentrism refers to the intellectually imperialistic tendency in much Western scholarship to assume that European and North American standards and values are the center of the moral and intellectual universe. From a Eurocentric perspective, Eastern thought is pathologized and marginalized. Eurocentrism has played a central role in the literature of psychoanalysis and Buddhism from Freud to the present.

The more sympathetic non-Eurocentric work of psychoanalysts Jung (1958), Horney (1945; 1987), Kelman (1960), Fromm (1960), Engler (1984), Rubin (1985; 1991; 1992; 1996), Roland (1988), Finn (1992), Suler (1993), and Epstein (1995) represent the second major trend in the literature on psychoanalysis and Buddhism; an attempt to take Buddhism more seriously. Although they have pointed to various aspects of Buddhism's salutary dimensions, including its ability to sensitize us to the inner life (Jung, 1958); enrich psychoanalytic listening (Rubin, 1985); improve affect demarcation and tolerance (Rubin, 1992, 1996); promote "well-being"–being fully awake and alive (Fromm, 1960); and expand psychoanalytic conceptions of subjectivity (Roland, 1988; Rubin, 1992; 1993; 1996; and Suler, 1993), they tend, with the exception of the work of Roland (1988), Rubin (1991; 1992; 1993; 1996) and Engler (1986), to neglect clinical issues and case material. There are thus few extant precedents for integrating psychoanalysis and Buddhism.

The two most compelling attempts to integrate Asian and Western psychology are Jack Engler's (1986) "developmental" model and transpersonal theorist Ken Wilber's "spectrum psychology." Both thinkers exhibit an exemplary mastery of both traditional psychological theory and spiritual disciplines as well as an integration of theory and practice.

Engler attempts to integrate conventional psychotherapeutic and contemplative spiritual disciplines by seeing them as complementary facets of a developmental continuum with the former representing "lower" stages of development and the latter representing "higher" stages. Developing a strong, cohesive sense of self is the "precondition" of the contemplative task of disidentifying from the illusion of substantial selfhood. Engler (1986) concludes: "You have to be somebody before you can be nobody" (p. 124). Engler's work makes a highly important contribution to the field of east-west studies by including a greater range of development than either psychotherapeutic or spiritual perspectives alone offer. Both psychoanalysis and Buddhism lack a full spectrum psychology. The former has little to say about psychological maturity and health. The latter neglects "earlier stages of personality organization and the types of suffering that result from a failure to negotiate them" (Engler, 1986, p. 49).

There is a tension in the developmental stage model between a complementary view of human development (one is first somebody and then nobody) *and* a complex, noncomplementary conception. In terms of the former: "Meditation and psychotherapy cannot be positioned on a continuum in any mutually exclusive way as though both simply pointed to a different range of human development. Not only do post-enlightenment stages of meditation apparently affect the manifestation and management of neurotic conditions, but this type of conflict continues to be experienced after enlightenment" (Brown & Engler, 1986, p. 212). In terms of the latter view: Brown and Engler conclude that "psychological maturity and the path to enlightenment are perhaps two complementary but not entirely unrelated lines of growth; or that they do represent different 'levels' or ranges of health/growth along a continuum, but with much more complex relationships between them than have previously been imagined" (p. 212).

Although Engler acknowledges that there are very complex interactions between conventional and contemplative stages and a "rigidly linear and unidirectional model is not at all what we have in mind" (Wilber et al., 1986, p. 7), the complexity of interaction between 'psychological' and 'spiritual' perspectives is not addressed or spelled out. The limitations of contemplative perspectives and the value of conventional psychological viewpoints are also neglected—especially the way the latter might enrich the former.

Transpersonal psychology was developed in the late 1960s by thinkers who felt that existing psychologies neglected the full range of human possibilities including transcendent states. Transpersonal psychology focuses on such things as altered states of consciousness and well-being, meditation, optimal psychological health, and the integration of therapeutic and spiritual disciplines. Ken Wilber, Roger Walsh, Frances Vaughan, Stan Grof, and Charles Tart are some of its esteemed practitioners.

Wilber's Spectrum Psychology attempts to create a marriage between Western psychological perspectives on human development and psychopathology, and

Eastern contemplative understandings of consciousness and optimal states of health. His work exhibits encyclopedic scholarship, an exemplary groundedness in contemplative practices as well as theory, and an openness to diverse psychotherapeutic and spiritual traditions. In Wilber's work the quest to integrate Eastern contemplative and Western psychotherapeutic thought receives its most comprehensive and sophisticated expression.

Central to the spectrum of psychology is what Aldous Huxley (1944) has termed the *philosophia perennis*, the "perennial philosophy," a doctrine about the nature of humankind and reality underlying every major metaphysical tradition. It represents a "reality untouched by time or place, true everywhere and everywhen" (Wilber, 1979, p. 7). According to Wilber, corresponding to the perennial philosophy there exists a "psychologia perennis," a "perennial psychology"— a "universal view as to the nature of human consciousness, which expresses the very same insights as the perennial philosophy but in more decidedly psychological language" (ibid.).

For Wilber, the crucial insight of the perennial psychology is that our "innermost consciousness is identical to the absolute and ultimate reality of the universe," which he terms *mind*, which "is what there is and all there is, spaceless and therefore infinite, timeless and therefore eternal, outside of which nothing exists. On this level . . . (one) is identified with the universe, the All—or rather . . . is the All" (p. 9). According to the perennial psychology this is "the only real state of consciousness, all others being essentially illusions" (ibid.).

The perennial psychology is the foundation of Wilber's "spectrum of consciousness" model. The central underlying assumption of Wilbur's model is that "human personality is a multileveled manifestation or expression of a single consciousness, just as in physics the electromagnetic spectrum is viewed as a multibanded expression of a single, characteristic electromagnetic wave" (p. 8). Consciousness, like light, exists on and is composed of various bands or spectrums, which develop through a series of stages, which can be correlated with corresponding states of self-organization and self-blindness. Different psychological and spiritual traditions address these different levels.

Wilber (1986) has proposed ten levels to the spectrum. In ascending order, they are: sensoriphysical, phantasmic-emotional, representational mind, rule/role mind, formal-reflexive mind, vision-logic, psychic, subtle, causal, and ultimate. It would distract from the central argument to define Wilber's terms. For our purposes it is sufficient to note that each stage of development has it own particular type of self experience, cognitive development, moral sensibilities, potential distortions, and pathologies. Each level is characterized by a different sense of personal identity ranging from the narrow and circumscribed sense of identity associated with the sensoriphysical level in which one identifies only with the realms of matter, sensation, and perception, to the ultimate level in which one is identified with the totality of the universe. According to Wilber, the great religious sages such as the Buddha and the esteemed twentieth-century Hindu saint Ramana Maharshi are exemplars of the highest level of the spectrum.

On this level one is identified with the universe, the "All," or rather, is the All. This level is not an altered or abnormal state of consciousness, but is "the only real state of consciousness, all others being essentially illusions" (1979, p. 9). One's "innermost consciousness is identical to the absolute and ultimate reality of the universe" (pp. 8-9).

Each higher stage is less "selfcentric" than its predecessors (Wilber, 1986). Each level can be correlated with corresponding ways of perceiving and misperceiving reality. Wilber maintains that different psychotherapeutic and spiritual traditions address and are best suited for different levels of the spectrum. Western psychotherapies—for example, psychoanalysis, Gestalt therapy, and transactional analysis—address pathology and lower levels of the spectrum while contemplative disciplines such as Buddhism are recommended for higher stages of the spectrum and the deepest kinds of transformation and liberation. For Wilber, psychoanalysis and Buddhism are complementary.

The value of Wilber's work, like Engler's (e.g., 1984), is at least twofold: it disentangles meditative states of heightened clarity, health, and freedom from psychotherapeutic reductionism. Wilber and Engler (1984) maintain that contemplative practices constitute a higher and advanced level of personality development "beyond ego" or the separate, autonomous, self-centered self that is the acme of mental health in most psychotherapies. Their second contribution is to offer guidance for meditators with psychological disturbances who are failing to make important discriminations in their meditation practice. Meditative practices, according to Wilber and Engler (1986), may attract individuals with self-disorders, by which I mean, people who experience themselves as brittle, fragile, worthless, vulnerable, and prone to self-esteem fluctuations. Meditators who experience self-issues of this sort—obviously not all meditators—may confuse their experiences of identity diffusion and depersonalization with genuine spiritual realization. For such individuals, Engler and Wilber recommend traditional therapy to shore up the self prior to pursuing meditation practice.

Psychoanalysis and Buddhism offer fertile possibilities for cross-pollination. Mutual enrichment, however, has been impeded by the restrictive perspective of previous studies which have adopted one of three monolithic viewpoints in characterizing their multifaceted relationship. These are what I would term the shotgun wedding, bridesmaid, and pseudo-complementary/token egalitarian models. I will briefly discuss each view before presenting my own alternative perspective.

Until relatively recently, much of the literature on Eastern and Western psychology has assumed either explicitly or implicitly, that Buddhism and psychoanalysis are antithetical and incompatible. It is claimed that they occupy positions of unavoidable disagreement, from which there can be no escape, except by embracing one and abandoning the other (Rinzler and Gordan, 1980). Since psychoanalysis and Buddhism have very "different visions" of the mind and human existence, any attempt to join them is a "shotgun wedding" which "does justice to neither." A synthesis is thus "almost impossible" (p. 52).

The most prevalent view of psychoanalysis and Buddhism is what I would term the bridesmaid stance in which psychoanalysis plays second fiddle to Buddhism. In the earlier Eurocentric literature *Buddhism* was often subordinate to psychoanalysis (e.g., Alexander, 1931). In its more recent Orientocentric guise writers emphasize Buddhism's value for psychotherapy (Boss, 1965; Trungpa, 1983; Deatherage, 1975) while neglecting the latter's value for Buddhism.

Orientocentrism does not refer to the "Orientalism" that literary and culture critic Edward Said (1979) critiques when he describes the tendency among Western commentators on the Orient to utilize a imperialistic discourse about Asia that fashions a distorted and reductionistic picture of "the East" in order to intellectually colonize Asia and psychologically fortify itself. Rather, it refers to the mirror opposite danger to Eurocentrism: the idealizing and privileging of Asian thought—treating it as sacred—and the neglect if not dismissal of the value of Western psychological perspectives. The potential contribution of psychoanalysis is then neglected.

The Zen master who told the student of Zen, who indicated that psychotherapy and Zen had similar effects in overcoming suffering, that the psychotherapist is just another patient (Matthiessen, 1987, p. 160) illustrates Orientocentrism. As does the absence of exploration concerning what value Western psychotherapies might have for non-Western thought in the preeminent, extant anthologies in the field of east-west studies—for example, Welwood's (1979) *Meetings of the Ways*, Tart's (1975) *Transpersonal Psychologies*, Boorstein's (1980) *Transpersonal Psychotherapy*, and Walsh & Vaughan's (1980) *Beyond Ego*. Orientocentrism is so unconscious that no one has even remarked on its presence! More on Orientocentrism shortly. When the bridesmaid perspective is operative, commerce between Buddhism and psychoanalysis occurs, but only in one direction.

The third way that psychoanalysis and Buddhism have been approached— arguably the most compelling perspective—is Wilber's "spectrum-of-consciousness" model and Engler's developmental model. The spectrum model has tremendous theoretical and emotional appeal, as it promises to integrate apparently irreconcilable psychological and spiritual systems. Chaos seems to be reduced and seekers after truth no longer feel like UN delegates without an interpreter.

The spectrum model, however, has several fundamental flaws. Development, according to this model, involves progressing through discrete and stratified stages ranging from disavowing aspects of one's identity to recognizing one's fundamental interconnectedness with everything. This presupposes, without actually demonstrating, that there is a uniformity to one's identity and stage of development and a separation and division of the psychological and spiritual.

The pathology of certain visionaries (Gordon, 1987; Schneider, 1987) and the prescience of some schizophrenics (Searles, 1972/1979) teaches us that human functioning is much more complex than such schematic accounts suggest. One can experience the highest stage on Wilber's scale—unity consciousness—perceiving the interconnectedness of human existence, while also operating, at times on "lower" levels; demonstrating myopia about one's body, feelings, or relationships. Some of the spiritual teachers embroiled in enormously egocentric and myopic behavior toward others around power, money, and sex, demonstrate less interpersonal sensitivity and morality than people who are apparently operating on "lower" levels. One could also be operating on "lower" levels of the spectrum in certain areas while experiencing "higher" facets in other areas. I have worked with schizophrenics, for example, who struggle with the deepest kinds of self-disorders and have also at times perceived insights associated with "higher" levels of development on Wilber's model. They also have not treated others so capriciously and insensitively as the spiritual teachers who have manipulated others for their own benefit.

Because of the asymmetrical nature of human development, we all operate on different levels depending on which particular area of human experience and issues we are confronting. One could be quite aware of one's mental life and be disconnected from one's body—as some spiritual teachers and analysts are—or one could be attuned to one's bodymind and relatively unaware of one's interpersonal relations and impact on others. The complexity and multidimensionality of human experience and development is obscured by linear, hierarchical, developmental models.

Wilber's model does not achieve genuine integration. The attempted "marriage" of psychological and spiritual perspectives is an asymmetrical affair, in which Buddhism (and other contemplative disciplines) are actually viewed as superior to psychological thought, offering a privileged and true description of how humans really are. A tacit inequality is hidden underneath the nominal complementarity. There is an illusory rapprochement in which psychoanalysis and Buddhism are discreetly segregated to separate and unequal realms of reality and one is granted a special status. Whereas psychoanalysis usually pathologizes non-Western thought, transpersonal theorists sometimes romanticize it.

Within the transpersonal ranks, what I have recently termed *Orientocentrism* (1991; 1993; 1996), not Eurocentrism, tends to predominate. When Orientocentrism reigns, then Buddhism is romanticized and uncritically overvalued and psychoanalysis is disparaged or neglected (Rubin, 1996). The partiality of the Buddhist worldview then remains unexplored and unconscious and the value of psychoanalysis is then neglected.

None of these perspectives on the relationship between the Western psychotherapeutic and Eastern contemplative disciplines—the shotgun wedding, bridesmaid approach, or pseudo-complementary view—is wrong, but they reduce to a single factor or characterization what is a complex relationship with a multitude of dimensions. There are ways in which psychoanalysis and Buddhism are antithetical, complementary, *and* synergistic. But they are not simply any *one* of these all the time.

BEYOND EUROCENTRISM AND ORIENTOCENTRISM

"Truth" suggested Anatole France, "lies in the nuances." The nuances are exactly what the standard approaches to Western psychotherapies and Eastern contemplative disciplines neglect and eclipse. The relationship between Buddhism and psychoanalysis is more complex than the existing accounts suggest, forming not a singular pattern of influence, but rather resembling a heterogeneous mosaic composed of elements that are—depending on the specific topic—antithetical, complementary, and synergistic. For example, the goals of psychoanalysis and Buddhism are antithetical; the former focuses on strengthening one's sense of self, while the latter views such an enterprise as the very cause of psychological suffering. Meditative techniques for training attentiveness complement and enrich the psychoanalytic perspective on listening, while the psychoanalytic account of defense and resistance enhances the Buddhist understanding of interferences to meditation practice. Psychoanalytic and Buddhist strategies for facilitating transformation are, at least in some ways, synergistic.

The Eurocentrism of traditional Western psychology and the "Orientocentrism" of more recent writings on psychotherapeutic and contemplative disciplines both inhibit the creation of a contemplative therapeutics or an analytic meditation because they establish an intellectual embargo on commerce between Asian and Western psychology. An alternative perspective is necessary for the genuine insights of each tradition to emerge. In contrast to the Eurocentrism of psychoanalysis and the "Orientocentrism" of much recent discourse on psychoanalysis and Buddhism, I will be recommending a more egalitarian relationship in which there is mutual respect, the absence of denigration or deification, submission or superiority, and a genuine interest in what they could teach each other.

The egalitarian relationship I am pointing toward is not meant to be a complementarity that erases differences or subsumes either psychoanalysis into

Buddhism or Buddhism into psychoanalysis in the act of detecting similarities. Since the advent of deconstructionism, the limitations of searching only for commonalities between two systems of thought appear more problematic. It misses what is most interesting, which is how they are *different*, what the common denominators eclipse, and how both systems are incompatible and mutually enriching.

The relationship between psychoanalysis and Buddhism is not without disagreements, points of contention, and conflict. But such turmoil can be healthy insofar as it impedes orthodoxy, dogmatism, and premature closure and can promote cross-pollination and growth.

What I have discovered since approaching psychoanalysis and Buddhism in this way is that both traditions have a great deal of merit, but neither provides a complete picture of human nature, transformation, and liberation. Each offers a valuable and incomplete perspective—neglecting indispensable elements included in the other. For example, Buddhist models of health could teach psychoanalysis that there are possibilities for emotional well-being that far exceed the limits described by psychoanalytic models, while psychoanalytic accounts of defensive processes and resistance enhance the Buddhist understanding of the interferences to the meditation practice and the growth process. Since neither tradition has the last word on these issues, both traditions could be enriched if their respective insights were integrated into a more inclusive and encompassing perspective—which currently does not exist—that takes into account their respective contributions and elucidates their blind spots, while attempting to bolster their limitations.

Once it is recognized that both traditions are valuable and incomplete, two questions emerge: What does each tradition illuminate? What does each tradition omit? With these two questions in mind I shall examine psychoanalysis and Buddhism along three dimensions common to any psychological, religious, or philosophical system: their (1) view of reality and model of ideal health; (2) their view of self; and (3) their conception of the process designed to reach its stated goals, which includes a theory of the obstacles to the process (e.g., Shapiro, 1989). Before addressing these questions let me give a brief overview of Buddhism. This will provide a context for the subsequent discussion.

Buddhism is the codification of the insights about human psychology developed by Gotama Buddha in the sixth century B.C. in India in the course of his meditative investigations of his own mind. The English translation of the Sanskrit word *budh* is "awakened." Whereas his contemporaries were "asleep" in a kind of socially sanctioned trance, unaware of the actual texture of their experience, the Buddha was awakened to the realities of birth and death. Classical Buddhism could be considered an ethical psychology of optimal health and wellness, rather than a theistic religion. Primary emphasis is placed on one's learning about and transforming the mind and body through one's own direct experience as opposed to faith in or devotion to a deity.

I shall briefly describe some essential facets of Buddhist psychology and practice as a reference point for the subsequent discussion. The central teaching of Buddhism is the Four Noble Truths. This doctrine delineates the symptoms, diagnosis, and treatment plan for alleviating human suffering. The First Noble Truth of Buddhism presents the salient characteristic of human life, *dukkha*, a Pāli word for a bone out of socket and a wheel off its axle. Awryness and unsatisfactoriness are inherent features of the universe. Life is dislocated and out of joint. No human being, according to Buddhism, escapes some sort of suffering and discontent. The Second Noble Truth presents the cause of suffering: desire, attachment, and craving, that is, the tendency of the mind to grasp or cling. Suffering, from a Buddhist perspective, derives from our difficulty acknowledging a fundamental aspect of life: that everything is impermanent and transitory. We fall in love and anticipate an everlasting joy and ecstasy and then the honeymoon phase ends. We believe that our favorite psychoanalytic theory is the capital *T* Truth, and then clinical experience demonstrates that something else is more motivationally important for a particular patient. Suffering arises when we resist the flow of life and cling to people, events, and ideas as permanent. The doctrine of impermanence also includes the notion that there is no single self that is the subject of our changing experience. The Third Noble Truth is that suffering can be completely eradicated. The Fourth Noble Truth provides a treatment plan, the Noble Eightfold Path, to address suffering and achieve ideal health. The Eightfold Path includes such things as right understanding or accurate awareness of the nature of reality; right speech, or speaking truthfully and compassionately; right livelihood, or engaging in work that promotes rather than harms life; right mindfulness, or seeing things as they are.

The central investigative method of Buddhism is meditation: the careful, nonjudgmental attentiveness to whatever is occurring in the present moment. Meditation often conjures up a host of distorting associations from otherworldly asceticism to narcissistic navel-gazing. Meditation is not religious dogma, self-hypnosis, regression, or pathology (Alexander, 1931).[1] Rather, it is an incisive technique for what I have recently come to think of as *experience-near self-investigation*.

There are two main types of meditation, *concentrative* and *insight*. (The analytic meditation found in Tibetan Buddhism could be viewed as a form of insight meditation.) In concentrative meditation one focuses on a single object, such as the breath, with wholehearted attentiveness. It is an exclusive state of mind. One excludes everything but the object one is concentrating on. When one notices that one's attention has wandered, one returns one's attention to the breath.

Concentrative meditation cultivates a high degree of mental focus. In the traditional Buddhist practice developed by the Buddha, one often begins with concentrative meditation. When the attentiveness is developed and stabilized, then one practices insight meditation. In insight meditation, one attends without attachment or aversion to whatever thoughts, feelings, fantasies, or somatic sensations one is experiencing. The purpose of such a practice, contrary to popular misconception, is not to make anything happen, such as silencing or emptying the chattering mind—but to relate to whatever is happening in one's experience (no matter how painful) in a very different way than we ordinarily do—with tolerance and a sense of inner spaciousness. To those of you who have never meditated, being present to what we are experiencing without aversion or clinging might sound like the simplest task. Given our normal state of distractedness it is actually enormously difficult. It requires discipline and practice to train the mind to be really present. One can practice meditation either in a retreatlike setting or in one's daily life. An analyst could, for example, meditate between patients. And an analysand could meditate at home or before a therapy session.

In order to meditate one sits physically still in an upright position, and pays attention to the immediate flow of one's moment-to-moment experience, attending to the breathing process, silently noting the experience of inhalation and exhalation at the nostrils or abdomen. The effort is not to control the breathing, but to be attentive to it. Meditation proceeds in stages. At the beginning it is difficult to even pay attention for five consecutive seconds. As meditators know all too well, as we attempt to pay attention to our breathing we become distracted. Memories, daydreams, anxieties, and insights arise. We replay old experiences or plan new ventures. There is an apparently endless flood of thoughts, feelings, and fantasies. One of these usually catches our attention and before we know it we have traveled down a path toward something far removed from the present moment. We have, for example, constructed a scenario that has never actually happened, or we have replayed something that happened many years ago. We are oblivious to the present moment.

As soon as one notices that one's attention has wandered, one resumes attending to the breath. After a few seconds our attention wanders again. Like a child who reaches for one toy, becomes bored, and reaches for another, and then another, the mind keeps jumping from one thought, feeling, or fantasy to another. Noticing that we have been inattentive slowly cultivates increased attentiveness and focus.

As attentiveness increases and becomes more refined, we can use the developing capacity to focus the mind to observe the nature of our consciousness. Like a movie that is slowed down, we can see how one frame of our consciousness leads into another—how particular feelings condition specific reactions. One might become aware, for example, that one is making expansive plans after feeling diminished. Or one might realize that one gets angry at one's child when one feels scared about the child's safety.

As our awareness becomes clearer and more focused, we experience a sense of psychological spaciousness: we do not become as entangled in reactive patterns of feeling and thinking. When praised, one might allow oneself to bask in its warm glow instead of automatically devaluing it. Psychological resilience is cultivated: when we are unsettled or distracted we regain clarity more quickly. We can begin to notice within the first few seconds that we are unthinkingly attacking ourselves, thus avoiding getting emotionally hijacked and caught in a downward spiral of self-contempt and self-destructive behavior.

Meditation lessens distractedness, quiets the inner pandemonium, and concentrates the mind. Fostering what Horney (1987) termed, "wholehearted attention" (p. 18), meditation cultivates precisely the quality that Freud (1912/1958) recognized was essential to psychoanalytic listening, namely "evenly-hovering attention." Unfortunately, Freud identified this state of mind, but never offered positive recommendations for how to cultivate it. His writings focused on the interferences to this sort of listening, not what to do to actually facilitate it (Rubin, 1985). Meditation can also reduce self-criticism, aid psychoanalysts and patients in tolerating a greater range of affect without the need to deny or decomplexify it, and foster the capacity to relate to self and other with greater openness and fluidity (Rubin, 1998).

At first glance, it might seem that speaking of psychoanalysis and Buddhism in tandem is advocating a forced and unproductive association. After all, several fundamental disparities between them exist. Buddhism is a spiritual system developed 2,500 years ago in India for attaining enlightenment; psychoanalysis is a psychotherapeutic system arising in Europe in the late nineteenth century addressing psychopathology and mental illness. To attain enlightenment Buddhism recommends recognizing the illusoriness of our taken-for-granted sense of self as a unified, static, unchanging, autonomous entity. Most analysts—with the exception of Lacanians—claim that strengthening the self is crucial to the psychoanalytic process. Buddhism emphasizes the necessity of letting go of all desires and self-centeredness, while psychoanalytic self psychology maintains that ideals and goals play a crucial role in psychological well-being.

Similarities between both traditions, however, make a comparison between them intriguing. Both are concerned with the nature and alleviation of human suffering and each has both a diagnosis and "treatment plan" for alleviating human misery. The three other important things they share make a comparison between them possible and potentially productive. First, they are pursued within the crucible of an emotionally intimate relationship between either an analyst-analysand or a teacher-student. Second, they emphasize some similar experiential processes—evenly hovering attention and free association in psychoanalysis and meditation in Buddhism. Third, they recognize that obstacles impede the attempt to facilitate change—for example, the self-protective strategies analysts have termed resistance and defensive processes in psychoanalysis and the "hindrances," "fetters," and "impediments" in Buddhism. In the next section I shall examine their respective worldviews and vision of ideal mental health.

PSYCHOANALYTIC AND BUDDHIST WORLDVIEWS AND VISIONS OF IDEAL HEALTH

Psychoanalysis and Buddhism are *stories* about and *strategies* for addressing human life. Treating Buddhism and psychoanalysis as *narratives* rather than as sacred *tradition*—by which I mean sources of absolute wisdom that provide a blueprint for how to live in the present—may shift the way we think about tradition in general and each tradition in particular. Instead of viewing either of them as Received Truths, universally valid for all times and places, we might conceive of them as human creations arising in particular historical and sociocultural contexts. The value of psychoanalysis and Buddhism thus resides in how well they help people in the present age live with greater awareness, tolerance, and care.

Tradition has two meanings: it means to pass on *and* it means a *traitor*. Tradition can be enslaving as well as enabling. It may give one an identity and an orientation in the world, even as it limits one's horizon of vision and stifles one's development. It is inhibiting because it assimilates the present into the past and predisposes us to look toward the past to solve dilemmas in the present. "Tradition is important just as history is important, not as a vise to squeeze the present into but as a steppingstone to grow from" (Kramer & Alstad, 1993).

Once tradition is no longer viewed as *sacred*, its essential *revisability* becomes more crucial. Buddhism as well as psychoanalysis, needs to be open to feedback about its limits, and to change, evolve, and grow so that it can respond to the living moment.

Let us return to the stories psychoanalysis and Buddhism tell about human existence. Stories are made, as the historian and cultural critic Hayden White (1973) notes, "by including some events and excluding others, by stressing some and subordinating others" (p. 6, note 5). "Emplotment" is what White terms this process of exclusion, emphasis, and subordination in the interest of creating a particular kind of story. Literary theorist Northrop Frye (1957) has identified four archetypal genres or types of plot structures—tragedy, irony, romance, and comedy. Each genre offers a conception of the world that is particular and partial, highlighting and omitting certain facets of the world.

Psychoanalysis is underwritten by a "tragic" view of the universe, by which I mean, it recognizes the inescapable mysteries, dilemmas, conflicts, and afflictions pervading human existence (Schafer, 1976). Tragic implies an acknowledgment that time is irreversible and unredeemable; that is, humans are beings moving toward death, not rebirth; choices entail conflict and compromise; and suffering and loss are inevitable. Religious consolations are quixotic in the tragic vision. A Buddhist's claims about enlightenment, that is, achieving permanent and irreversible cessation of egoism, vanity, self-deception, and suffering, would seem illusory in a tragic vision.

Psychoanalytic views of health emerge directly from its tragic view of the world. Psychoanalysis is essentially a psychology of *illness* that focuses on what is wrong with people. It is no accident that health does not appear in the Standard Edition of Freud. Freud (Breuer & Freud, 1895/1958) claimed that the best humans can do is transform "neurotic misery" into "common human unhappiness." Psychoanalysis neglects wellness or exceptional states of health and functioning. Health, in the less arid and less depressogenic mood of contemporary psychoanalysis, involves self-integration and self-enrichment—the development of a cohesive, integrated, and multidimensional self and the cultivation of more complex and enriching modes of relatedness. But states of health, wellness, compassion, and wisdom that are central to Buddhism are neglected even in this view of health in contemporary psychoanalysis.

Buddhism adopts a "romantic" view of the world. "Romance" refers not to romantic involvement, infatuation with another, or idealized love, but rather to a view of the world that personal and familial conditioning can be transcended and that ultimate meaning on a grand design can be achieved. In the romantic vision, life is viewed as a quest involving the hero's or heroine's "transcendence of the world of experience, his [or her] victory over it, and his [or her] final liberation" (Frye, 1957, p. 8). Given the emphasis on the pervasiveness of suffering in Buddhism, it may seem odd to claim that Buddhism is emplotted in a romantic narrative. Buddhism's *diagnosis* of the human condition is tragic. But its *prognosis* is romantic. That Buddhism is a romantic narrative about human existence is demonstrated by its belief in the possibility of getting beyond one's psychological conditioning and experiencing transcendence and unqualified fulfillment.

The Buddhist view of health is enlightenment, which is defined differently in each of the three main Buddhist traditions. To Zen Master Dōgen, the founder of Sōtō Zen, enlightenment meant "intimacy with all things" (e.g., Rubin, 1996, p. 83). An esteemed Tibetan Buddhist monk-psychiatrist has described enlightenment as "no unconsciousness" (Lobsang Rapgay, personal communication). In classical Indian Buddhism, enlightenment is described as completely purifying the mind of "defilements," for example, greed, hatred, and delusion, which is said to result in the transcendence of psychological conditioning, the total cessation of suffering, and the presence of profound love and compassion. An enlightened meditator in that tradition is said to be without any trace of egoism and self-deceit, in a permanent and irreversible state of clarity, equanimity, loving-kindness, and wisdom (Rubin, 1996).

The times we live in demand both a sobering recognition of the fragility and tenuousness of our condition and a decisive and a progressive or visionary response to the enormous challenges that we collectively face. Optimism is a better strategy for change than pessimism (Joel Kramer, personal communication). Pessimism often breeds paralysis, which inhibits the motivation to change. Ungrounded optimism, however, can result in an illusory and disabling conception of reality.

With his notion of "pessimism of the intellect, optimism of the will," the Italian Marxist Antonio Gramsci (1971, p. 175, note 75) provides one possible way of theoretically integrating the stories psychoanalysis and Buddhism tell about reality and ideal health so that they might speak to the concerns of late-twentieth-century citizens confronting meaningless, disconnection, and self-alienation.

Psychoanalysis is a "hermeneutics of suspicion" (Ricoeur, 1970), by which I mean, it questions and often demystifies (or attempts to demystify) conventional and unquestioned assumptions about motives and meanings. Psychoanalysis can help Buddhists detect where they neglect unconsciousness and are being self-deceptive—where, for example, self-abasement in a Buddhist meditator can masquerade as spiritual asceticism. Psychoanalysis can temper Buddhism's unqualified belief in self-transcendence. Buddhist teachers are often presented as being beyond self-deceit. For those spiritual seekers who are experiencing an idealizing transference, such a possibility is enormously reassuring. The claim that a Buddhist teacher is without unconsciousness is about as likely as an analyst never experiencing countertransference again. Psychoanalysis teaches Buddhism that psychological conditioning and emotional strife cannot be transcended or eliminated. Psychoanalysis can enlighten Buddhists about where unconsciousness and transference and countertransference live in its theories, institutions, and practices. That Buddhism has pockets of unconsciousness is suggested by three things: (1) the residues of pathology found in enlightened meditators (e.g., Brown & Engler, 1986), (2) the rash of scandals in Buddhist communities, and (3) the nature of consciousness. Rorschach studies of enlightened meditators at Harvard suggested that these meditators had intrapsychic conflict, struggles with dependency, and needs for nurturance; fear and doubt regarding relationships; and fear of destructiveness (pp. 188–189). In recent years there have been numerous scandals in Buddhist communities involving Buddhist teachers from both Asia and the United States (those supposedly self-realized beings who are paragons of self-awareness, health, and virtue) illegally expropriating funds from the community and sexually exploiting nonconsenting female students (Boucher, 1988). Few people have confronted these scandals directly. Typically they are denied or rationalized. One way of attempting to do this and sidestep and ignore the disturbing implications of this immoral behavior is to assert that Western Buddhists have insufficiently internalized Buddhism and its ethics because they have grown up in a non-Buddhist culture. But the fact that these scandals involve indigenous Buddhists from Buddhist countries, as well as "homegrown" American Buddhist teachers, casts doubt on this explanation. These scandals among Buddhist teachers suggest that these teachers have areas of self-blindness and egocentricity. The nature of mental life also casts doubt on Buddhist claims about the permanent and irreversible transformation of consciousness and the eradication of conflict. Since mental life is fluid and partially unconscious there is no final resting place of complete self-awareness and inner peace. Conflict and suffering cannot be eliminated from mental life.

Buddhism's romanticism, its belief in radical possibilities of self-transformation, can temper the excessive pessimism in psychoanalysis' psychology of illness. The trace of the tragic psychology of illness in psychoanalysis emerges implicitly in its neglect of such topics as creativity, spirituality, and optimal mental and physical health.[2] The psychoanalytic view of health is, according to Buddhism, a suboptimal state of being; an arrested state of development.

Buddhism can challenge the limitations of a psychoanalytic view of self that is excessively self-centered and restrictive (Rubin, 1996; 1998). This egocentricity emerges when we consider relationships and morality in psychoanalysis. While a successful psychoanalytic treatment obviously fosters greater empathy for and attunement toward others, there is a tendency in psychoanalysis to cultivate an egocentric sense of self, in which one views the other as an *object* that does (or does not) fulfill the needs of the self, rather than a *subject* with its own separate values and needs. Analysts within the relational fold usefully highlight the relational nature of human development and treatment. But the legacy of a one-person, nonrelational view of patients emerges when moral issues arise in treatment. At such times the questions analysts ask often predispose patients to adopt a self-centered way of thinking about morality. If a patient is struggling, for example, with whether to take in his or her aging mother-in-law, I suspect many analysts would not tend to ask How would your decision impact on the network of relationships you are embedded in, but rather, What do you think and feel and need to do? The question assumes and pulls for an egocentric stance toward morality rather than a relational one (Rubin, 1998). Buddhism can encourage psychoanalysts to think about morality in a less self-centered way so that the needs and claims of the other as well as the self are given more weight. Buddhism can also teach psychoanalysis that the integrated self can foster a constricted way of living. The experience of meditation practice points toward a more uncongealed and unfettered sense of self and way of living.

Buddhism points toward possibilities for self-awareness, freedom, wisdom, and compassion that Western psychology in general, and psychoanalysis in particular, has never mapped. In other words, the Buddhist vision of health goes beyond the love and work Freud felt were essential to health, or the authenticity and creativity that were central to Winnicott's vision. It also goes beyond the humor, creativity, awareness of mortality, and wisdom that Kohut espoused, or the relational sensitivity and competence that interpersonally oriented clinicians value.

PSYCHOANALYTIC AND BUDDHIST APPROACHES TO THE MIND AND VIEWS OF THE SELF

Psychoanalysts and Buddhists examine self-experience from radically different vantage points that lead to very different conceptions of it. The meditative method involves a solitary individual paying careful, detailed attention to whatever he or she experiences in the present moment. I'd like to stress three facets of the meditative method: (a) the meditative process is a private, noncommunal[3] examination of one's consciousness; (b) one utilizes a microscopic lens in examining one's experience; (c) the meditative method, to borrow the language of linguistic theory, is synchronic, that is, one studies one's mind cross-sectionally—one examines oneself in the present moment rather than historically.

Examining one's immediate experience with the microscopic, "zoom lens" attentiveness cultivated by meditation lessens inner distractedness, quiets the inner pandemonium, and concentrates and focuses the mind. "Wholehearted attention" (Horney, 1987, p. 19) promotes greater receptivity and attunement to internal and interpersonal experiences. This fosters a clearer and more spacious perspective on one's experience. It can aid one in reducing self-criticism and tolerating a greater range of feelings without fleeing from them or getting lost in them. This is obviously of great benefit to both the spiritual seeker and the person in therapy. Psychoanalysts who meditate would have greater affect tolerance and would listen more attentively and empathetically to their patients. They might also have a less narcissistic relationship to their own favored theories, committing to particular ways of organizing the multidimensionality of the patient's material without being attached to the ultimate Truth of their conceptions. Analysts who meditate might thus hold their theories more lightly rather than tightly (Rubin,

1998). Patients who meditate would reduce self-criticism, tolerate a greater range of feelings, and relate to self and others with greater flexibility and openness.

The non- or antiself that Buddhism "discovers" is directly related to its way of investigating self-experience. When self-experience is examined microscopically one is predisposed to see the discontinuities in one's experience; an apparently unrelated flow of separate states of consciousness rather than a solidified self.

Meditative approaches to the mind are myopic as well as illuminating. They have blind spots that eclipse certain facets of self-experience. In exploring humans with a microscopic perspective, meditation promotes "near-sightedness," by which I mean, meditation neglects historical influences on the person arising from the distant past including the shaping role of unconsciousness, transference, and character. The essentially isolative and noncommunal aspect of the meditative experience ensures that there is a neglect of the kind of public dialogue, feedback, and validation that characterizes disciplines such as Western science and psychoanalysis. I say neglect because certain schools of Buddhism such as Zen offer a slight corrective for this with the emphasis on working with a meditation teacher. But the isolated nature of the meditative process still exists. And the Buddhist teacher does not systematically examine or work through transferences, relational enactments, and countertransference. These phenomena remain relatively unconscious in Buddhism.

There are several problems with the meditative method. First, Buddhism has an ambivalent relationship to emotional life. On the one hand, the meditative method counsels nonjudgmental attentiveness to whatever one experiences. This fosters greater openness to experience and helps the meditator access formerly unconscious thoughts, feelings, and fantasies. On the other hand, in some meditative traditions such as classical Buddhism, afflictive emotions, such as greed and hatred, are viewed, as "defilements." The goal of meditation, from this Theravāda perspective, is to "purify" the mind of "defilements." (In Tibetan Buddhism the goal is transformation). Trying to purify the mind establishes an aversive relationship to experience. Thought and emotions are viewed as obstacles that interfere with experiencing a deeper reality. Then we are unconsciously predisposed to devalue our experience; to wish to transcend or get rid of it, rather than determine its shaping power and learn what it might teach us. During the first meditative retreat I ever participated in, a wealth of formerly unconscious thoughts and feelings arose during my meditations. I asked one of the Buddhist teachers how to handle this material. "Don't do anything," he counseled me, "just let go of it."[4]

Letting go has its value when one is hypervigilant and overcontrolled, or caught in obsessive thinking or excessive worrying. But when we let go without investigating the meaning of our experience—like the Buddhist teacher recommended to me—then the unconscious ways that we conceive of and relate to ourselves and others can remain hidden. For patients who have experienced severe trauma, such as sexual abuse or physical torture, and who have "survived" by not registering or disconnecting from and segregating their experience, integrating formerly disavowed experiences seems crucial to the healing process. Prematurely detaching from such experiences makes it more difficult to understand some of the forces that motivate us in the present. Our lives are then restricted.

Psychoanalysis examines the self diachronically and "telescopically," that is, it investigates self-experience historically. It utilizes a more wide-angle lens, a more generalized and unfocused mode of introspection, to examine the way the distant past influences the present. When one studies the self in this way, one is predisposed to "see" a substantial agent shaped by his or her past. Understanding our past gives us a powerful tool to transform the self in the present. While Western psychotherapy goes deep into the roots of mental conditioning, exploring the past can become a way of evading responsibility for living in the present. The psychoanalytic approach to the mind can be "far-sighted," by which I mean that it may eclipse certain near-at-hand aspects of the self. In seeking the historical roots of our difficulties in living, psychoanalysis tends to neglect the shaping role of conditioning that arises in the present moment (e.g., Kramer & Alstad, 1993). This is, of course, less true of analysts who place more emphasis on the intersubjective nature of the analytic process and the "here-and-now" facets of the patient's material or the analytic relationship.

Eastern meditative disciplines teach us that psychological conditioning is caused by experiences in the present as well as the past. Meditative traditions alert us to what I would very provisionally term the "contemporaneous" unconscious, by which I mean, the unconsciousness that we experience in the present. When we speak of the "unconscious," we ordinarily refer to formative experiences from the past that we are unaware of in the present. But the unconscious is not only the repository of early traumas and forgotten memories. It is also being continually created in the present by selective processes of perception and attention that filter the way information is taken in and kept out. All perception involves a selective process. One of the most powerful unconscious selective filters involves keeping out of our awareness that which causes discomfort to us. An area of extreme discomfort for most of us is anything that clashes with our ideals and self-images (Kramer & Alstad, 1993). The contemporaneous unconscious, unlike Freud's dynamic unconscious derived from our distant, familial past, is created in the present moment. It is composed of whatever thought or conduct—for example, our self-centeredness, laxity, or competitiveness—that does not match our cherished views of ourselves. These phenomena are not registered by us in the present because they would make us feel bad about ourselves. Not seeing how we sometimes think and act in ways that contradict our values and ideals ensures that we do not feel badly about ourselves. It also ensures that these facets of our experience tend to be sequestered from our sense of ourselves and thus remain unconscious.

Buddhism teaches psychoanalysis that it also neglects what I have termed non-self-centered aspects of self-experience. Non-self-centered subjectivity is implicated in a wide range of adaptive behaviors ranging from art to psychoanalytic listening to intimacy. It is an unconstricted state of being, a non-self-preoccupied, non-self-annulling immersion in whatever one is presently doing. There is heightened attentiveness, focus, and clarity. Action/response is unconstrained by self-concern, thought, or conscious effort and restrictive self-identifications and boundaries are eroded. This facilitates a greater sense of freedom and an inclusiveness of self-structure. When excessive self-preoccupation wanes—as may occur, for example, while one is deeply immersed in playing a musical instrument, watching an engrossing cultural event, playing with a child, or making love—one may experience a heightened sense of living.

Neither psychoanalysis nor Buddhism recognizes that there is no immaculate perception. The self (or anti/no-self) that they "discover" is intimately related to how they investigate it. The telescopic approach to self-experience employed by many psychoanalysts yields a substantial self shaped by a particular history. Examining self-experience microscopically as Buddhist meditation does, reveals the fluid and unfolding nature of identity, the way we are shaped anew, moment-by-moment.

We need a bifocal conception of self that realizes that the self is both a substantial, embodied, historical, agent as psychoanalysis suggests, that perceives, chooses, and acts, and a fluid, uncongealed process that is created afresh by changing states of consciousness in the present. Each conception of self is useful in particular circumstances. At certain times of the day when we have to evaluate among conflicting values and choose a particular moral course we need to fixate the self and see it as a substantial agent with a history and a hierarchy of values. When listening to a patient in therapy, observing art, or appreciating nature, we sometimes need to unconstrict our sense of self and see it as an open and unfolding process.

PSYCHOANALYTIC AND BUDDHIST PATHS

In this final section of my paper I shall discuss the relationship of the psychoanalytic and Buddhist approaches to change. The process of change in psychoanalysis involves the illumination, transformation, and expansion of the patient's subjective world (Stolorow et al., 1987). Psychoanalysis has identified three dimensions that are central to change, namely, cognitive insight, the affective bond to the analyst, and the integration of formerly dissociated experience (e.g., Friedman, 1978). I shall use this model as a point of reference in organizing the vast yet important topic of how psychoanalysis and Buddhism conceive of change and how each discipline might help or hinder people in their quest for self-transformation.

Since most of us may be more familiar with the psychoanalytic process than the Buddhist one, I shall devote more attention here to Buddhism. Buddhism helps and hinders one in the process of change. Meditation, as I suggested earlier, can foster the cultivation of self-introspective abilities. Meditation practice helped a woman I shall call Maureen, a long-term practitioner of Buddhist meditation, cultivate enhanced self-observational capacities—it increased her attentiveness and self-awareness. Meditation practice aided Maureen in becoming unusually attentive to nuances of her inner life such as latent motives, formerly disavowed intentions, and subtleties in the way she related to me. When she discussed relationships, for example, she demonstrated great insight into the possible patterns of interaction and the hidden motives and meanings that might be operative. This enabled her to track her reactions to me and others and often detect inchoate perceptions and fantasies. While meditating, for example, she became aware of formerly disavowed feelings of betrayal at the way her parents "gaslighted" or betrayed her and covered it up.

Not only did her receptivity to inner and interpersonal life increase, her attitude to her experience changed. The meditative spirit of attending to experience without judgment or aversion gradually replaced the self-critical stance exemplified by her characterologically contemptuous father. This led to greater affect tolerance. She had a highly developed capacity for tolerating and living in and through a range of affects without having to foreclose or simplify either the confusion or the complexity. She was able, for example, to examine such things as ambivalence and anger without criticizing herself, reducing the complexity of these experiences, or clamoring after premature understanding. As she accepted herself more, emotional warts and all, she developed deeper acceptance of others.

Cognitive insight can develop as a result of meditation. Maureen gained greater insight into the formerly unconscious disappointment, deprivation, and rage she felt toward her critical and emotionally unavailable parents. Her cognitive insight about the way she had subverted what she called her "voice" so as to remain connected to and not threaten the fragile emotional tie to her parents emerged more clearly for her because of her refined capacity in meditation to attend to her experience with nonjudgmental awareness. As patients who meditate develop the capacity to view their own experience—even troubling facets such as deprivation and shame—with understanding and acceptance—they can more easily integrate formerly disavowed experience.

Meditation also aids the analyst in a variety of ways. Listening to ourselves and our analysands is both the essential tool of psychoanalytic inquiry and the foundation of psychoanalytic technique. And meditation deeply aids analytic listening. The analyst who meditates develops greater self-introspective abilities. Meditation fosters greater access to formerly unconscious material as well as greater receptivity to subtle mental and physical phenomena. The analyst notices thoughts, feelings, fantasies, images, and bodily sensations that he or she is ordinarily unaware of (Rubin, 1996). To cite one example among many: while involved in intensive meditation practice, I have much greater access to and clarity about my own dream life, including frequent occurrences of lucid dreaming.

Meditation practice also promotes greater tolerance for whatever we experience, including affect. By developing the ability to open to the texture of experience with less attachment and aversion, meditation aids the therapist in more skillfully handling affect. The analyst can literally sit with and through a greater range of affect without the need to shield him- or herself by premature certainty or intellectualized formulations. There is then a greater tolerance for complexity, ambiguity, and uncertainty. There is less pressure to know and to do. Not-knowing is then a more comfortable state of being for the analyst. The analyst experiences more "beginner's mind." "In the beginner's mind there are many possibilities," notes Shunryu Suzuki (1970), "in the expert's mind there are few" (p. 21). The analyst who has a beginner's mind takes less for granted, is more receptive to the unknown, and more capable of being surprised.

The analyst's creativity is then enhanced. The analyst is less filled with preconceptions about treatment, the therapeutic relationship, or life in general. The analyst is freer to question, wonder, and doubt. The analyst relates to analysands less habitually, repetitively, and self-centeredly. Such an analyst also has a deeper respect for differences, and is more tolerant of a wider range of internal and interpersonal phenomena. This creates an analytic environment that decreases the patient's vulnerability and shame.

By aiding the therapist in tolerating a wider range of experiences and reactions without fear or judgment, these experiences can be utilized as grist for the self-investigative mill. This opens up unexpected possibilities for learning and growth.

Meditation also fosters what Buddhists term *nonattachment*, a nongrasping state of mind in which one hold one's viewpoints less tightly. The nonattachment that meditation practice develops also cultivates greater freedom in the analyst. Meditation practice has personally helped me adopt a more fluid relationship to the theories that I utilize to organize and make sense of the complex and over-determined clinical actualities. It has helped me employ theoretical and clinical

maps that I find illuminating while simultaneously recognizing their ultimate pro-
visionality and the inevitability of continually revising them. In cultivating perceptual acuity, attentiveness, and nonattachment, meditation fosters awareness of,
and deautomatization from, previously habitual patterns (Deikman, 1982); including some of the unresolved issues from one's own analysis that create difficulty or conflict for the clinician in conducting therapy.

Buddhism fosters the process of change in another way. It widens the field
of psychoanalytic practice to include our lives outside the session. The Buddhist
eightfold path, for example, right speech, or the effort to speak in a way that is
truthful and useful (eschewing gossip, backbiting, and so forth) and right livelihood, work that enriches rather than detracts from human life, emphasizes that
the stage of our practice is, to borrow from Shakespeare, all the world—including
and beyond the therapist's office. Buddhism emphasizes that everything in daily
life—from the way we speak to our family and colleagues to the work we do and
the values we live by—is grist for the meditative mill. And Buddhism encourages
us to give morality and values a more central role in our lives.

Buddhism hinders as well as facilitates the change process. It interferes with
it in several ways. While meditative methods make the thoughts, feelings, and
fantasies more available to us for scrutiny, the Buddhist stance of detaching from
experience rather than exploring its *meaning*, discourages us from using what we
have discovered during our meditations to study ourselves. We feel more when we
meditate, but we do not do enough with it. Buddhism, to cite one possible example from many, can foster lucid dreaming even as it encourages the dreamer to detach or let go of the dream rather than exploring and elucidating its meaning and
significance in one's life. Psychoanalysis can aid us in getting more mileage from
the inner experience that meditation so wonderfully makes available to us. So
after becoming aware of our inner experience through meditation, we then need
to utilize psychoanalytic methods to investigate what we have become aware of.
And psychoanalysis teaches Buddhism that it is crucial for self-transformation
that one explore areas in one's life that meditation neglects, such as the shaping
role of one's past, unconsciousness and character, our views of self and others, our
strategies of self-protection, and the nature and quality of our relationships.

Buddhism occurs in the context of an emotionally intense relationship between a teacher and student. But neither the student nor the teacher reflect on
interpersonal dynamics, transference and countertransference, or relational enactments. And it is not a relationship that is designed to illuminate and transform
the patient's characteristic ways of relating to self and other. The Buddhist teacher
might relate to the student in such a way as to challenge the student's internalized
and limiting beliefs about herself and others. But the absence of a relationship

designed to investigate and illuminate the patient's recurrent ways of relating to self and the world makes it impossible to understand and transform the patient's transference or work through archaic self-defects.

By systematically analyzing transference phenomena and relational reenact-ments, psychoanalysis can illuminate ways of being that may either go unnoticed or be submerged in Buddhism—such as a student's idealization of his or her teach-ers and his or her concomitant self-submissiveness (e.g., Tart & Deikman, 1991). In Buddhism, this dynamic may remain unexamined, and the student's self-devaluation and deferentiality may never get resolved and may play itself out in various other relationships.

As the crucible for the reemergence of archaic transferences, the psycho-analytic relationship can aid in the process of aborted development being re-cognized, reinstated, and worked through. Since it omits the crucial task of self-*construction*, Buddhism's model of working with self-experience is a necessary but incomplete way of healing the fault line that some of the people we work with struggle with. Such people need self-creation and self-*amplification* as well as self-*deconstruction*. When one's life is haunted by absence, emptiness, and virtuality, not misplaced desires and attachments, one needs to build a *new* life based on one's relational and avocational values and ideals, not simply detach from a bad one—one based on attachments to illusory notions of self and reality. Working through a self-void and building a meaningful life is very different from letting go of illusory conceptions of self. Such a person would thus need psychoanalysis as well as meditation in order to work through their directionlessness and build a meaningful life.

Rudyard Kipling believed, perhaps like many of us, that "East is East and West is West and never the twain shall meet." In *East, West*, a recent collection of his stories, Salman Rushdie (1994) offered an opposite perspective: "I too have ropes around my neck, I have them to this day pulling me this way and that, East and West, the nooses tightening, commanding choose, choose . . . Ropes I do not choose between you . . . I choose neither of you and both. Do you hear? I refuse to choose." "East" may be East and "West" may be West, but in my experience, if we are open to what psychoanalysis and meditation might teach us and allow the twain to meet, then our lives and the lives of those we work with, might well be transformed and greatly enriched.[5]

NOTES

1. This is, of course, not true of analysts such as Jung, Horney, Kelman, Fromm, Roland, Coltart, Finn, Cooper, Magid, and myself, among others, who discerned value in Eastern contemplative practices (e.g., Rubin, 1996).

2. There are exceptions to this claim. Winnicott, Milner, Gedo, Phillips, and Oremland, among others, have been interested in the nature of creativity. But there is a pervasive tendency in psychoanalysis to view this topic pathologically and reductionistically. Freud's study of Leonardo Da Vinci was termed, for example, a pathography. In recent years there has also been a greater interest in spirituality in psychoanalysis. But again this is an exception rather than the rule.

3. Sangha, the community of like-spirited spiritual seekers, is central to Buddhism. Nonetheless, meditation practice, even done in a Buddhist community (or with a group of Buddhists outside a community or retreat context), involves paying attention to one's own *inner* experience, which is an essentially isolative process and practice.

4. This may be less true of Zen, in which there seems to be a greater emphasis on experiencing rather than transcending experience. If one cannot let go of aversive experience, such as physical pain in Zen practice, then one is encouraged to be the pain. Many meditators have experienced the way pain shifts or evaporates when one does this. But this strategy may not work as well with certain experiences that our patients struggle with such as intense self-criticism or severe trauma. The Dalai Lama was shocked to hear that Americans suffered from "self-directed contempt" (p. 196). He told a group of American scientists and mental health professionals that this experience was absent from Tibetan culture (Goleman, 1997).

5. This is adapted from an earlier work (Rubin, 1996, 1998). The first and final section introduces new material and extends this previous work. This paper was enriched by the thoughtful feedback of Barry Magid, Uwe Gielen, Susan Rudnick, and Seth Segall.

REFERENCES

Alexander, F. (1931). Buddhistic training as an artificial catatonia: The biological meaning of psychological occurrences. *Psychoanalytic Review, 18,* 129–145.

Boorstein S. (Ed.). (1980). *Transpersonal psychotherapy.* Palo Alto, CA: Science and Behavior Books.

Boss, M. (1965). *A psychiatrist discovers India.* London: Oswald Wolff.

Boucher, S. (1988). *Turning the wheel: American women creating the new Buddhism.* San Francisco, CA: Harper and Row.

Breuer, J. & Freud, S. (1958). *Studies on hysteria.* In J. Strachey (Ed. and Trans.), *The standard edition of the complete psychological works of Sigmund Freud,* Vol. 2, (pp. 255–305). London: Hogarth Press and the Institute of Psychoanalysis. Original work published in 1895.

Brown, D. & Engler, J. (1986). The stages of mindfulness meditation: A validation Study. Part II: Discussion. In K. Wilber, J. Engler, & D. Brown (Eds.), *Transformation of consciousness: Conventional and contemplative perspectives on development* (pp. 17–51). Boston: Shambhala.

Burtt, E. (1955). *The teachings of the compassionate Buddha.* New York: New American Library.

Deatherage, G. (1975). The clinical use of 'mindfulness' meditation in short-term psychotherapy. *Journal of Transpersonal Psychology, 7,* 133–144.

Deikman, A. (1982). *The observing self: Mysticism and psychotherapy.* Boston: Beacon Press.

Epstein, M. (1995). *Thoughts without a thinker.* New York: Basic Books.

Engler, J. (1984). Therapeutic aims in psychotherapy and meditation: Developmental stages in the representation of self. *Journal of Transpersonal Psychology, 16,* 25-61.

Finn, M. (1992). Transitional space and Tibetan Buddhism: The object relations of meditation. In M. Finn & J. Gartner (Eds.), *Object relations theory and religion* (pp. 87-107). Westport, CT: Praeger Press.

Fromm, E., Suzuki, D.T., & Martino, R. (Eds.). (1960). *Zen Buddhism and psychoanalysis.* New York: Harper and Row.

Freud, S. (1958). Recommendations to physicians practicing psychoanalysis. In J. Strachey (Ed. and Trans.), *The standard edition of the complete psychological works of Sigmund Freud,* Vol. 12, (pp. 228-226). London: Hogarth Press and the Institute of Psychoanalysis. Original work published in 1912.

Friedman, L. (1978). Trends in the psychoanalytic theory of treatment. *Psychoanalytic Quarterly, 47,* 524-567.

Frye, N. (1957). *Anatomy of criticism: Four essays.* Princeton, NJ: Princeton University Press.

Goleman, D. (1997). *Healing emotions: Conversations with the Dalai Lama on mindfulness, emotions, and health.* Boston: Shambhala.

Gordon, J. (1987). *The golden guru: The strange journey of Bhagwan Shree Rajneesh.* Lexington, KY: The Stephen Greene Press.

Gramsci, A. (1971). *Selections from the prison notebooks.* (Q. Hoare & G. Smith, Eds. & Trans.), New York: International Universities Press.

Hoffman, Y. (1975). *The sound of one hand clapping.* New York: Basic Books.

Horney, K. (1945). Our inner conflicts. New York: Norton.

Horney, K. (1987). *Final lectures.* New York: Norton.

Jung, C. G. (1958). Psychology and religion: West and East. In: *Collected Works,* Vol. 11. Princeton, NJ: Princeton University Press.

Kelman, H. (1960). Psychoanalytic thought and eastern wisdom. In J. Ehrenwald (Ed.), *The History of psychotherapy.* New York: Jason Aronson. 1976.

Kornfield, J. (1977). *Living Buddhist masters.* Santa Cruz, CA: Unity Press.

Kramer, J. & Alstad, D. (1993). *The guru papers: Masks of authoritarian power.* Berkeley, CA: Frog Press.

Matthiessen, P. (1987). *Nine-headed dragon: Zen journals 1969-1982.* Boston, MA: Shambhala.

Ricoeur, P. (1970). *Freud and philosophy: An essay on interpretation.* New Haven, CT: Yale University Press.

Rinzler, C. & Gordon, B. (1980). Buddhism and psychotherapy. In: G. Epstein (Ed.), *Studies in non-deterministic psychology* (pp. 52-69). New York: Human Sciences Press.

Roland, A. (1988). *In search of self in India and Japan: Toward a cross-cultural psychology.* Princeton, NJ: Princeton University Press.

Rubin, J. B. (1985). Meditation and psychoanalytic listening. *Psychoanalytic Review, 72,* 599-612.

Rubin, J. B. (1991). The clinical integration of Buddhist meditation and psychoanalysis. *Journal of Integrative and Eclectic Psychotherapy, 10,* 173-181.

Rubin, J. B. (1992). Psychoanalytic treatment with a Buddhist meditator. In: M. Finn & J. Gartner (Eds.), *Object relations theory and religion: clinical applications* (pp. 87-107). Westport, CT: Praeger.

Rubin, J. B. (1993). Psychoanalysis and Buddhism: Toward an integration. In: G. Stricker & J. Gold (Eds.), *Comprehensive textbook of psychotherapy integration* (pp. 249–266). New York: Plenum Press, pp. 249–266.

Rubin, J. B. (1996). *Psychotherapy and Buddhism: Toward an integration*. New York: Plenum Press.

Rubin, J. B. (1998). Psychoanalysis is self-centered. In: *A psychoanalysis for our time. Exploring the blindness of the seeing I*. New York: New York University Press.

Rushdie, S. (1994). *East, West*. New York: Pantheon Books.

Said, E. (1979). *Orientalism*. New York: Vintage Books.

Schafer, R. (1976). *A new language for psychoanalysis*. New Haven, CT: Yale University Press.

Schneider, K. (1987). The deified self: A 'centaur' response to Ken Wilber and the transpersonal movement. *Journal of Humanistic Psychology, 27*, 196–216.

Searles, H. (1979). The function of the analyst's realistic perceptions of the analyst in delusional transference. In: *Countertransference and related subjects* (pp. 196–227). NY: International Universities Press. Original work published in 1972.

Shapiro, D. (1989). Judaism as a journey of transformation: Consciousness, behavior, and society. *Journal of Transpersonal Psychology, 21*, 13–59.

Smith, H. (1986). *The religions of man*. New York: Harper and Row.

Stolorow, R., Brandchaft, B., & Atwood, G. (1987). *Psychoanalytic treatment: An intersubjective approach*. Hillsdale, NJ: The Analytic Press.

Suler, J. (1993). *Contemporary psychoanalysis and eastern thought*. Albany, NY: State University of New York Press.

Suzuki, S. (1970). *Zen mind, beginner's mind*. New York: Weatherhill.

Tart, C. (1975) (Ed.). *Transpersonal psychologies*. New York: Harper and Row.

Tart, C. & Deikman, A. (1991). Mindfulness, spiritual seeking and psychotherapy. *Journal of Transpersonal Psychology, 23*, 29–52.

Walsh, R. & Vaughan, F. (Eds.) (1980). *Beyond ego: Transpersonal dimensions in psychotherapy*. Los Angeles, CA: Jeremy Tarcher.

Welwood, J. (Ed.) (1979). *Meeting of the ways: Explorations in east/west psychology*. New York: Schocken.

White, H. (1973). *Metahistory: historical imagination in nineteenth century Europe*. Baltimore, MD: Johns Hopkins University Press.

Wilber, K. (1979). Psychologia perennis. In: J. Welwood (Ed.), *Meeting of the ways: Explorations in east/west psychology*. New York: Schocken.

Wilber, K. (1986). The developmental spectrum and psychopathology; Part I, Stages and types of pathology. *Journal of Transpersonal Psychology, 16*, 75–118.

Wilber, K., Engler, J., & Brown, D. (Eds.) (1986). *Transformations of consciousness: conventional and contemplative perspectives on development*. Boston, MA: Shambhala.

Yokoi, Y. (Ed. and Trans.) (1976). *Zen Master Dōgen: An introduction to selected writings*. New York: Weatherhill.

CHAPTER 3

The Buddha Teaches an Attitude, Not an Affiliation

Belinda Siew Luan Khong

> There are some who believe that Buddhism is so lofty and sublime a system that it cannot be practised by ordinary men and women in this workaday world of ours. . . . However noble and pure Buddhism may be, it would be useless to the masses of mankind, if they could not follow it in their daily life. . . . But if you understand the spirit of Buddhism correctly (and not only its letter), you can surely follow and practice it while living the life of an ordinary [human being].
>
> —Rahula, *What the Buddha Taught*

Occasionally, I am asked, "Am I a Buddhist"? My reply is usually, "No, I am not a Buddhist, but I am informed by the Buddha's teachings." To me, this is not a question of semantics, since one of the popular misconceptions concerning the Buddha's teachings is that to understand and practice his teachings, one has to adopt the Buddhist religion. That is, one has to follow the beliefs, dogmas, traditional observances and rituals that belong identifiably to the religion of Buddhism as opposed to those followed by Christians, Moslems, or Hindus (see Batchelor, 1997; Rahula, 1987). One reason for this misconception is that most people understand the form of Buddhism better than its substance. I believe that the Buddha teaches an attitude rather than an affiliation, and that this state of mind can be acquired by any individual irrespective of his or her race, culture or religious orientation.

In this chapter, I propose to examine some of the Buddha's teachings and explicate the kind of attitude that he promotes. The discussion focuses on the eightfold path and, in particular, meditation. I explore the practice of mindfulness in Buddhist meditation and its pivotal role in the Buddha's teachings. Finally, I examine the therapeutic application of these ideas and their contributions to psychology. Anecdotes and clinical vignettes are discussed to illustrate the applications and contributions.

AN ATTITUDE NOT AN AFFILIATION

What is the attitude that the Buddha promotes? It is one of acceptance and letting go, and is grounded on "seeing, knowing and understanding" (Rahula, 1978, p. 6). That this kind of attitude is developed through personal effort and taking personal responsibility rather than through relying on an external source or an orientation is made explicit in the Buddha's advice for people "not to depend on others for your salvation [but to] develop your self-confidence to gain it" (Dīgha-Nikāya. II.100, *Treasure of the Dhamma*, 1994, p. 290).

This approach is best illustrated by the story of the young man who left home to become a monk based on what he had heard about the Buddha's reputation. One day he encountered a stranger who delivered a discourse on truth that he found convincing and accepted. It was only subsequently that the recluse realized that the stranger was in fact the Buddha (Majjhima Nikāya, 140, cited in Rahula, 1978, p. 6). The story demonstrates that according to the Buddha, to understand the truth, it is irrelevant whether the teacher is the Buddha or that the teachings originated from him. As Rahula (1978) explains, what is important is seeing and understanding the truth for oneself, rather than following a set of beliefs based on "blind faith."

Rahula (1978) notes that the human qualities and emotions that the Buddha encourages such as love, charity, compassion, tolerance, and patience are not sectarian as they are neither Christian, Buddhist, Hindu, nor Moslem. They come from developing the right attitude and not the right affiliation. In this context, Abhinyana's (2000) exegesis of the term "Catholic" is instructive. According to Abhinyana, if we label a person a Catholic, using this term in its noun-form, we are simply describing a follower of a particular religion. On the other hand, if we use the term *catholic* in its adjective form, such as having "a catholic point-of-view," it means possessing a "universal, liberal, broad, wide-open" attitude (p. 20). Citing Mother Theresa as an example, Abhinyana notes that she is a catholic in its adjective-form, for labeling her a saint or a devil would not change what she is. Similarly, being a buddhist in its adjective-form is the attitude that the Buddha encourages.

ATTITUDE AND EXPERIENCE

As pointed out earlier, the attitude that the Buddha promotes can be developed through knowing and seeing, and not just believing. What this means is that the Buddha encourages insight and understanding based on direct experience rather than from intellectualizing or following certain beliefs.

The crux of this approach is captured in his famous discourse to the members of the Kālāma Clan, in which he encourages his audience not to accept anything on mere reports, including religious texts, on theoretical considerations, from external appearances, or even from the consideration that it is disseminated by a teacher. Instead he counsels them to accept and follow things based on their own experience: "When you know for *yourselves* [italics added] that certain things are unwholesome (*akusala*), wrong and bad, then give them up. . . . And when you know *for yourselves* [italics added] that certain things are wholesome (*kusala*) and good, then accept them and follow them" (Anguttara Nikāya, I.187, *Treasure of the Dhamma*, 1994, p. 292). According to Rinpoche Tarthang Tulku (1990), Buddhism is about understanding reality and verifying this understanding through our own experiences, or as one of his students paraphrases it succinctly, "Studying myself not a religion" (quoted in Tarthang Tulku, 1990, p. 11).

THE ATTITUDE PROMOTED IN THE BUDDHA'S TEACHINGS
The Eightfold Path

The importance of acquiring insight and understanding through direct experience is a common theme in many of the Buddha's teachings, and is especially emphasized in the fourth noble truth (the eightfold path). According to Batchelor (1997), while the term "Buddhism" suggests another belief system, "dharma practice" points to a course of action. Batchelor notes that the eightfold path is neither particularly religious nor spiritual as it encompasses everything we do and signifies "an authentic way of being in the world" (p. 10). The eightfold path comprises the following (Dhammananda, 1987, p. 90; Dhamma, 1997):

Wisdom	*Morality*	*Mental Culture*
1. Right Understanding	3. Right Speech	6. Right Effort
2. Right Thought	4. Right Action	7. Right Mindfulness
	5. Right Livelihood	8. Right Concentration

In this path, the Buddha enunciates a set of practices that the individual can adopt to overcome his or her own suffering. The word *right* (*sammā*) used to qualify each factor of the path does not imply moral judgments concerning sin and guilt, or arbitrary standards imposed externally. The path is neither hierarchical nor prescriptive, as the Buddha does not dictate what is right or wrong. Instead he speaks of skillful (wholesome) or unskillful (unwholesome) actions, and explains that the path merely serves as a guideline or a "raft" for helping people take personal responsibility (Majjhima Nikāya, 1.260, *Treasure of the Dhamma,* 1994, p. 69). As Thich Nhat Hahn (1998) explains, through our own awareness and understanding, we ascertain what is right (beneficial) or wrong (nonbeneficial). Hence the word "right" is synonymous with "harmonious," that is being in harmony within and without (Punnaji, 1978, p. 46). From this perspective, it can be said that the eightfold path grounds our mental attitude. Adopting the right attitude frees one's mind from remorse and helps one to acquire peace of mind. Or in layman's term, "helps one to be comfortable with oneself, one's thoughts, speech, actions, etc."

The kind of attitude that the Buddha promotes can be illustrated in relation to action. Action is commonly perceived as involving activity, that is "doing something," as opposed to exercising restraint. The Buddha recommends that each of us take the responsibility to cultivate an attitude (right understanding, right thought) of seeing what is an appropriate response (right action, right speech, right livelihood) in each situation. Most of us are familiar with the power of speech to hurt or to soothe. If one refrains from using unskillful speech, notwithstanding the opportunity to do so, one is said to be practicing right speech and right action. Similarly, there will be occasions when friendly and meaningful advice are helpful and other occasions when keeping "noble silence" is appropriate (Dhamma, 1997). Hence depending on the circumstances, restraint is not passivity or indifference, but right action. This is similar to the Taoist idea of "*wei-wu-wei,*" that is, action through nonaction (Khong & Thompson, 1997). The litmus test of what is "right" is the psychological impact it has on your and the recipient's mental well-being.

Ajahn Sumedho explains the psychological effect of adopting this kind of attitude:

> If you do something kind, generous and compassionate, the memory makes you happy, and if you do something mean and nasty, you have to remember that. You try to repress it, run away from it, get caught up in all kinds of frantic behaviour—that's the kammic result. (quoted in Snelling, 1992, p. 70)

The main thrust of the Buddha's teachings is to help the individual to develop *respond-ability,* that is the ability to be aware of what unique response is called for in each unique situation and to act accordingly (Khong, 1999). The idea is to let go of "what should be" (Trungpa, 1988, p. 14) and to respond spontaneously to changing circumstances. In order to cultivate this attitude, self-awareness and self-understanding are invaluable. According to the Buddha, through the practice of meditation or mental culture, the individual can develop wisdom and insight, that is, the clarity of mind to see things as they really are.

Meditation

The mental culture referred to in the eightfold path is now popularly associated with the practice of meditation. However, the word *meditation* itself is not used in classical Buddhist texts (Rahula, 1978). This omission is not accidental, for as Epstein (1995) points out, what is important in Buddhist psychology is not the formal practice of meditation, but the cultivation of "certain critical qualities of the mind" (p. 105), such as clarity and openness. According to the Buddha, the mind is naturally pure, but becomes clouded by our psychological responses and emotions. If the mind is trained to become clear and calm, we can learn to overcome our own suffering.

In mental culture, two types of meditation are recommended, namely tranquillity (*samatha*) meditation and insight (*vipassanā*) meditation. While both forms of meditation are practiced today, tranquillity meditation, more commonly referred to as concentration meditation, is not unique to Buddhism. This kind of meditation is taught in many ancient Indian traditions that encourage the individual to seek calmness and equanimity through concentration. What is unique to Buddhism is insight meditation (H.H. the XIV Dalai Lama, 1997; Rahula, 1978). Although the Buddha promotes tranquillity meditation as a means of enabling the mind to quiet down, he emphasizes the importance of insight meditation in helping people to understand reality and deal with their own problems. Rubin (1996) notes that the Buddha's teachings pertaining to meditation have been preserved relatively intact in the Therevāda tradition, which has vipassanā meditation as its core practice. The present discussion focuses on insight meditation as practiced in this school.

In the development of mental culture, the eightfold path points to the importance of maintaining right effort, right concentration, and right mindfulness. These three factors represent the kind of attitude that is conducive to meditation. Right effort involves applying the right amount of effort to prevent negative thoughts from arising and developing positive thoughts. In this context, effort does not suggest willed action, but rather maintaining moment-to-moment awareness and an open attitude toward changing sensations and experiences (Bodhi, 1994). As Dhammananda (1987) explains, meditation, like love, is a spontaneous experience, and cannot be forced or acquired through strenuous effort.

Right concentration involves sustaining attention on one object to the exclusion of others. In Buddhist meditation, there are about forty traditional objects of meditation, the most commonly employed being the breath and loving-kindness (mettā). By not allowing other stimuli to compete for attention, this practice of "one-pointedness" reduces the mind's tendency to ruminate and enables it to calm down (Buddhaghosa, 1956; Goleman, 1984). Coupled with right effort, right concentration helps the meditator to experience a state of tranquillity and equanimity.

When the mind is calm, there is space for the development of insight or vipassanā. Vipassanā means learning to see clearly (Young, 1994). The important ingredients of insight (vipassanā) meditation are mindfulness and observation (Rahula, 1978). The cultivation of right mindfulness is so important to the Buddha's teachings, that it has been described as the "heart of Buddhist meditation" (Nyanaponika, 1992). As such, I propose to deal with mindfulness at some length.

Unlike in tranquillity meditation, where the practitioner is encouraged to let go of thoughts that impinge, with insight meditation, the meditator is encouraged to be mindful of whatever enters the mind. Nyanaponika (1992) explains mindfulness as "the bare and exact registering of the object [of attention]" (p. 32). Normally, we infuse what we perceive with subjective judgments and associative thinking. Mindfulness helps us to silence this internal dialogue, and to "see things as they really are," without labeling them good or bad.

Buddhist practice is based on the four foundations of mindfulness (Satipatthāna Sutta, Treasure of the Dhamma, 1994, p. 277). This means developing continuous awareness of the (1) body (e.g., posture, breath) (2) feelings (whether pleasant, unpleasant or neutral) (3) mind (thoughts, emotions, intentions, volitions, and so forth) and (4) mental objects (mental phenomena relevant to awakening, such as the seven factors of enlightenment and the five hindrances to meditation) (Goleman, 1984; Nyanaponika, 1995). According to the Buddha, if we are mindful of each phenomenon as it arises, we can learn to differentiate, for example, between the injured arm and its damaged condition (body), the unpleasant nature of the associated pain (feelings), the anger and annoyance at the perpetrator (mind), and the way pain affects our ability to achieve meditative concentration (mental objects) (Nyanaponika. 1992, p. 33). On the one hand, Young (1994) explains that with this insight, we can experience pain as physical pain without turning it into emotional suffering. On the other hand, if a person does not differentiate between these different experiences, then suffering arises, which is pain multiplied by all the extraneous additions. In short, mindfulness increases the individual's awareness of the circuitous nature of the mind expounded by the Buddha in the idea of dependent origination, of how one thing leads to another, and enables us to learn to separate our responses and feelings about the situation from the situation itself.

Why does mindfulness occupy such a central position in the Buddha's teachings? The Buddha has repeatedly advised people to accept things only when

Suffering is pain multiplied by all extraneous additions.

Bare attention;

they have experienced them for themselves. Insight meditation, especially mindfulness, gives the practitioner a method and the internal resources to do this. For example, the Buddha encourages people to adopt an attitude of seeing and accepting things as they really are. Mindfulness allows the meditator to freely observe and experience what unfolds without needing to change or justify it (Gunaratana, 1991). In this way, we gain insight into the true nature of things. Through bare attention, we learn to see things as they really are, without the leveling effect of subjective judgments and preconceptions. The earlier example of the injured arm illustrates this attitude. This is similar to the Heideggerian notion of *releasement,* which involves waiting for, rather than willing things to happen (Heidegger, 1959/1966). According to Heidegger, waiting does not imply inactivity or indifference, but rather being open to what is encountered. In this way, instead of interpreting things or subjecting them to the will, we learn to let things be as they are.

Meditation also allows practitioners to verify the Buddha's teachings for themselves. Take the example of change or impermanence (*anicca*). According to the Buddha, everything including our own existence is in a constant state of flux, and change is in the nature of things. By encouraging people to appreciate the transitory nature of all phenomena, the Buddha's intention is to help people to adopt an attitude of seeing change as fundamental and unavoidable, and to accept it gracefully (Khong, 1999). As Puriso (1999) notes, intellectually we can understand that things are impermanent, but understanding impermanence intellectually is far removed from coming to terms with it. Hence, the Buddha advocates meditation as a way of helping people experience impermanence. Mindfulness brings the meditator into direct confrontation with the continual presence of change and impermanence in a profound way (Nyanaponika, 1992). During meditation, when we experience within ourselves how everything is constantly changing, "rising and falling," and how no phenomenon, whether mental or physical stays the for two moments, we gain insight into impermanence. This insight helps us to appreciate that change is in the nature of things and that clinging to anything that possesses such a characteristic will inevitably lead to suffering (*dukkha*). Therese's experience is a good illustration: *Experience change universally*

Therese was diagnosed with cancer and experienced difficulties in coming to term with her illness. She was particularly concerned with the changes in her physical appearance, especially the loss of her hair resulting from chemotherapy treatment. Therese was encouraged to simply observe and experience change in nature. She reported being mindful of the falling leaves from a deciduous tree and the changing nature of passing clouds. Therese explained that her experience with impermanence in nature was deeply moving, and she gained the insight that change is

No phenomenon (mental or physical) stays the same for two moments.

Everything is constantly Changing

natural and inevitable. Learning to experience change universally, she found it easier to accept personal change.

APPLICATIONS AND CONTRIBUTIONS

Meditation, Rahula (1978) explains, does not mean assuming a particular posture, trying to attain a mystical state, or withdrawing from society. Similarly, the attitude that the Buddha teaches is not restricted to when one is meditating. It constitutes an attitude that one takes toward life constantly. In this section I discuss how we can develop and apply this attitude and the Buddha's teachings in the therapeutic context, and explore their contributions to psychology and psychotherapy.

One of the main contributions of Buddhist practices is their usefulness as a prophylactic measure. In meditation, especially with mindfulness practice, the meditator is encouraged to objectively observe the workings of the mind and emotions without trailing after them, or adding value to them. In this way, we can prevent a problem from developing or a present condition from deteriorating. Goleman (1988) explains that in general, psychotherapies seek to break the hold of past conditioning on present behavior and personality, whereas meditation aims to alter "the process of conditioning per se so that it will no longer be a prime determinant of future acts" (p. 173). By learning to separate our responses from the core events themselves, we can make space for, and not identify with our reactions.

How can this kind of attitude contribute to psychology and psychotherapy? Clearly there are parallels between Buddhist meditative practices and various psychotherapies that focus on behavior, cognition, and phenomenological seeing. These include behavior therapy (de Silva, 1990), cognitive and cognitive-behavioral therapies (Kwee, 1990; Mikalus, 1990; Rapee, 1998), and daseins-analysis, an existential-analytical therapy developed by Medard Boss (Boss, 1963, 1979). Within the limited scope of this chapter I will focus on cognitive therapy and daseinsanalysis.

Mikalus (1990) notes that currently most cognitive, and cognitive-behavioral therapies focus on the products of the mind, such as thoughts and images. The aim of these therapies is to change cognitive distortions into more realistic thinking (Burns, 1980; Rapee, 1998), or change overt behavior, which then produces changes in cognition (Mikalus, 1990). There are obvious parallels with the Buddhist approach of understanding the workings of the mind. Although some therapists working in this area recommend attentional training exercises similar to that of tranquillity meditation (Rapee, 1998), they have overlooked the importance of mindfulness practice.

In daseinsanalysis, Boss emphasizes phenomenological seeing based on the phenomenological approach employed by the German philosopher, Martin Heidegger. Heidegger (1936/1971) recommends that we set aside our propositional way of understanding things, and just experience what we encounter, returning "to the things themselves" (*Zu den Sachen Selbst*) (Heidegger, 1927/1962, p. 58). Daseinsanalysts encourage clients to set aside theoretical and intellectual constructions and to accept and experience the phenomenon as it is perceived. This is similar to the Buddha's teaching of learning to see and accept things as they are.

Despite these parallels between the above-mentioned therapies with Buddhist practices, there is a major difference. In my view, these psychotherapies tend to stay within the realm of thinking and intellectualization. Kwee (1990) notes that in cognitive therapy, the emphasis is on evaluating rationally. For example, clients are helped to identify irrational thoughts and beliefs, and replace them with more realistic or rational ones (Rapee, 1998). With daseinsanalysis, Boss explains Heidegger's phenomenological seeing as "fundamental thinking . . . looking at, contemplating . . . in the sense of just opening your eyes so that all the meaningfulness which makes up a certain thing may show itself to you" (quoted in Craig, 1998, p. 37). In this regard, Abe (1985) notes that Heidegger "did not depart from thinking itself, and tried till the last to stay in a kind of thinking" (p. 119), that is, meditative thinking as opposed to scientific and calculative thinking.

As I noted previously, the Buddha promotes a change of attitude based on direct experience rather than on intellectualization. I have illustrated this experiential approach earlier with Therese's case. This emphasis on developing insight derived from experience is missing from the other psychotherapeutic approaches that I have discussed, and points to the way that Buddhist ideas and practices can complement and contribute to psychotherapy.

The Buddha advocates paying bare attention to our thoughts, feelings, and sensations as they arise, without falling into the habitual tendency of judging or criticizing them. The idea behind mindfulness is to become continually aware of and to "name" our thoughts, feelings, and emotions objectively and accept them fully for what they are. In acquiring this awareness and understanding, the person develops the freedom to break the hold of compulsive habits. Epstein (1995) explains that "training in this attitude of mind is why mediation is practiced" (p. 102). Let me illustrate with the case of Mary.

Mary was experiencing depression resulting from her relationship problems with family members. When taken through the process of her thinking and emotions across different situations, Mary was able to identify the internal dialogue and feelings that contributed to her depression. For example, when the family inquired how she was coping, Mary felt anger (*"they are so nosy"*), frustration ("*nobody understands*"), and sadness ("*I feel incompetent*"). These feelings resulted in her habitual responses of justification and negative retorts. In most of her family interactions, Mary tended to remain in this small arc, swinging from negative feelings to negative responses and vice versa.

During therapy, she was encouraged to just observe, experience and make space for her feelings (i.e., to see "anger as anger," and "sadness as sadness"), without judging or repressing them or carrying on an internal dialogue ("*Why do I feel like this*," or "*I shouldn't feel so angry*"). By learning to just be with her feelings, and not attempting to change or justify them, she was able to see how one feeling gave rise to another, how anger, for example, gave rise to frustration, then to sadness, and ultimately to depression. In order to break this cycle, Mary was encouraged to be mindful of her bodily sensations as these feelings were being experienced. She reported, for example, that her "stomach felt all knotted up." Finally, Mary was encouraged to put in place a circuit breaker such as counting or simply watching her breath. In this way, she was able to break the vicious cycle of ruminative and associative thinking that had previously resulted in her feeling depressed for many hours or days. By putting in place a circuit breaker before she reacted, Mary was able to see the situation for what it was ("*They are genuinely concerned about me*," "*I don't need to justify my feelings*").

According to the Buddha, if we can understand and experience how one thing leads to another (dependent origination), and how every action produces a reaction (karma), we can step out of our habitual patterns of responding so that things can be otherwise. The practice of mindfulness schools the individual in the art of acceptance and letting go, the key elements in the attitude that the Buddha encourages. For example, Mary reported that she "loves the idea of just accepting my feelings. It is so simple but it is such a relief. It's a relief to recognize my feelings and to accept them and let them go."

Although Mary was not asked to think about the irrationality of her thoughts and to replace them with more rational ones, or to see the phenomena as they are being experienced, nevertheless she was able to accomplish all of these by just being mindful of her thoughts and feelings, and not allowing them to spiral. According to Mary, learning to separate her emotions from the situation and to acknowledge and make space for her feelings without feeling guilty or the need to justify them, gave her a sense of emotional freedom, and the ability to cope more effectively. She was now better able to articulate and discuss her problems with her family. In this way she was able to respond more appropriately.

Epstein (1995) explains that the Buddha teaches us a new way to be with our feelings, thoughts, and so forth. By simply observing our thoughts and feelings as they arise and labeling them objectively, we uncover strengths and weaknesses that have hitherto remained veiled and learn to deal with them accordingly (Nyanaponika, 1992). As Goleman (1990) notes, in meditation the client's free association has been found to be "particularly rich in content" and the patient "more able to tolerate this material" (p. 25). He adds that these materials are not limited to what the therapist and client find problematic, but includes whatever comes to mind. Adam's case illustrates these points directly:

Adam was recently divorced and his wife had custody of their children. Adam had difficulty letting go of his feeling of anger toward his wife. He was encouraged during meditation to just experience and accept this feeling of anger and other feelings and thoughts as they arose, and to let them be by not reacting to or trying to change them. By simply permitting his anger to be, Adam uncovered other emotions and feelings that had previously been set aside or not admitted to. First, he was able to identify feelings of loneliness, and subsequently, his own negative attitude. He became aware that the reason he was unable or unwilling to let go of his anger was due to his fear of loneliness. He was also mindful that his attitude was a major contributor to his state of loneliness. In accepting and letting each of these feelings go, he was able to see himself as he really was, a person with an attitudinal problem, and deal with it accordingly. Through mindfulness, Adam learned to let go of material that he could let go of, and to begin dealing with those which he could not. This proved to be a meaningful starting point for his process of self-understanding.

Although cognitive and cognitive-behavioral therapies and daseinsanalysis share with Buddhist psychology the common goal of helping people to adopt a different attitude toward their problems, we can see from the above examples that Buddhism employs a unique approach. Even though Boss recommends that people maintain a meditative or open attitude toward what they experience and accept things for what they are, he did not articulate a method for cultivating this attitude. Hanna (1993) summarizes this paradox well when he points to the "catch-22" position, wherein if one is not already intuitive, one might not be able to assume an attitude that calls for further intuition. Similarly, it can be argued that cognitive therapies presuppose that a person who has irrational thoughts and beliefs possesses the capacity to set aside these thoughts and beliefs. It is difficult for people to acquire a meditative attitude. Even Boss himself acknowledges that it requires mental discipline and training. He notes that "in order to see things like this you have to exercise your thinking until you get it. It took me years. And I also had personal help from Martin Heidegger himself—for about twenty-five years" (quoted in Craig, 1988, p. 27). Batchelor (1990) explains that if the kind of silence required for developing a meditative attitude eludes us, it is helpful to adopt methods that can help us develop it. In my view, Buddhist meditation affords us techniques, currently absent in most psychotherapy, for fostering this attitude.

Buddhism starts from the premise that if one experiences this attitude personally, then one is better able to accept it intellectually. Kwee's (1990) reference to an ancient Chinese proverb that reads, "I see and I remember. I do and I understand" (p. 53) is a pithy explanation of why the Buddha emphasizes experience. Hence, in the eightfold path, the Buddha counsels that right understanding and right thought (the cognitive component) are to be developed contemporaneously with right speech, right action, right livelihood (the behavioral components) and right effort, right mindfulness, and right concentration (the experiential components), as all the eight factors are interrelated and each provides the foundation for the others.

From the above discussion, it can be seen that when meditation, and in particular mindfulness, is practiced alongside other complementary therapeutic approaches, the result is an incisive and powerful "tool" for empowering clients to understand and deal with their problems with less reliance on the therapist. Additionally, as meditation can be practiced at almost any time and place, it is particularly helpful to clients outside the therapeutic context. The idea is not to replace psychotherapy with meditation, but to recognize that they can coexist and complement each other, and that when used efficaciously, meditation is a powerful adjunct for developing good mental health and well-being.

CONCLUSION

Kwee (1990) opines that meditation is suited for therapy, particularly when it is divorced from its esoteric contexts. This holds true for most of the Buddha's teachings. As Rahula (1978) notes, "Buddhism is a way of life" (p. 81), and to become a Buddhist, there are no external rites or ceremonies to follow, but one merely needs to understand and practice the Buddha's teachings. As I have argued, the Buddha teaches an attitude and this attitude can be developed by each individual through self-discovery and self-understanding, a process that calls for personal responsibility and effort rather than an affiliation.

REFERENCES

Abe, M. (1985). Zen and western thought (W. R. LaFleur, Ed.). Honolulu: University of Hawaii Press. Meditative thinking vs scientific/calculative think -

Abhinyana. (2000). Great expectations, great disappointments. Buddhism Today. 15(2), 16–20.

Batchelor, S. (1990). The faith to doubt. Berkeley: Parallax Press.

Batchelor, S. (1997). Buddhism without beliefs. New York: Riverhead Books.

Burns, D. (1980). *Feeling good: The new mood therapy*. New York: Signet Books.

Bodhi, B. (Ed.). (1994). *The vision of Dhamma. Buddhist writings of Nyanaponika Thera* (2nd ed.). Kandy: Buddhist Publication Society.

Boss, M. (1963). *Psychoanalysis and daseinsanalysis* (L. B. Lefebre, Trans.). New York: Basic Books.

Boss, M. (1979). *Existential foundations of medicine and psychology* (S. Conway, & A. Cleaves, Trans.). New York: Jason Aronson.

Buddhaghosa, B. (1956). *The path of purification* [Visuddhi Magga]. (B. Ñānamoli, Trans.). Singapore: Singapore Buddhist Meditation Centre.

Craig, E. (1988). An encounter with Medard Boss. In E. Craig (Ed.). Psychotherapy for freedom: The daseinsanalytic way in psychology and psychoanalysis [Special Issue]. *The Humanistic Psychologist, 16*, 24-58.

H.H. the XIV Dalai Lama. (1997). *The four noble truths*. (G. T. Jinpa, Trans.). Hammersmith: Thorsons.

de Silva, P. (1990). Meditation and beyond: Buddhism and psychotherapy. In M. G. T. Kwee (Ed.). *Proceedings of the First International Conference on Psychotherapy, Meditation & Health* (pp. 165-182). London: East-West Publications.

Dhamma, R. (1997). *The first discourse of the Buddha*. Boston: Wisdom Publications.

Dhammananda, K. S. (1987). *What Buddhists believe* (4th ed.). Kuala Lumpur: Buddhist Missionary Society.

Dhammananda, K. S. (Ed. and Trans.) (1994), *Treasure of the Dhamma*. Malaysia: Buddhist Missionary Society.

Epstein, M. (1995). *Thoughts without a thinker*. New York: Basic Books.

Goleman, D. (1984). The Buddha on meditation and states of consciousness. In D. S. Shapiro & R. N. Walsh. (Eds.). *Meditation: Classic and contemporary perspectives* (pp. 317-360). New York: Aldine.

Goleman, D. (1988). *The meditative mind*. Los Angeles: Jeremy. P. Tarcher.

Goleman, D. (1990). The psychology of meditation. In M. G. T. Kwee (Ed.). *Proceedings of the First International Conference on Psychotherapy, Meditation & Health* (pp. 19-35). London: East-West Publications.

Gunaratana, H. (1991). Mindfulness in plain English. Singapore: Singapore Buddhist Meditation Centre.

Hanna, F. (1993). The Transpersonal consequences of Husserl's phenomenological method. *The Humanistic Psychologist, 21*, 41-57.

Heidegger, M. (1927/1962). *Being and time*. (J. Macquarrie & E. Robinson, Trans.). Oxford: Basil Blackwell. (Original work published 1927).

Heidegger, M. (1959/1966). *Discourse on thinking: A translation of Gelassenheit*. (J. M. Anderson & E. H. Freund, Trans.). New York: Harper & Row.

Heidegger, M. (1936/1971). The origin of the work of art. In A. Hofstadter, (Trans.), *Poetry, language, thought* (pp. 17-81). New York: Harper & Row.

Khong, B. S. L. & Thompson, N. L. (1997). Jung and Taoism—A comparative analysis of Jung's psychology and Taoist philosophy. *Harvest: Journal for Jungian Studies, 43*, 86-105.

Khong, B. S. L. (1999). *A comparative analysis of the concept of responsibility in daseinsanalysis and Buddhist psychology*. Unpublished doctoral dissertation. Macquarie University. Sydney, Australia.

Kwee, M. G. T. (1990). Cognitive and behavioural approaches to Buddhism. In M. G. T. Kwee (Ed.), *Proceedings of the First International Conference on Psychotherapy, Meditation & Health* (pp. 36–53). London: East-West Publications.

Mikalus, W. (1990). Mindfulness, self-control, and personal growth. In M. G. T. Kwee (Ed.), *Proceedings of the First International Conference on Psychotherapy, Meditation & Health* (pp. 151–164). London: East-West Publications.

Nyanaponika, T. (1992). *The heart of Buddhist meditation.* Kandy: Buddhist Publication Society.   5 *hindrances* to *meditation* p. 33

Punnaji, B. (1978). Buddhism and psychotherapy. *Buddhist Quarterly, 10,* 44–52.

Puriso, B. (1999). Mind training. *Buddhism Today, 14,* 6–14.   *Impermanence; come to terms w/ it*

Rahula, W. (1978). *What the Buddha taught* (rev. ed.). London: The Gordon Fraser Gallery.

Rapee, R. M. (1998). *Overcoming shyness and social phobia.* Killara, Australia: Lifestyle Press.   *Cognitive / behavioural therapies*

Rubin, J. B. (1996). *Psychotherapy and Buddhism. Toward an integration.* New York: Plenum Press.

Snelling, J. (1992). *The Buddhist handbook.* London: Rider.

Thich Nhat Hahn. (1998). *The heart of the Buddha's teachings.* Berkeley: Parallex Press.

Trungpa, C. (1988). *The myth of freedom and the way of meditation.* Boston: Shambhala.

Tarthang, T. (1990). *Openness mind.* Berkeley: Dharma Publishing.

Young, S. (1994). Purpose and method of vipassana meditation. *The Humanistic Psychologist, 22,* Spring, 53–61.   *ability to experience pain as physical pain*

Myth of Freedom   *& are not turn it into emotional suffering.*

CHAPTER 4

On Being a Non-Buddhist Buddhist
A Conversation with Myself

Seth Robert Segall

> In my mind, the arguers never stop—
> the skeptic and the amazed—
> the general and the particular in their
>   uneasy relationship.
>
> Then the robin sings.
>
> Then the bulb of the lily becomes the stalk,
> the stalk opens into a handkerchief of white light.
>   —Mary Oliver, *The Leaf and the Cloud: A Poem*

Bertie: You have to admit this is an odd idea for a dialogue.

Ānanda: Why do you think so?

Bertie: Well, first of all, it's a <u>dialogue with yourself</u>. Frankly, the very idea sounds more than a little narcissistic. What makes you think other people will be interested in *your* internal dialogue? In addition, the idea of making a Western psychological understanding of Buddhism the central concern of this dialogue has, to be honest, only limited appeal. Who is your audience? Will it appeal to psychologists? Will it appeal to Buddhists? What's worse, you can hardly call yourself an expert on Buddhism! How long have you been a practicing Buddhist?

Ānanda: This is my seventh year.

Bertie: So what makes *you* such an expert?

Ānanda: I'm not claiming to be an expert, at least not an expert on Buddhism. I am <u>an expert</u>, however, <u>at being a novice Buddhist</u>. Maybe other novice Buddhists might be interested? Or maybe those just seriously curious about Buddhism? It also seems to me that this type of dialogue has its virtues. After all, who knows me better than you do? You won't let me get by with any of my usual sophistry! In addition, my faith and your skepticism may provide just the right contrapuntal balance as we thread our way through the psychological, philosophical, and moral twists and turns of our conversation.

Bertie: All this talk of "me" and "you" might be confusing to our readers, providing we actually have any. Maybe they'll suspect that we are a multiple personality?

Ānanda: Actually, the whole question of who "I" am and who "you" are is a wonderfully Buddhist question, don't you think? If Buddhism is about anything, it's about identity. There are psychologists who think that identity itself is dialogical in nature (Hermans and Kempens, 1993) and that none of us are unified, solid, unchanging "wholes;" we all embody sets of contradictions and are less integrated than we like to think we are.

Bertie: Let's put that question aside for now. Maybe the best place to begin is by introducing ourselves. For the sake of this dialogue, who am "I" and who are "you?"

Ānanda: Well, I'm the Buddhist part of us. I'm committed to a life of mindfulness, equanimity, compassion, and loving-kindness. I'm the part of us that gets up and meditates daily, goes on meditation retreats, follows *The Five Precepts* (the Buddhist ethical precepts for laypersons concerning killing, stealing, improper speech, sexual immorality, and intoxication), teaches meditation to medical and psychiatric patients, and devours Buddhist texts. Buddhism is the center of my life, and a source of great happiness and joy for me.

Bertie: I worry about you! I'm the part of us that thinks getting taken in by half-baked philosophies is your worst quality. I've seen you taken in before by religious and political beliefs that you later grew tired of and repudiated. Remember your flirtation with Orthodox Judaism in your adolescence? Remember the political radicalism of your young adulthood? Remember your middle-aged neoconservatism? What's left of any of those?

I'm the part of us that was trained as a research scientist. I'm the part of us that is agnostic, skeptical, logical, discriminating, critical, and iconoclastic. I worry about a religion like Buddhism. It claims to be based on the word of the historical Buddha, yet its earliest known texts were written hundreds of years after the Buddha's death (Skilton, 1994). Its various schools and sects dramatically disagree on what the central texts and tenets of Buddhism are. Some Buddhist sects demand intellectual and spiritual subservience to "enlightened" gurus or masters whose "enlightenment" is not only impossible to prove, but is downright suspect given their behavior. I find that there are tenets in Buddhism that seem to contradict each other, and others that seem simply implausible. In addition, Buddhist texts often seem to be repugnantly misogynist and puritanical!

If you look at the historical record, Buddhists have done no better than Jews, Christians, Moslems, Hindus, or atheists in terms of the morality of their behavior. Many of the great Japanese Zen masters of the last century supported the Japanese war effort in World War II, and at least one expressed outright anti-Semitic sentiments (Victoria, 1999). In the seventeenth century there were fierce battles between Karma-pa and Gelug-pa Tibetan Buddhist monks (Shakabpa, 1984). In our own lifetime several well-known American Buddhist teachers have slept around with their students or have had substance abuse problems. Let's face it: Buddhism is just another religion, and religion is always an escape from uncertainty, an attempt to explain the inexplicable with the implausible. Why leave the Jewish religion you were born into to just to join another illogical escape from life's ambiguities that once again requires reliance on spiritual and textual authority?

Ānanda: I understand your concerns so I'd better explain what I mean by being a Buddhist. Maybe "Buddhist" isn't the right word for what I am. Maybe I'm a "neo-Buddhist" or a "non-Buddhist Buddhist." In fact, the very idea of having an identity as a Buddhist seems to be an oxymoron given Buddhist concerns about the hazards of identification. I have been trying to use "Buddhism" as a convenient label that would provide readers with some rough-and-ready shorthand image of me, but I'm now afraid that the label imparts as much misinformation about myself as information.

I would agree with all of your criticisms of Buddhism and then some: we have no certain knowledge of what the historical Buddha actually said and thought. Everything we know about him is filtered through texts written after his death, and these texts were certainly written by authors who had their own particular point-of-view or institutional interest to promulgate or protect. Many of the *Mahāyāna Sūtras*, texts which allege to be the teachings of the Buddha, were probably written a millennium or more after the Buddha's *parinirvāna*, but even parts of the older *Theravāda Pāli Suttas* were written and compiled long after the Buddha's death (Skilton, 1994). We have no way of knowing what is actually the word of the Buddha.

Moreover, even if we were to know for sure what the word of the Buddha was, we would have no basis to assume that his understanding of the world was infallible. We would have to understand the Buddha was an ordinary human being (is there any other kind?) who lived in and was conditioned by a particular historical era, a particular social class, and a particular set of family dynamics. We would not want to take his opinions on neuroanatomy, astrophysics, or macroeconomics as being necessarily wiser or better than whatever opinions Moses, Jesus, Mohammed, Confucius, or Aristotle might have had on those topics. We can safely assume that even the greatest thinkers get more things wrong than right; we should assume the same for the historical Buddha.

I would also agree with you that there are concepts in Buddhism that seem nonsensical and contradictory. For example, how can one reconcile the idea of the reincarnation of human beings with the idea that human beings have no essential self? If there is no essential self, what is it that gets reborn? In addition, reincarnation is an idea that can only be accepted on faith; it's hard to imagine any objective evidence that impartial observers might agree proves its existence. It is impossible to prove that it is a more likely outcome than rotting in the grave or going to Hell. All one could say is that one prefers the idea of reincarnation because it is more aesthetically pleasing, or that one prefers it because the Buddha said it, and one puts one's faith in the Buddha.

I have trouble with my native Judaism because it requires similar suspensions of logic. One is asked to believe in a supernatural Being who stands outside of the material world, and whose existence leaves no material footprint. One is asked to believe that this Being dictated the Torah to Moses, even though all available evidence suggests that Moses never wrote the Torah (Friedman, 1997), and that it, like the Buddhist Sūtras, is a compilation of the works of various authors who had their own unique agendas to pursue. One is asked to assume that this Being is very much concerned with whether or not one mixes meat with dairy products, or whether one has trimmed the foreskin of one's penis. None of this makes very much sense, and I am unwilling to state, like the second-century Christian Apologist, Tertullian, that "*credo quia absurdum est*" ("I believe because it is absurd"). So, don't worry. I'm not about to replace the superstitions of Judaism with the superstitions of Buddhism with its colorful heaven and hell realms and celestial beings.

Bertie: But take away the infallibility of the Buddha, any knowledge of what the Buddha actually said, and the folk beliefs, superstitions, rituals, and practices that partly define Buddhism as it evolved in each of the particular Asian localities in which it emerged, and what is left? Can this kind of deracinated Buddhism even be called Buddhism at all? Maybe it's just an American New Age "Spirituality for Atheists" that is influenced by Buddhism in a vague or partial way, but really doesn't deserve to be called Buddhism at all?

Ānanda: Let's not quibble over semantics. I could be content to call it "Ānandaism" and name it after myself, but that seems to be taking far too much credit for something that is not at all original with me. I think that after one has removed what is speculative and irrational from Buddhism there is still something distinctively unique that can only be identified as "Buddhist," and which is qualitatively different from the core of other religious and philosophical traditions. Why not give the Buddha credit for those ideas that the narrative tradition of Asia identifies with him? And if there are religious purists who would want to write me out of the Buddhist community for my reformist views, so be it. I will still identify the core beliefs that illuminate my life as having originated in Buddhism.

Bertie: I now have some idea of what you *don't* identify as being part of your Buddhism or neo-Buddhism, but I can't really say I have the vaguest idea of just what you think your Buddhism *is*. You seem to have conceded a great many points to me, but I'm a dyed-in-the-wool rationalist, not a Buddhist. Where exactly do we differ?

Ānanda: I'll leave it to you to define where we differ, but you're right in saying that it's time I talked about what my Buddhism is, rather than defining what it isn't.

Bertie: It *is* about time. Get on with it.

Ānanda: To begin with, Buddhism means a commitment to the practice of *mindfulness*.

Bertie: I'm not quite sure what you mean by "mindfulness."

Ānanda: It's the practice of opening oneself up and being receptive to the flow of sense perceptions, emotions, and thought processes in each given moment while attempting to hold judgment in abeyance. This is done with no other goal than to be as present as one can possibly be within each and every moment. One does this with an intimate attention that is very different from a scrutinizing, objective stance. Rather than being a distant observer of a set of experiences, one is a participant-observer, and what one observes is not only the sense impressions of the "outside" world, but also one's own subjective reactions to that world.

I'm afraid, however, that these words are inadequate to convey the wholeness of this kind of awareness. Not only is one not an objective observer, but at times it becomes palpably apparent that there is no separate observer, nor is the "outside" world outside; the observer, the body, and the world are all part of one ongoing process. In these moments of unimpeded awareness there is a wonderful sense of lightness of being, and a sense of the rightness to things just as they are. In these moments when the sense of a separate self that needs defending, approval, status, or justification is nowhere evident, one is open to being present and responsive to the world in a deeply caring way. This is what I mean by mindfulness: seeing events as they are with minimal interference from a separate ego that needs to control both self and world; being intimately in touch with the moment as it is, and open-heartedly responsive to it.

Bertie: Thanks for your explanation. What you say is appealing, but I wonder if it really makes sense. There are a number of assumptions that need to be explored to see if they make sense or are just wishful nonsense. Are you open to taking a logical look at this?

Ānanda: I have no choice but to accept you as my partner in this dialogue. You are, after all, part of me. I couldn't believe anything without you scrutinizing it, challenging it, and picking it apart. While you make for a rather prickly bedfellow, I do appreciate you at times. You have kept me out of more trouble in life than I care to admit! So sure, let's do it. But let's be careful not to get into argument just for argument's sake. Let's make sure we are not just quibbling over definitions. Whatever we choose to argue about must be about distinctions that make a difference; distinctions that make a difference in terms of the kinds of choices we human beings are forced to make all the time. They must have, as William James used to say, "cash value." In fact, the more I think about it, let's not argue at all. You like arguing, but I don't. Instead, let's just agree to investigate this together as two friends.

Bertie: It's a deal. And while we're handing out compliments, let me say that I appreciate having your illogical but well-intentioned presence around too. I appreciate your warmth and your ability to connect with people that I seem to lack. I am always discovering the points that differentiate and separate me from other people, and am incessantly busy dissecting and questioning those very moments that could, if allowed to blossom, become moments of intimacy, love, and wonder.

But enough of this mutual admiration; frankly, it makes me a little uncomfortable. Let's get down to thinking clearly about "mindfulness." You seem to be describing a process that is somewhat similar to the process of introspection that was the primary source of data for nineteenth-century German and American psychologists, and the eighteenth-century British empiricists. It also bears some similarity to Husserl's (1921/1973) *epoché*, the phenomenological method for freshly observing the contents of experience prior to conceptualization and abstraction. I have no doubt that there is a lot one can learn from attending to the stream of consciousness.

Meditation, if it is a type of meditation that emphasizes mindfulness, frees our attention to include a sensory world that is usually largely neglected. Most of the time our attention is directed to the world outside our skin. This makes evolutionary sense; after all, most of the objects of our desire or threats to our continued existence emerge from that external world. Our inner life becomes important to us in an evolutionary sense only when attention to it improves our chances of achieving our goals in the external world. Our minds privilege information coming to us through our eyes and ears above information coming from our nose, mouth, or skin since our eyes and ears provide us with our earliest intimations of spatially distant goals and dangers. Sensory information from inside our skins only gets attended to when learning new motor skills, or when the discomfort and pain of injury and illness inform us that something has gone seriously awry within.

When we meditate, we sit in a quiet space with eyes either closed or fixed on an unchanging field. Visual and auditory input is minimized, and the mind must content itself with turning itself toward the less attended to senses. Even here, at least initially, there is little occurring. Breathing is the only major source of movement and change, and the mind settles on attending to it as the most interesting object. Given little to occupy it, however, the mind soon turns to generating its own entertainments, chattering away about its memories, intentions, hopes, and fears. If one adopts a mental set of minimal goal-directedness and minimal censorship, one can watch the whole passing parade of one's primary concerns. One can also watch one's emotional, physiological, and cognitive responses to external and internal sensations as they arise. In this way, one can become deeply acquainted with one's habitual patterns of psychophysiological activity and reactivity.

So far we are in agreement. Quiet watchfulness and attentiveness to one's own mental and physical processes can be a source of important knowledge and increased self-awareness. A human being who knows him- or herself well is better able to act effectively in the material world.

I can also see this sort of quiet introspection as having a beneficial effect on one's "nerves." As one sits quietly, one's body is thrown into a restful state, just as it is in relaxation training and quiescent hypnosis (Edmonston, 1991). One can imagine a general shift from sympathetic to parasympathetic autonomic tone with a slowing of heart rate and respiration, a drop in metabolism and the secretion of stress hormones, and a general relaxation of the skeletal muscles. I can imagine most meditators might experience this state as pleasant and restorative. There might even be general health benefits from practicing this regularly including a reduced elevation in blood pressure, decreased muscular pain, and a decrease in the medical symptoms of stress-related illnesses. All this can be easily verified or disproved by empirical research (e.g., Benson, 1975 and Kabat-Zinn, 1990).

But these are all practical and material benefits that might arise from meditation. Your own interest in meditation is not about these kinds of practical gains, however, if I am reading you correctly.

Ānanda: That's right. In fact, to the extent that one is doing meditation to achieve these sorts of material and practical gains, one is not really doing meditation at all. Meditation is best characterized by nondoing and nonstriving.

Bertie: Again with the paradoxes! But let's get back to your claims about mind-fulness: You seem to be stating that when one meditates mindfully one loses a sense of the boundaries that separate mind from body and self from other; that one becomes aware of self-as-process indistinguishable from the external world; that notions of inner and outer lose their relevance. Is that correct?

Ānanda: Yes.

Bertie: Well, here is where we begin, I think, to diverge. First of all, does the med-itator really experience a oneness with the world and a loss of boundaries, or does the meditator only indulge in having ideas about oneness? One can directly per-ceive "hot" and "cold," and "bright" and "dark," but can one perceive "oneness," or is "oneness" a concept, a conclusion, an act of imagination and speculation?

Second, does this experience of "oneness" have any value? Why is it impor-tant to have it? You seem to imply that when one is in this state of "oneness" and "egolessness" (if that is what it genuinely is) that one somehow sees things more clearly and as they genuinely are. Is this really so? You also seem to imply that in this selfless state our response to the world seems more loving and caring. Is that really true? If it is really true, is it necessarily good? There seems to be something terribly sappy and naive about this kind of notion. As if all one needs is to love the world! The world is dangerous and unfair. At times, anger at injustice and the force necessary to stop it are more relevant than love to moral action.

Ānanda: Let's start with your first question: Can one directly experience "one-ness" itself, or can one only entertain the thought of "oneness?" The answer to your question is both "yes" and "no" depending on how the question is inter-preted. First, "oneness" is clearly a concept, and as such it is something to be thought about rather than a direct object of experiencing. One does not sit down in stillness and come across the object "oneness" except as an idea. What one can experience is the intimate and direct presence of other objects without any sense of separation of observer from observed. There is only the process of observation itself, which is an interactive reciprocal process with no observer separate from that process. There is seeing, but no seer and no thing seen; hear-ing, but no hearer and no thing heard. So I would say that "oneness" is a process or mode of experiencing rather than the object of experiencing. Descartes, by the way, made a fundamental mistake when he wrote, "I think, therefore I am." The experiencing of thinking does not prove the existence of the thinker. If Descartes had been a Buddhist meditator he might more accurately have said, "Thoughts occur." Period.

On a conceptual level, the whole idea of the oneness of experience is inti-mately related to the idea of the illusory nature of a separate and enduring self.

Objectively, we understand that we are both part of nature and one with nature. Conversely, whatever gifts we have are a natural expression of the state of the universe. If we are intelligent, then we live in a universe with the potential for the emergence of intelligence, since we are not separate from or outside of the universe. If we are conscious, then consciousness must be a phenomenon that arises as a function of the natural world.

As an organism and as a being there is no place where I start or end, and no time when I started or will end. My skin is not a boundary that separates me from the universe; it is an organ that connects me to it. There is no demarcation where the atoms and electromagnetic fields of my skin end and the atoms and electromagnetic fields of the universe begin. There are no atoms that make up "me" that are separate from the atoms that make up the universe. In fact "my" atoms and "my" energy are always in a process of exchange with the matter and energy that lies "outside" my skin. Through breathing, eating, defecating, urinating, sweating, metabolizing, sloughing off the outer layer of skin, and expending thermal and kinetic energy I am interchanging self and world. At the end of a decade of living, are there any atoms "in me" that were "in me" at the beginning of the decade, or have all atoms been exchanged with the environment? I "began" as one cell, and that one cell recruited the carbon, hydrogen, oxygen, nitrogen, phosphorous, calcium, and potassium atoms in the extracellular environment into becoming part of the design of "me." But that one cell that was "my beginning" itself did not start with me but started with my parents, and they in turn received their genetic material from their parents and so on *ad infinitum*, so there is no place or time where a separate "me" began. I am an expression of an ongoing dynamic process that began with the Big Bang. I flow out of that primordial explosion of being through an unbroken line of causes and effects in the same way that the stars and galaxies do.

I think we are very much like a whirlpool (Beck, 1993) in the ocean. We can identify and point to the whirlpool as a "separate" entity that we can observe. It is a pattern of energy and matter that emerges for a time, persists for a time, and then dissolves, much like ourselves. But the water of the whirlpool is not separate from the sea. The water in the whirlpool at one point in time is not the same water that is in the whirlpool at another point in time. The whirlpool is constantly exchanging its substance with the ocean of which it is always itself an inseparable part. And there is no Inner Whirlpool that gives the whirlpool its whirlpool-ness. It has no separate enduring nature apart from its existence. Similarly, we are an ongoing process without any inner "me" that gives us our identity.

The same is true for the entity I label as "my mind." I might wish to think of it as a fixed thing that begins and ends with my personal history. I might like to locate it as an entity that exists behind my eyes and between my ears. If I believe in mind as a kind of nonmaterial mental "stuff," however, no mental entity can have a physical locus. If I am a physicalist, however, I might try to identify mind with the integrative activity of my central nervous system.

My central nervous system, however, is not really separate from the rest of my body. Its neuronal fibers extend to and interact with every organ I possess. The nervous system's sensory end organs pick up kinetic and chemical energies from the body and transform them into information. Nor is my central nervous system separate from the "external" environment: The nervous system's sensory end organs pick up electromagnetic, kinetic, and chemical energies from the "outer" world and transform them into information, too. My senses are constantly taking in information from the physical and social world; and right now the information I am transmitting through these words is transforming your nervous system. We are connected, too.

The central nervous system is part of the body, and as such, it too can be characterized by the whirlpool analogy. My nervous system did not begin with "me," but with my ancestors's germ plasm, and with the extracellular minerals and molecules that were transformed into nervous system tissue as I grew from one cell to an organism of trillions of cells. It continues to exchange its constituent elements with elements from the environment through the circulation of the cerebrospinal fluid and blood. The ideas it struggles with originate in the larger culture in which it swims. They are absorbed from linguistic structures, the mythology of the culture, and the mores, rituals, prejudices, and wisdom passed from generation to generation. They exist within the buzz of the media, the texts of the academy, and lore of one's clan. They grow out of the thousand daily acts of assimilation and accommodation that our mental structures make as we encounter the physical stuff of the world and the social stuff of human interaction. Every word and idea in this dialogue was invented by someone else, heard from someone else, thought of by someone else before "me." There is no separate mind that I possess that is apart from the sea of the culture in which I live, a culture which is itself interacting with other cultures, transforming, and changing. No beginning. No end. No fixity.

Bertie: Enough. I get the point. I concede that as an organism and as a mind (whatever "mind" may be) I am a part of the universe and the informational sea with only arbitrary points demarcating "me" from "you," "them," and "it." I also concede that the entity I identify as "me" did not begin in time, but is the end result of an infinite regress of causes going back to the Big Bang, if not before. Surely, though, I come to an end when I die?

Ānanda: I do not see why that is so either. Whatever ideas and influences I emit that touch another human being become part of the culture and informational sea too, and they have their effects that continue to ripple through the universe after my death. The elements that make me up continue on and are transformed into plants and minerals and other sentient beings. Maybe my germ plasm continues on as well if I have children. If I don't exist as an entity separate from the universe, then I had no beginning, and I have no end either. What happens to my consciousness? Well, my consciousness is not really "mine," is it? It is part of the integrative activity of the universe, and I have no idea what happens to it after the demise of this particular form that seems to be so separate, but isn't.

Bertie: Your idea that we are not separate from the universe makes sense to some extent, but it does have its limits. There is *some* sense in which I am this unique separate being. I mean, I can feel the world through my hands, but not through your hands. I can see the world though my eyes, but not through yours. I can think my thoughts, but I can only imagine what your thoughts are, and even when you vocalize them aloud, I can only hazard a guess as to whether you are telling the truth or not. I have special knowledge about "me" that is private and internal, and no special knowledge about the existence of rocks, trees, or other people such as yourself. I am *this* very particular being. In addition, the direct knowledge I have about the physical and social universe is only about *this* local space just around me. I can see and hear around me for a several hundred feet, maybe several thousand feet, but while I am here in Connecticut, USA, I have no direct knowledge of what is going on at this moment in Beijing, China, or on Alpha Centauri.

Ānanda: I think there may be times when we do in fact have knowledge at a distance. At least there are a great many people, perhaps the majority of the human race, who claim to have had some experience at some time in their lives of knowledge at a distance, for example, a person who claims to have knowledge of the exact moment when a family member died, even though the death occurred halfway around the globe. People who have such anomalous experiences find them terribly persuasive, and I want to at least leave open the possibility that such events can occur (Cardeña, Lynn, and Krippner, 2000). So there may be some mechanism which can circumvent distance and time and give us certain kinds of knowledge about the state of the universe elsewhere and elsewhen.

Nevertheless, your point is well taken. Most of our experience, the overwhelming majority of it, is of this body and of conditions that can best be described as local. So that even though we have no beginning or end, no point of demarcation from the universe as a whole, we, as a rule, only have the experience of being *this* particular entity here and now. At any given moment my experience is

usually *this* particular local experience here and now, not an experience of everything and everywhen. Meditation always puts us in intimate contact with the particular *this-ness* of experience, and not with some abstract *everything-ness*.

The fact that our sensory experience is limited and that we do not have sensory feedback from everything, everywhere, and everywhen does not undermine
the argument of unity with all things, however. For example, suppose that I were
to argue that I really am separate from my environment; that I am this skin-
encapsulated organism, and that what lies within the skin is definitely "me." Even
within this domain of a separate "me," however, there would be areas of which I
would have no awareness. For example, brain tissue itself is devoid of sensory
nerve endings. I also receive little to no conscious information about a multiplicity
of internal physical states including the elevation of my blood sugar and blood
pressure or the acidity of my saliva. Even many "mental" events seem outside of
the range of my consciousness. In the process of speaking to a friend, I make frequent "decisions" about whether or not to add an /s/ to the end of a verb. There is
a simple rule for adding or not adding an /s/, but most of us could not verbalize
what that rule is without some thought (it is added in the third-person present
tense), and we are certainly not aware of the process we go through as the brain
makes these choices. Much of the brain's linguistic and perceptual processing is
often described as "preattentive" (Neisser, 1967) and occurs without awareness or
even the potential for access to awareness. Does that mean these processes aren't
"me?" Is "me" only to be identified with my consciousness and volition? Not only
is our consciousness local, but even within what might seem like the locality of
"me-ness" it remains spotty. If we try to limit "me" to what is within my skin, then
who I am remains unclear even within that delimited domain.

Bertie: I accept your argument that we are an integral part of the entire universe,
an ongoing process of the universe, but I am definitely having problems with the
implications of all this for my own sense of identity, for my understanding of who
"I" am. Surely there must be something I can identify as "me." The idea that I am
a very specific "me" is the thing I am most sure of in this world. My specific consciousness, and the local world that is reflected in it, is the only thing I absolutely
know for certain. In your whirlpool metaphor the whirlpool is nowhere separate
from the sea, yet there *is* still an identifiable entity called a "whirlpool" that can
be visually and conceptually abstracted from the sea. It seems to me that you are
trying to undermine this sense of "me-ness" with your arguments.

Ānanda: I am not trying to undermine anything. I am only trying to examine
our shared experience of "me-ness" a little more intimately. What do you suppose
this kernel of me-ness that you are talking about is?

Bertie: Well, I suppose I am talking here about the part of me that *has* experiences, or that *makes* choices. So I guess I am identifying the core of "me-ness" with consciousness and volition.

Ānanda: So then, do you also *have* a body instead of *being* a body? Your body is not your consciousness or your volition.

Bertie: But I have consciousness of my body, and I can move my body through my volition. Or at least that's the way I experience things. My body is more intimately associated with my consciousness and my volition than a chair is, or someone else's body. Those things I cannot have kinesthetic awareness of and I don't have volitional control over. I agree with you that talking about *having* a body as opposed to *being* a body is problematic, but I don't really identify myself with my body so much as with my consciousness and my volition. I feel as if I go around in my body rather than being my body; that my body is part of the network of me-ness, but not the very core or center of that network in the way that my consciousness is. I can imagine being disembodied, having an out-of-body experience, for example, and still being me. I cannot imagine what it would be to be me without a mind, however.

Ānanda: So you *have* a body but you *are* your mind? And do you *have* a brain, or *are* you your brain?

Bertie: I can see all the problems that you are trying to get at here. I identify myself with the product of the activity of the brain, but not with the brain itself. My mind is me but not my brain. This commits me to a kind of dualism that I don't really believe in, a separation of mind and matter, the Cartesian res *cogitans* and res *extensa*. The only world I intellectually believe in is the physical world, but when it comes to the thing I identify most as "me," I identify myself with something that isn't physical. It certainly is a muddle and a conundrum.

Ānanda: It certainly is. But it sounds like you agree with me in principle that mental and material processes must be aspects of a unitary reality?

Bertie: I agree, but not because I can really understand how it can be so. I agree only because the only alternative is a dualism that seems even less comprehensible.

Ānanda: And I agree with you that the question of how consciousness and material processes co-arise is not something we can currently address satisfactorily. I suspect, however, that the answer may be clearer once we have a clearer idea of what exactly materiality is. Is matter made of quarks? Is it made of vibrating superstrings? Physicists struggle with how best to comprehend matter, but any final answer they come up with must, it seems to me, also be able to account for the existence of consciousness.

Leaving the mind-body question aside, however, the same problem with possession and being exists when we talk only about conscious experiences themselves. Do we *have* experiences or *are* we our experiences? *Having* an experience implies there is someone, an observer, who possesses the experience: a "little man," or *homunculus*, inside our head who watches the read-out of our sensory processes. Even neurologically sophisticated thinkers sometimes make the mistake of thinking that, for example, what goes on in the sensory cortex does not become an "experience" until that information is relayed to the frontal lobe, almost as if the frontal lobe was the homunculus's home address. The idea of a homunculus is like the idea of the "inner whirlpool" that might theoretically give the whirlpool its whirlpoolness. Gilbert Ryle (1949) derided it over a half-century ago as "the dogma of the ghost in the machine," and philosophers have not been able to bring that ghost back to life in the decades since. The fundamental problem with the homunculus is that he creates a problem of infinite regress: If we have experiences because the little man inside our head views our sensory readouts, how does the homunculus accomplish this task? Does he also have a little man inside his head watching the readout of his experiences? I think you can see the problem. It seems logical to assume that there is no observer separate from the experience (cf., Dennett, 1991). No one is having the experience. The experience alone exists. We are bioexperiential happenings, and our experiences are just manifestations of our being as we happen along with the universe. This becomes palpably evident as we practice meditation. We look for traces of that ghost everywhere, but he or she is nowhere to be seen. There is no hearer, but only sound; no seer, but only vision.

Bertie: Then there is no one inside who wills things to happen either; there's no volition.

Ānanda: That's right.

Bertie: Hold it just one moment! Let's explore what that statement "no volition" means. I find that even harder to accept than the idea of "no experiencer." It seems I am most me when I make choices and when I will things to happen.

A few years back I made the decision to become a vegetarian. That was a hard decision. I enjoy the taste of meat and am sometimes tempted to renege on my original decision. But I think that making animals suffer is wrong when there are alternative ways to meet my nutritional needs. And so, despite my thought that I would enjoy occasionally eating meat, I don't. Each time I shop in the supermarket or order in a restaurant I remake that decision.

I make similar decisions every day: the decision to control my expression of anger toward others; the decision to remain faithful to my wife; the decision to not spend money frivolously, but to pay for my children's education and save for retirement; the decision to try to speak as honestly as possible; and so on. These decisions define who I am and what my life is about. I believe I am an active agent in the world, and that my choices make a difference in the world and have moral resonance. I believe I ought to act in a morally responsible manner. Your belief in a universe without morally responsible agents who make choices and will their own behavior would make all this meaningless.

Ānanda: You seem to be making a two-part argument: First, that you experience "yourself" as a "chooser." There seems to be a process of choosing that you go through that implies your existence as an agent. Second, that without a "you" who is an agent, morality becomes a meaningless proposition. Is that right?

Bertie: That just about sums it up.

Ānanda: May I separate those propositions out and take them one at a time?

Bertie: Be my guest.

Ānanda: Let's first examine the idea that you experience "yourself" as a "chooser." What exactly do you become conscious of when you make a choice? Let's use your example of deciding not to eat meat.

Bertie: Well, first I experience a hunger pang in my stomach and become aware that I am hungry. I go to a restaurant and look at the menu. I read the menu and see the words *roast beef*. My stomach growls and I have the idea that it might be pleasant to go ahead and order the dish. Then I think about my decision to be a vegetarian to save animals from suffering and think that if I order the roast beef I am abandoning that moral decision. Maybe I think that no one knows me in the restaurant and that if I cheat this one time no one will notice. I can always go back to being a vegetarian tomorrow and still appear moral to anyone who might judge my actions. Then I think that there is no one out there who cares whether I eat meat or not, no one external to me that I have to impress. I am making this decision because of my own wish to be a moral being, and I would know about my cheating and disapprove of it.

Then I tell myself, well this cow is already dead and my eating it does not contribute at all to its death. It wasn't killed for me. If I don't eat it someone else will, and if no one eats it, the cow's death would have been wasted and its suffering would have benefited no one. Then I counter that argument with the idea that I am really rationalizing here: my ordering the beef would encourage the restaurant to buy more beef, and make the death of some cow in the future more likely.

Then I have the thought that this vegetarianism is a lot of crap. That lions, for example, kill antelope for food, that nature is red in tooth and claw, that predator and prey is the nature of the universe, and that I should just go ahead and do what nature has intended me to do. In eating vegetables I am also engaged in killing: for example, if the vegetables are not organically grown, they may have been treated with an insecticide that killed insects, or insects may have been killed in the plowing and harvesting process. For all I know vegetables may be sentient beings also, and I am taking their lives. We live by killing: in my blood stream right now my white blood cells are attacking bacteria. I should just accept that I am a killer and go ahead and order that roast beef. The thought also occurs to me that I am a hypocrite in that I am wearing a pair of leather shoes and a leather belt which some cow died for, so whom am I kidding with my vegetarianism?

Then I counter that argument with other arguments: that I know that cows suffer pain and appear as if they might possess consciousness, but I don't know that vegetables and insects experience pain, and I am less inclined to think of them as conscious. We must begin making distinctions and decisions somewhere. If I am somewhat hypocritical, so be it. I'll think through the shoe and belt issue another time. The roast beef decision is the one before me right now. In the end, I order a vegetable dish and I experience some sense of pleasure for being moral, consistent, and strong-willed in the face of temptation.

Ānanda: Yikes! Has anyone ever told you that you think too much?

Bertie: You have. Many times.

Ānanda: Let's take a closer look at the process you have just outlined. It seems to me that every step of the way you feel physical sensations (hunger pangs), hear sounds (stomach growls), experience thoughts that alternate and come and go and have past reinforcement histories behind them, and experience mental images of various outcomes (pleasant tastes, enhanced self-esteem). These thoughts have different valences and strengths based on your past experiences with and attachments to teachers, parents, and esteemed others, and on your own direct reinforcement history. One thought leads to another as a whole network of associations is charged, presumably by electrical and chemical processes within the brain. Eventually one of these thoughts "wins out" and leads to action: it is the "stronger" thought. Your past reinforcement history gives more valence to being a moral being than to being a sensualist connoisseur of beef products. But where in this chain of sensations, sounds, thoughts, and anticipated mental images of future pleasures is there a sensation of "you?"[1]

Bertie: Well, there was an alternation of thoughts going on as if there was an internal argument. Finally I leaned more to one side than the other, and gave that side a bit of a "push," lent it more energy, and made the decision based on morality rather than selfish pleasure. Don't you think I deserve some reward for it?

Ānanda: There was this alternation of thoughts, but I rather think one thought drew upon its argumentative cousin by an associational process. There wasn't another consciousness inside arguing with you. That only happens in fictional dialogues like the one we are engaged in here.

More important, I am interested in the idea that you gave the "winning" idea an extra kind of "push." Did you experience this act of "pushing" and "making effort," or did the "decision" just happen somewhere along the line?

Bertie: Well, in this case I think the decision just kind of happened. But surely there are cases in which one does make a mental "push." We have thoughts we don't want and we try to push them out of our mind; or maybe it is a cold dark morning, and we've had a late night, and we need to push ourselves a bit to get out of bed and meditate. Isn't that the way it is?

Ānanda: I'm not at all sure that's the way it is, although I agree that's the way it seems. Let's take the case of having an unwanted thought and trying to push it out of one's mind through mental effort. First of all let's agree that minds have no "inside" and no "outside," and that there is no "place" from which or to which an unwanted thought can be pushed. Agreed?

Bertie: Agreed.

Ānanda: So what do we really mean when we talk about pushing a thought "aside" or "out?" This is something that patients who suffer from psychiatric disorders such as obsessive-compulsive disorder or posttraumatic stress disorder know a great deal about. Patients with obsessive-compulsive disorder struggle to rid their minds of unwanted images, thoughts, and impulses, while people with posttraumatic stress disorder struggle to block the repetition of traumatic memories. These patients expend enormous amounts of energy trying to block mental content through either narrowing the focus of awareness or through a process of distraction. Unfortunately the unwanted thoughts never really go away; they just keep popping back up, like those weighted inflatable dolls we used to knock down in childhood, because there is no other "place" for them to go to. When we are talking about pushing a thought away, we are really talking about refocusing the mind on some other mental content for a while, in the hope that while we are doing so whatever mental process that has ignited the unwanted thought burns itself out. Sometimes this is just what happens, and there is relative peace until the process that generates the unwanted thought is somehow rekindled again.

But I want to focus this investigation more on the processes of narrowing and distracting the mind. What happens when "we" do it and who is the "we" that is doing it?

It's my belief that this is a process that just occurs without anyone doing it. Two trains of thought compete for dominance: one the thought that is experienced as distressing, the other the thought that we should avoid the distressing thought and attend to another mental content, and whichever train is most energized wins. The degree of energization does not stem from some Internal Decider who throws his weight in one particular direction or another, but from a whole host of variables including inherited inclinations, fluctuations in a variety of physiological states, psychological reinforcement histories, and organismic appraisals of the likely pleasurable or painful consequences of pursuing one train of thought or the other. Some of these processes are conscious and some are not, but the process in its entirety is an organismic process of an integrated atomic/molecular/biological/psychological organism responding within a complex socioenvironmental field. Our sense of ourselves having been the Decider is probably only semireal, in much the same way that the "folders" on a computer "desktop" are only semireal.

Bertie: I just had the amusing thought that we seem to have switched roles. I am the rational scientific part of us, and you are the Buddhist part, but here I am arguing in favor of some sort of mental ghost in the machine, and you are being the radical empiricist. Strange, no?

Ānanda: Not really. Buddhism is a form of radical empiricism. The Buddha taught that one should not to take his word on his authority, but that one should see things for oneself. And seeing means radically seeing with nothing taken for granted. In the *Kālāma Sutta* he is quoted as having said:

> It is proper for you . . . to doubt, to be uncertain. . . . Do not go upon what has been acquired by repeated hearing; nor upon tradition; nor upon rumor; nor upon what is in a scripture; nor upon surmise; nor upon axiom; nor upon specious reasoning; nor upon a bias toward a notion that has been pondered over; nor upon another's seeming ability; nor upon the consideration "this monk is our teacher." (*The Instructions to the Kalamas*, 1981/1994, para. 4)

Bertie: But let's just suppose for a moment that you are right here, and that my moral decisions are not chosen by an inner me but are the outcome of a calculus of physiological processes which are being pushed at and pulled at by information streaming in from the environment. We are, then, a kind of wet computer, or to use William Burroughs's (1966) term, a "soft machine." If one knows the programming and the inputs and the state of the computer, one can predict the outcome. What happens to our concept of morality then? Our choices are only illusory, as they have been predetermined by everything that happened before. They could have been predicted if only we had a complicated enough computer and knew the initial state of the universe and all the laws of the universe at the moment of the Big Bang.

Ānanda: Yes. This is analogous to the Buddhist law of karma: all actions, including mental acts, are conditioned and are themselves the conditioners of future actions. There is no escape from it. If actions are not linked together by cause and effect, then they are random: they just happen without a cause. Random actions are not moral actions either. One could hardly give someone moral credit for a random act that "just happened."

Bertie: But if we accept what you say, that all human choices are determined by genetics and past conditioning and the effects of previous and current physical and biological factors rather than freely chosen, why would anyone strive to be more moral? Why wouldn't people say, "I might as well just do what is the most fun for me regardless of how it affects other people. If I act that way it is just because I was predestined to act that way. I can't choose any other course but the way I choose." If people don't make choices but only act out their programming, why are some actions meritorious and others censorious?

Ānanda: First, I do not think people "deserve" credit or blame for the way that they act, if by "deserve" we mean that there is some cosmic scorekeeper who keeps a record of our meritorious actions like so many gold stars. Credit and blame are social consequences of actions that serve to condition future responses. As such they have an important role to play in learning, but they are not rewards for the process of choosing through free will, only consequences of past choice and determiners of future choice.

Second, I think that the pursuit of selfish pleasure at another's expense is not the road to happiness but the road to misery. Sense pleasures are fleeting and empty, and the people we harm in our pursuit of them often end up resenting us and treating us accordingly. Amoral hedonism is a poor recipe for happiness. All wisdom traditions, including Buddhism, recognize this and most people grow to understand this truth through the fruits of their own experience over time. It is part of the psychobiological process that we call maturation.

Third, trying to reconcile the objective truth of causation with the experiential truth of choice is very difficult. The Buddha insisted, however, that we try to find a middle way between these irreconcilables, and that dismissing the reality of either causation or choice is an error. I think the only way to do this is to understand that our everyday functioning requires us to talk in terms of choice, but that the language of choice does not give us the deepest understanding of the way things are. In this sense, the experience of choice is, as I suggested earlier, analogous to the "desktop" metaphor in a computer graphical user interface: it makes life easier to talk about "desktops," "folders," and "files," but at a deeper level there are only photons or electrons that either change state or don't in a binary fashion. The desktop is semireal: one can see it and do things on it, or so it seems. At another more privileged level of discourse, however, there is no desktop. One is reluctant to see causation and choice in this way because even though cause-and-effect is an inescapable conclusion of an objective stance toward events, subjectively it still always "feels" as if one is choosing. This parallels the experiential fact that however much physics may tell us that physical objects are mostly empty space, we cannot help living in a world in which they appear solid.

I think it can be worthwhile to explore this process of choosing in a little greater depth. Most of our behavior occurs without much a sense of being conscious of it or the reasons for it. We mostly operate on automatic pilot. A moment ago I noticed my hand rubbing my eye. I didn't "choose" to do it. Some part of my brain must have registered some irritation around my eye, and my hand was there in an instant. Most of the time that my hand is touching my face I am not even aware I am doing it. Similarly, I don't usually "choose" to swing my arms when I go for a walk, or even decide what to look at and notice while on that walk. Our experience of most behavior is that it just happens. When we retrospectively try to come up with the reasons why we did one thing or another, often our answers are only guesses based on what we think we must have been experiencing. Our guesses are often no better than an outside observer's guesses (c.f., Kirsch & Lynn, 1999).

So when do we become aware of "choosing" our behavior? When a snafu has developed in the usual automatic pilot program. When the usual way of resolving a problem nonconsciously is not working and a metaphorical warning light blinks on. It may be that there is a conflict between two equally strong behaviors, or an awareness that the behavior we are about to engage in has had painful consequences in the past, or an awareness that what we are about to do is in conflict with a high priority goal. When that warning light blinks on, the brain allocates more workspace to the problem and puts more of the brain's computing power in service of its solution. The brain does this because it has learned in the past that when conditions like this occur, allocating more resources to the problem usually leads to a happier outcome. As a fuller range of associations, memories, and acquired problem solving algorithms are brought to bear, we are more likely to succeed. This is the process that we experience as choosing which feels so different from our automatic pilot behavior. But the main difference between the "choosing" behavior and the "automatic" behavior is the greater degree of resources involved, not some newly acquired freedom from cause and effect. A bigger computer is being used to solve the problem, but the solution still relies on the structure of the brain and our past experience.

I might also add that one additional reason why the experience of "choosing" feels "free" is that we are unaware of most of the antecedent processes that go into making a choice. The brain does not receive feedback about most of these ongoing antecedent processes, and their final product, a particular "thought," for example, just seems to pop into our heads from the void, uncaused as far as we are aware.

Bertie: Your argument makes sense to me. I'm afraid that as a committed empiricist and materialist I really have no choice but to agree: choice is only apparent choice and is not free of conditioning.

But let's return to my main concern about how to understand moral action in a world without free choice. It appears to me that this type of determinism renders morality meaningless. *moral*

Ānanda: I don't think this concern of yours is valid. First of all, every human culture has an idea of morality. Morality is as universal as other human activities, such as language, tool making, spirituality, decorative activity, music, and dance. Cultures may disagree on whether specific acts within specific contexts are moral or not, but all cultures have an understanding of moral ideas such as fairness, courage, loyalty, compassion, honesty, and so on. These might be innate ideas that are wired into our brains. Our brains seem prewired, for example, to acquire language (Chomsky, 1965) or to have a perceptual appreciation of small numbers (Piaget, 1952). I see no a priori reason why certain moral ideas might not also be prewired in some proto-form. Alternatively, moral ideas could be memes (Dawkins, 1976) of such high survival value that they have managed to spread universally. Last, it's also possible that these are ideas that are just incredibly easy to acquire *de novo* from experience given the structure of our brains.

Whatever the case, young children seem to have a rudimentary idea of fairness very early on. As the child develops, his or her moral ideas become more integrated and differentiated, more abstract and less concrete, and increasingly decentered from the self, but there is a kind of proto-fairness that is there almost from the beginning.

For the sake of our discussion let's arbitrarily decide that these universal moral ideas are hardy and useful memes. Moral ideas are extraordinarily useful memes because they enhance the likelihood that a society will function well. Moral ideas facilitate trust, cooperation, compromise, and other forms of prosocial behavior that are necessary for a society's survival, and since man is a social animal, they indirectly promote individual survival and the passing on of one's genetic inheritance. A society that inculcates these memes in its members's off-spring by reward and punishment is therefore going to have a cultural edge over one that does not. When there is greater social cooperation and greater empathic behavior, there is also reduced individual and communal suffering.

Morality still exists as an extremely important part of our existence even if our moral choices are the result of our past exposure to these memes and their re-inforcement history. Punishing immoral behavior and rewarding moral behavior still makes sense as a way of increasing the likelihood that these memes will be used by a given individual, even though they aren't the result of the free choice of the individual.

Your other argument of concern is that if people didn't believe in the fun-damental reality of free will they could just "choose" not to make any effort and goof off because whatever occurs is predetermined anyway. I have three points to make about this:

First, I'm not sure that this is a real problem. I don't believe in the funda-mental reality of free will, but I still make what seem to be moral efforts. Maybe your fear that people will just goof off is a fantasy.

Second, there is no way to know in advance what our decisions are going to be. To do so we would need to build an enormous computer that could take into account the location, spin, and momentum of every subatomic particle in the uni-verse. The computer would also need to take into account all of the interactions of these particles. Last, it would also need to take into account the effect of its own observations on all of these particles and their interactions. My fantasy is that even if such a computer were possible to construct it would end up having to be larger than the universe itself. We could call this fantastic computer the General Observing Device, or GOD for short. Since it's too large for the universe, we could stick it into some kind of extra-universal virtual space called the Huge Extra-Actual Virtual Environmental Nexus, or HEAVEN for short.

Since we can't build such a computer in actuality, we can never predict with certainty what we will decide. Saying that our behavior is always predeter-mined is really an argument based on generalizing from past experience; it's not empirically provable. We can only know what was predetermined retrospectively and on principle.[2]

So while on a theoretical level free will does not exist, and the Internal Chooser does not exist, on a day-to-day experiential level we go about the process of what seems like moral choosing. And however we might ultimately characterize that unfree conditioned process, it seems to be a beneficial one for the individual and for his culture.

If our internal decision-making process is not free from *causality*, it can be relatively free in other senses of the word. We can imagine choices that are relatively free from the salient pushes and pulls of immediate stimulus context, or are relatively free from the influences of parental, social, or religious authority, or are relatively free from short-term self-interest. Our capacity to have larger segments of our brains go "on-line" as part of the process of "making" decisions makes these kinds of relative freedoms possible, and these freedoms are the crucial freedoms from a moral point of view.

Bertie: I want to go back to your previous metaphor about how theoretical physics indicates that solid objects are not really solid, but that we live experientially in a world of solid objects. You suggest that this is similar to the fact that objectively there is no Internal Chooser or free will, but that subjectively we live in a world of making choices. I agree with the similarity, but the very similarity of these two metaphors suggests a flaw in the argument I believe you are trying to make. No one urges human beings to see the world of solid objects as insubstantial. No one says: "You are living in delusion. Your world is not solid. Wake up before it is too late!" When one is dealing with everyday reality, there are no pernicious consequences from perceiving objects as solid. Only in the physics lab does the ultimate truth about solidity have consequences. Buddhism seems content to allow us to live in this solid world.

One the other hand, Buddhism wants us to wake up to the insubstantiality of the Inner Experiencer and Chooser. Why is this insight so important? The absence of the Inner Chooser is probably only important in the neuroscience or artificial intelligence laboratory, not in everyday life. Why not allow this illusion to stand? What's the problem?

Ānanda: There are real existential and ethical consequences that flow from our erroneous view of selfhood. On an existential level, the existence of this inner self separates us from the rest of creation; we believe we are different from stars, rocks, ferrets, and daisies; we believe ourselves to be this free mental thing that stands outside of materiality and causality. When we experience ourselves as a process that is one with the universe, however, our sense of existential loneliness and estrangement drops away.

Our sense of existential estrangement underlies some of our most destructive behavior. When we harm the environment or another being we feel we are harming something other than ourselves. When we wake up to our existential continuity with Being, we realize that when we harm others we are harming ourselves.

This separate self we are constantly trying to protect and aggrandize is the source of much of our cruelty towards others. We are always worrying about the status of this self as if it was a currency whose value was floating in a free market: "What's the value of my self at this moment?" In contemporary free-market societies the self seems to fluctuate in value from moment to moment. The resulting insecurity means we are always trying to enhance our value through the accumulation of wealth, power, and status, through the pursuit of perfection, through ceaseless defensiveness and self-promotion, and through the defeat and humiliation of our rivals. The anxious self, worried about its own insufficiency, is at the root of most human cruelty.

Bertie: Now here's a bit of philosophical irony: A moment ago I was arguing that morality was impossible without a self, and now you are arguing that the self is a moral nemesis!

Ānanda: There are also psychological consequences to our erroneous view of the self. Our clinging to a separate, enduring self can become a false refuge from existential anxiety and can impede a genuine awakening to our human condition. We often hear exhortations from within the self-help community to "express ourselves," "love ourselves," "be our true selves," and "discover ourselves." These exhortations have genuine value when they encourage the undoing of habitual self-abnegation, self-hatred, or self-obliviousness. They become hindrances, however, when they encourage glorification of the self, or pursuit of the self as an end-goal in life. The self is a will-o'-the-wisp, an insubstantial ghost, only semireal, and not even "mine;" it cannot be a refuge from life's exigencies.

The Buddha believed that trying to take refuge in insubstantial, transient, and ultimately unsatisfying things was the root cause of human suffering. The belief that "if only I had this I would be happy" is reborn in the human heart in each and every moment: "If only one had more money," or "a better job," or "a better partner," or was "more beautiful," or "talented," or "healthier," and so on, ad infinitum. This belief in psychological rescue and refuge in ultimately unsatisfying things leads us to waste our lives in their pursuit, or leads us to berate and hate ourselves for failing to obtain or be them. The Buddha believed that if one clearly saw that the self was insubstantial, one would not cling to self, and that this would assist one in ending suffering.

Bertie: I'm not sure what you mean by "not clinging to the self?"

Ānanda: One would not take pride, for example, in being intelligent, and use that personal characteristic as a way of feeling either existentially sufficient or superior to others. Intelligence is not a static, fixed thing: we act intelligently one moment and stupidly the next. Intelligence is not permanent: at any moment it can be impaired by age, injury, or disease. Intelligence is also not "ours"; we cannot take credit for it: It is a function of our parents' genes, adequate nutrition, gifted teachers, the inculcation of good study habits, and the knowledge passed on to us from past generations. So there is no reason to cling to it: it is something that is here due to previous causes and conditions and is ephemeral. It is the same with every trait that we take to be part of the self: our kindness, our beauty, our courage, our strength. All of it is due to causes and conditions, and will vanish with changing causes and conditions; none of it is ours. We can be happy it is here, but it can't be our refuge.

Bertie: But if the self is illusory, why is it universal? What purpose does it serve in evolutionary terms?

Ānanda: I think calling the self "illusory" is going too far.

Bertie: Huh? I thought that was the point you have been trying so hard to make! Just when I begin to agree with you, you switch premises! That's not playing fair!

Ānanda: I never said I was trying to disprove the existence of the self, only that I was trying to examine our experience of what it means to be or have a self. I am content to say that the self is not what we usually think it is and that it has no separate enduring existence as an entity: the self is a reification of an ongoing process that is not localized inside our skin and does not belong to us. But it has a semireal existence. Just like those computer desktop "folders" have a semi-real existence. They are not really "folders," but they serve a purpose.

You are asking a good question when you ask about the universality of the self: all human beings above a minimal level of intelligence develop a sense of self, regardless of culture. It's also clear that they do so at a very early age, although the sense of self continues to elaborate and develop across the life span. The universality of the self suggests that we are biologically predisposed to develop one, and that this self must have important survival value for us as a species. This sense of self and agency are also deeply imbedded within language which has a semantic structure based on the distinctions between agent, action, and object. While some think that our sense of self grows out of the semantic structure of language, it seems more likely that a proto-self emerges prior to language acquisition, and that both the self and the semantic structure of language have similar roots in the structure of human experience given our biological makeup and our interaction with the world.

Some of the earliest roots of the self lie in mammalian behaviors such as territoriality, possession, and the social structure of the pack. It's easy to intuit the survival values of those behaviors and their role in natural selection. It is also easy to tie identity formation to the welfare of the family and clan; identity is in part determined by the reflected appraisals and ascribed roles of family and clan, and in turn serves as a locus of social responsibility for parents and teachers as they enculturate the child.

In addition, however, there is something dramatically self-evident about the self/other distinction. As soon as living cells acquire a membrane, a behavioral distinction arises between inside and outside. This distinction is reflected in activities as basic as the amoeba's protoplasmic streaming toward and engulfment of food and its streaming away from chemically noxious environments. As soon as we can move toward and away from what is other in order to survive, as soon as digestion and elimination are established as processes around which life organizes, we have the basis for the differentiation between outside and inside, self and other.

Bertie: You do realize, don't you, that you have just made the case for the biological inevitability and evolutionary value of the distinction between self and other? I rather think that undermines Buddhism's view of the self as illusory (or *semi-illusory* as you now insist) and its belief that it ought to be transcended.

Ānanda: Not at all. The fact that we are biologically predisposed to view things in a certain way, and that it might be useful to do so for some purposes, doesn't mean that it is the only, or even the most useful, way to view things. We are biologically predisposed to see objects as solid, and it is in many ways useful to do so; but objects are mostly empty space, and viewing them as solid prevents us from making other kinds of use of the material world. It looks to us as if the Earth is flat and that the sun moves around it; for most purposes that suits us well, but it is woefully inadequate for other purposes. As our social and intellectual evolution progresses, and as our species continues to interlink across the globe and reach beyond it, and as we begin to alter our environment and genetic makeup in radical ways, and as we develop technologies that can lead to our own extinction, prior ways of seeing things may no longer serve us. In our ancestral world of open space and small competing clans with only limited powers of control and destruction, the old view of self and other may have been good enough. Now, perhaps, a view of understanding what connects us, the unity of all things, a vision of interbeing, becomes imperative if we are to survive as a species. That is why I think that the *Dharma* (the Buddha's teachings) has come to be as important as it is in the West at this time. It is our survival raft. The Dharma is a set of memes that has been lying around for several millennia waiting to take root in whatever soil is ready to receive it.

Bertie: I understand your point, but I wonder if what you suggest is really possible. The subject-object dichotomy and our sense of selfhood seem so deeply programmed into our own makeup that the possibility of transcending it seems impossible to me. Even if it can be transcended for moments at a time, one can't possibly live one's whole life that way.

Ānanda: I don't know if it is possible or not. I know from my own experience that moments of transcendence are possible. My Buddhist teachers tell me that they know from their own experience that it is possible to spend more than just moments transcendently. The Buddhist literature tells us that there have been fully transcendent beings, and I think that there is no goal more worthwhile than discovering for oneself how much this might be possible.

Bertie: I wonder whether you are right in placing so high a value on the goal of self-transcendence? It seems to me that there are other goals that are more worthwhile: taking care of one's family, raising one's children, increasing social justice, working toward world peace, making beautiful art. As I think about it, all of these are more important than self-transcendence. Isn't cultivating self-transcendence more than a bit self-centered and self-indulgent? Isn't it the "Me Generation" writ large and cultivating its own navel?

Ānanda: I don't think so. The kind of transcendence I am talking about is the awakening to interbeing and interconnectedness, and a decentration of the self. It is the transcendence of the self and the liberation from it rather than the cultivation of or enhancement of it. The end result of that transcendence and decentration is the extension of one's caring to an ever-widening circle of Being: one's caring for one's family and for all beings who come across one's path, and for the environment that is one's dwelling place. Real compassion grows out of connection: the understanding that there is no difference between self and other, and that in helping someone else one is helping oneself and all beings. I sometimes think the main outcome of my own meditative practice has been the potential for the deepening of my attention to and appreciation of what life gives me to take care of on a moment-to-moment basis. For me this has meant more intimate attention to and caring for my family, my home, my friendships, and my work as a psychotherapist, as a supervisor, and as an administrator.

Bertie: But didn't the Buddha advocate leaving one's family and one's household responsibilities and withdrawing from the world? Didn't he in fact desert his wife, his newborn son, and his future kingdom to become an ascetic? Didn't he name his son *Rāhula*, a name that translates into English as "fetter?" How does that square with what you are saying?

Ānanda: You raise an intriguing point here. Although the Buddha's wife and child eventually became members of the *sangha* (the Buddhist monastic community), and although the Buddha left his family in palatial luxury as he went off in pursuit of enlightenment, there is no evidence that the Buddha had any special relationship with them; there is no evidence that he treated them differently than he did any other members of the *sangha*, as family rather than as followers; there is no evidence of any special attachment or intimacy; there was certainly no further sexual contact with his wife.

Some early Buddhist texts maintain that complete awakening and liberation can only occur for monastics who have abandoned household and family to enter the "homeless life." There is a path of practice for householders that emphasizes the practice of virtue; that path leads to better karma and "rebirth," and even to the guarantee of eventual enlightenment within a future lifetime; it does not lead, however, to the realization of *nirvāna*, complete awakening, in one's present lifetime.

Mahāyāna Buddhism reacted against the dualism it perceived in Theravāda Buddhism's setting nirvāna and the world of appearance apart. It also reacted against what it perceived as the selfishness of striving for individual awakening; instead it argued for the *bodhisattva* ideal of working for the awakening of all beings. Nevertheless, the path to enlightenment in Mahāyāna Buddhism (and, subsequently, Vajrayāna Buddhism) is still that of the monastic or the hermit. While the Zen variant of Mahāyāna Buddhism does not uphold a distinction between practice and everyday life, it still does not, at least in its traditional forms, view the householder's life itself as a complete path to liberation and enlightenment. In Japan, Zen priests only began to marry during the Meiji restoration, and at least one biography of a beloved contemporary Zen master suggests that his practice did not extend deeply into his family life (Chadwick, 1999).

There are historical precedents in Vajrayāna Buddhism for enlightenment outside of monastic and celibate life, but these examples do not point to the exigencies of the householder's life as a path in itself. For example, Marpa, the eleventh-century *siddha* who was the first Tibetan in the *Kagyu* lineage, managed a farm, was married, and had seven children. Marpa didn't view family life and agricultural work themselves, however, as an integral part of the path to enlightenment. Marpa rarely plowed the fields himself, and his wife viewed it as undignified for a great siddha to do so. His situation was such that he could afford to leave farm and family to go study in India for extended periods of time, and he could also conduct a three-year retreat on his property with his family while letting others attend to the farming (*The Life of Marpa*, 1986).

The reason for the privileging of the monastic or hermit's life is that awakening is liberation from all forms of clinging to phenomena. The householder's path of earning a living, maintaining a home, maintaining a marriage, and raising a family is seen as too intensely involving and demanding to allow for the slow, careful, intensive work of liberation through the meditative path. In addition, the activities of providing for and maintaining a family can naturally fan the flames of acquisitiveness, possessiveness, jealousy, dependent or obsessive attachment, and us-against-them protectiveness. In contrast, the monastic life theoretically simplifies life's demands: one's only possessions are one's razor, robes, a needle and thread, and one's begging bowl. Only one meal a day is needed, and that is obtained though begging rather than through labor. There are none of the difficult responsibilities of child rearing or maintaining a romantic relationship to be fretted over and resolved. One can devote one's full time and attention to meditation and learning the Dharma.

The idea that one's everyday household, workaday, and family life can be the focus and nexus of Buddhist practice seems to be a distinctively Western and twentieth-century idea. It can be seen as an extension and elaboration of the Mahāyāna denial of a duality between nirvāna and the world of appearance, and the Mahāyāna concern about the selfishness of the pursuit of individual liberation. Traditionalist critics could well argue, however, that this kind of twentieth-century Westernization of Buddhism is based on the uniquely American delusion that one should and can have everything: money, status, sex, power, *and* awakening too. There is a distinct danger that Buddhist awakening is being watered down into just another commodity one should acquire and have (and if one doesn't have it, perhaps one can sue one's teacher for malpractice?).

While the dangers of an easy Buddhism, one in which one can become awakened without sacrifice, are very real, there is still much that is intuitively appealing about the idea of the householder's life as a path to awakening; it cannot be dismissed out of hand, even if it contradicts the Buddha's endorsement of the homeless life. The idea of maintaining mindfulness of clinging and aversion as one goes about one's daily activities is an extension of the Buddha's advice to monks in the *Satipatthāna Sutta* (1995) that they practice mindfulness in all of their activities: sitting, walking, eating, and so on. The commitment one makes to the well-being of one's spouse or children can be seen as a field for the practice of the five ethical precepts. The self-sacrifice required of family life allows one to mature in one's understanding of what it means to do what is called for free from the demands of enhancement of self. As one struggles with what it means to be committed to other beings and emotionally bonded to them without clinging, one's understanding of respect and loving-kindness and compassion for another is enriched. Similarly the struggle with how to earn a living within the ethical precepts, and one's efforts to make work meaningful and mindful, can also be an enlarging, humbling, and enriching part of the path to awakening.

Western Buddhism has been exploring a path that includes both meditation and the household life, and in doing so is creating a new form of practice.

The inclusion of daily meditation and times for longer meditative retreats as part of one's household life is an effort to find a balance and compromise between the insights gained through meditation and the insights gained through creative engagement with the world. It remains to be seen whether this form of practice can lead in itself to full awakening, or whether it leads only to an enhancement and enrichment of life; in either case it does no harm.

It is also possible that monastic life is not necessarily any better at producing fully awakened beings than family life. While I have met monastics who manifest a high degree of awakening and who inspire respect and devotion, I have yet to meet a monastic (or anyone else) who is a fully enlightened being. In addition, one can point to monasteries throughout the world where acquisitiveness, selfishness, and attachment are as much of a problem as they are in secular life. I am not saying this to disparage monastic life: there can be an important place for monastic life in Western Buddhism. What I am suggesting is the possibility of a plurality of paths which can be accorded the same deep respect and which include lay practice.

Bertie: I think we are getting sidetracked here. Let's set aside the issue of whether lay practice can lead to full enlightenment or not, or whether it is equal in value to monastic practice. This question doesn't really interest me all that much.

Ānanda: Okay. What does interest you?

Bertie: I am interested in the question of whether Buddhism leads to full engagement with life, or whether it is an escape from life. It seems to me that one doesn't really need Buddhism to make a serious commitment to a goal, whether it is to be a loving husband and father, a devoted artist, or an impassioned advocate for political and economic justice or world peace. One just makes an existential commitment to these goals and gives it one's full energy and attention. Making a commitment to meditation and awakening may actually detract from the energy one could invest in these other goals. More important, I worry that Buddhism could offer a quietist escape from social responsibility, an easy way out from having to deal with the messy and seemingly intractable conflicts that are at the core of social existence.

Ānanda: It's all very well and good to make a serious commitment to a goal, whether to being a better husband or to creating world peace. The question is, after one has made a commitment to these things, how does one go about manifesting that commitment? What is being a better husband? How does one create peace? Doing these things requires more than a commitment. Both require moment-to-moment mindfulness of one's situation, one's responses to the situation, and the likely consequences of one's responses. Both require transcendence of one's small self to identify with a larger entity, either as part of a couple, or as part

[handwritten margin note:] Once commitment made, ? is how does one go about manifesting that commitment

of the world community. Both require a willingness to let go of clinging to one's preferences and a responsiveness to doing what the situation one finds oneself in requires. Both require a compassionate heart and a willingness to listen deeply to the other. These are all themes of Buddhist practice, and as such, Buddhist practice can contribute to one's ability to be successful in these goals.

Bertie: I think you are maybe being dishonest with yourself. I want to return to an earlier question as to whether what you are really espousing is Buddhism or not. I think what you are doing is adopting some Buddhist ideas about mindfulness, emptiness, nonself, and interbeing that happen to dovetail with Western ecological insights, quantum physics, cognitive science, phenomenology, and existentialism. I think you are melding them together, however, into a philosophy that is no longer authentically Buddhist at its core. The aim of your philosophy seems to me fundamentally different from the aim of the Buddha's philosophy: Your philosophy is about engagement with life and living one's life in a philosophically justified way. The Buddha was interested in disengagement from life and the ending of rebirth, not about finding a meaningful life in the world. In many ways your belief system seems more Jewish than Buddhist: it celebrates and blesses creation and places the highest value on ethical life. In contrast, Buddhism seems disenchanted with creation and seeks annihilation.

Ānanda: And I think you are making the mistake of thinking there is this thing called Pure Buddhism, and that I am diluting this Pure Buddhism by mixing it with both Judaism and more contemporary Western ideas.

There is no such thing as Pure Buddhism. Buddhism has always been a philosophy in active dialogue with preexisting cultural themes. Tibetan Buddhism is the end product of a dialogue between Indian Mahāyāna and Tantra, Chinese Ch'an, and Pre-Buddhist Tibetan Bön beliefs and practices. Zen is a distillation of the dialogue between Indian Mahāyāna and Chinese Taoism filtered through the lens of Japanese culture. What could be more different than the spare aesthetic of Japanese Zen and the colorful profusion of Tibetan Vajrayāna? Which is truly Buddhist? Even Theravāda Buddhism itself arose as one of several protestant-like responses to Brahmān practice, and it incorporated much of the preexisting Vedic cosmology and prescientific understanding of the natural world within itself. Western Buddhism is just the latest version of this ongoing dialogue, and it is only natural that it be a dialogue with the Judeo-Christian tradition, as well as with Science and Existentialism.

Bertie: Perhaps, but I still think you are evading my main point: Your philosophy is a philosophy of full engagement with the world and Buddhism is a philosophy

Nonidentification

Entitled to my anger but not entitled to transforming it

of withdrawal from the world. You have turned Buddhism on its head to suit your own purpose.

Define Buddhism

Ānanda: I don't think so. I think the real Buddhist message is mindfulness in each moment, nonidentification with the perceptions, sensations, thoughts, cravings, and aversions that arise in each moment, and the realization in each moment of the transience and interdependence of all phenomena. This mindfulness and insight leads to a life in which one no longer pursues self-aggrandizement, permanence, the accumulation of goods, or the pursuit of transient pleasures; as a consequence, one lives compassionately and wisely in harmony with the world doing what each situation requires. It does not require withdrawal from the world, but the release of one's grasp on it. That's Buddhism.

Bertie: Well, I don't know enough about Buddhism to argue this point any further. I still have my suspicions here, but let's just leave it at that. Since I am not a Buddhist, I don't really feel a need to strike any blows for the purity of the religion. I suppose if Orthodox or Hasidic Jews can't agree that Reform Judaism is a valid Judaism, then Buddhists are probably free to endlessly debate what is real Buddhism. Maybe, though, you have just gone from being a Reform Jew to being a Reform Buddhist? No orthodoxy for you, huh?

Ānanda: There is some truth in that. I am a modernist, and clinging to ancient traditions is not all that appealing to me, whether they be Jewish or Buddhist. I can appreciate the aesthetic of traditionalism, but it's not a path I can authentically walk.

Bertie: I want to thank you for explaining your Buddhism to me. I still have many reservations and doubts about your arguments. I can't say that you have entirely convinced me, especially around the issue of moral choice and free will and the illusory (ahem) I mean semi-illusory nature of the self, but I think I now understand what your Buddhism is.

Ānanda: Not really.

Bertie: You're really impossible, you know? You can never simply agree to anything I say! Just what are you trying to get at here?

Ānanda: What you have at best is an intellectual appreciation of a particular aspect of Buddhism as it relates to an understanding of the self. But Buddhism is not mostly philosophy; it's mostly practice. If you don't practice it, you don't understand it. It's like trying to understand what vanilla tastes like by reading a cookbook. Buddhism is not mostly about thinking. It is about the practice of

Buddhism is not mostly philosophy; it's mostly practice mindfulness moment-to-moment

mindfulness moment-to-moment. It is something one does; something one lives. In fact all this talking and thinking about Buddhism verges dangerously on not being very Buddhist at all: It's just more discursive thought, mental chatter that takes the mind away from stillness. The actual nature of reality is too subtle, elusive, and nonlinear for language to capture. As soon as we say something about the way things are we have distorted the truth. *actual nature of reality is too subtle, elusive & nonlinear for language to capture*

Bertie: So how does one get *real* understanding?

Ānanda: By ceasing identification with this intellectual chatter. By sitting quietly and being still. By practicing being attentive to each moment as it is without judgment or clinging. As the Buddha says, "*ehipassika*," come and see for yourself.

NOTES

1. I am indebted to Toni Packer for this analysis, and also for her comments on this manuscript. A similar description of Packer's analysis is described in Tollifson (1996).

2. I do not want to get into a full discussion of the nature of cause and effect because it is irrelevant to the main thrust of our discussion. The British empiricist philosopher David Hume argued that cause and effect can never be directly observed, but can only be understood as a belief about the future based on past observation that "whenever 'x' has happened in the past, 'y' has followed." Furthermore, quantum physics informs us that we cannot make definite statements that "if 'x,' then 'y'" but can only make probability statements about the state of the world (if "x," then a 99.999 chance of "y"). There appears to be a certain degree of randomness built into the very nature of the universe. In addition, the Heisenberg uncertainty principle limits what we can really know about quantum events since we can never know both the location and momentum of a particle at the same time. It would appear then that our GOD computer could only make probability statements about our likely "choices" rather than absolutely certain statements. But randomness is not at all the same thing as free will. We want our moral choices to be made according to reason and not randomness. So let's put aside the probabilistic nature of cause and effect for the moment, and discuss it as if it were something more solid. (The nonsolidity of cause and effect, by the way, is just another example of the Buddhist concept of *śūnyatā*—the essential emptiness or insubstantiality of all phenomena, whether the solidity of objects, the self, choice, or cause and effect. Let's just keep it in the back of our minds that cause and effect are not quite what we think they are, just like our separate sense of being a self is not quite what we think it is.

REFERENCES

Beck, C. J. (1993). *Nothing special: Living Zen*. San Francisco: HarperSanFrancisco.

Benson, H. (1975). *The relaxation response*. New York: William Morrow.

Burroughs, W. (1966). *The soft machine*. New York: Grove Press.

Cardeña, E., Lynn, S. J., and Krippner, S. (Eds.). (2000). *Varieties of anomalous experience: Examining the scientific evidence*. Washington, DC: American Psychological Association.

Chadwick, D. (1999). Crooked cucumber. New York: Broadway Books.

Chomsky, N. (1965). Aspects of the theory of syntax. Cambridge, MA: The MIT Press.

Dawkins, R. (1976). The selfish gene. Oxford, England: Oxford University Press.

Dennett, D. (1991). Consciousness explained. Boston: Little Brown.

Edmonston, W. (1991). Anesis. In S. J. Lynn and J. Rhue (Eds.), Theories of hypnosis: Current models and perspectives (pp. 197–237). New York: Guilford Press.

Friedman, R. E. (1997). Who wrote the Bible? San Francisco: HarperSanFrancisco.

Hermans, H. J. M. & Kempens, H. J. G. (1993). The dialogical self. New York: Academic Press.

Husserl, E. (1973). Phenomenology (R. Palmer, Trans.). In R. Zaner and D. Idhe (Eds.), Phenomenology and existentialism (pp. 46–70). New York: Capricorn Books, G. P. Putnam's Sons. (Original work published in 1921.)

Kabat-Zinn, J. (1990). Full catastrophe living: Using the wisdom of your body and mind to face stress, pain, and illness. New York: Delacourt.

Kirsch. I & Lynn, S. J. (1999). Automaticity in clinical psychology. American Psychologist, 54, 504–515.

Neisser, U. (1967). Cognitive psychology. New York: Appleton-Century-Crofts.

Oliver, M. (2000). The leaf and the cloud: A poem. Cambridge, MA: Da Capo Press.

Piaget, J. (1952). The child's conception of number (C. Gattegno & F. M. Hodgson, Trans.). London: Routledge & Paul.

Rubin, J. B. (1996). Psychotherapy and Buddhism: Toward an integration. New York: Plenum.

Ryle, G. (1949). The concept of mind. London: Hutchinson.

Satipatthāna Sutta (1995). The middle length discourses of the Buddha: A new translation of the Majjhima Nikāya (B. Ñānamoli & B. Bodhi, Trans.) (pp. 145–155). Boston: Wisdom Publications.

Shakabpa, W.D. (1984). Tibet: A Political History. New York: Potala Corporation.

Skilton, A. (1994). A concise history of Buddhism. Birmingham, England: Windhorse.

The instructions to the Kalamas. The Kalama sutta: The Buddha's charter of free inquiry. (1994). (Soma Thera, Trans.). DharmaNet Edition. Retrieved January 14, 2001 from the World Wide Web: http://watthai.net/talon/Wheel/wheel8.htm. Republished from The Kalama sutta: The Buddha's charter of free inquiry. (1981). (Soma Thera, Trans.). The Wheel Publication Number 8, Kandy, Sri Lanka: Buddhist Publication Society.

The life of Marpa the Translator. (1986). (The Nalanda Translation Committee under the direction of Chögyam Trungpa, Trans.). Boston: Shambhala.

Tollifson, J. (1996). Bare bones meditation. New York: Bell Tower.

Victoria, B. (1999). Yasutani Roshi: The hardest koan. Tricycle, 9, 60–65.

CHAPTER 5

Finding the Buddha/Finding the Self
Seeing with the Third Eye

Jean L. Kristeller

Buddhism is said to be the most psychological of the religions—and the most religious of the psychologies.

—attribution unknown

On my meditation stand is a slender bronze Buddha figure, about a foot tall, seated on a lotus pad inscribed with *om mani padme hum*, the Sanskrit mantra of enlightenment, around the base. I searched for this figure several years ago on a trip to Nepal, going into small dark shops that reminded me of the travelogue/spiritual journal *Shopping for Buddhas* (Greenwald, 1996). Finally, on the side of a tiny but airy courtyard, I found a much larger shop, lined with tiers of Buddhas. The setting and the ambience reflected a sense of pride and joy in the work. Among these finely crafted Buddhas, one drew me—and then I realized he was missing the third eye. As I hesitatingly pointed this out to the person assisting me, he offered that this could be taken care of. To my surprise, I was directed to carry my Buddha out into the courtyard and up a narrow ladderlike staircase to an attic garret where, with a sense of awe and unexpected privilege, I watched my third eye being inscribed by the craftsman.

Why it was missing I don't know. The craftsmen were more likely to be Hindus than Buddhists, although the process of transcendent "seeing," symbolized by the third eye, is important to both. Nepal, the only official Hindu country in the world, is also magical for the presence of living Buddhism in the Kathmandu valley and other places. This is not only due to the Buddhist history and presence of a substantial Tibetan community in the valley; our Nepali hosts' homes often had extravagantly large gold Buddhist figures in the living room— while close by hung a picture of the household Hindu deity. Buddhism felt as alive in Nepal as it had in Japan, where I had first seen the face of the Buddha almost 30 years earlier.

I have other Buddhist figures in my home (in my office, in the bathroom, in the front hall), and in my university office. They create a presence that meets a need, although it took me a number of years to recognize and acknowledge that this need was real and valid, and that my Buddhas represented more than a collection of travel souvenirs. It is this "third eye," this representation of a alternate way of seeing, of creating a space that allows a different sense of self and transformation to occur, that has engaged me. Buddhism has gradually, over 30 years, allowed me to meld a sense of spiritual being with an understanding of psychological growth. I have grown into it as it has grown into me, and in writing this account, I have had the opportunity to explore and then acknowledge the profound impact Buddhism has had on my development—both as a psychologist and personally.

When I was first invited to contribute this chapter about my personal development as a "Buddhist psychologist," I was flattered but conflicted. Although at times I have called myself a Buddhist because of my meditation practice and the appeal of many aspects of the philosophy, at this moment I do not really consider myself a Buddhist—nor a Buddhist psychologist—because I question some of the basic belief structures of Buddhism. Furthermore, it seemed inappropriate and disrespectful to friends and colleagues who are much more serious scholars and practitioners of Buddhism and meditation to claim this for myself. It would also be disrespectful to my own intellectual roots that are as equally grounded in logical positivism, cognitive-behavioral perspectives, humanistic psychology, and other contemporary psychological theories. Nevertheless, in challenging myself to respond to this invitation and to write about the significance of Buddhism for me and its relation to my professional life, I have had to examine more closely how I have come, at this point in my career, to be doing most of my research on meditation and spirituality. Some of the influences are extremely personal, others are cultural. Some have to do with growing up in the 1960s and 1970s, some with an opening up of clinical psychology to consider multiple perspectives, and much with the growing interest in mind-body connections; some with a particular moment in history, in that I grew up in a family that was a mixture of New England Yankee and Jewish-German, but which also had exposed me, more unusually, to Japanese culture at an early age.

Therefore this chapter is a story with several threads: a journey that has led me to try to integrate "seeing with the third eye" into rational logical positivism; an effort to make sense of my attraction to Buddhism from within my personal background; the pull of meditation practice both for myself personally and as a therapeutic technique; and, most recently, a growing awareness and acknowledgment of a spiritual path that began in Buddhism but has expanded past that. I am increasingly persuaded that "seeing with the third eye" is a fundamental and universal human capacity, a distinct mode of processing of experience. Despite the limitations of Buddhist psychology as a science-grounded perspective, I believe it speaks more clearly to these processes, to date, than do our Western psychological constructs. Furthermore, because Buddhism expands the frame of the value of such seeing beyond spiritual growth to other aspects of optimal health and self-regulation, it opens the opportunity to consider this aspect of human capacity not only from a religious perspective, but more broadly as a psychological process. Finally, without my exposure to Buddhism and meditation practice, I have little question that I would be doing different work as a psychologist, and be finding less satisfaction in my own personal life.

I will try to address within this chapter three aspects of my experiences with Buddhism: my relation to Buddhism as a source of spiritual connection and belief; my experience with meditation as personal practice, as a therapist, and as a focus of my own research; and my growing regard for the intellectual contributions of Buddhism to psychology. Since the original path I took into Buddhism was quite personal, direct, and spiritually directed, I shall begin with these threads, and then move to practice. Consideration of Buddhist principles that I have found particularly useful as a *psychology* are woven throughout.

The timeline of this account is somewhat nonlinear. My connection with Buddhism occurred after my first experience with meditation practice, but these two threads—of spiritual growth and practice—have continuously interacted and fed each other for over 30 years. Both have been informed by, and then influenced my development as a psychologist. Only as I have worked gradually through the years with both sides—the experiential and the intellectual understanding—have I felt able to grasp the fundamental truths behind the concept of seeing with the third eye, the critical importance to both psychological and spiritual growth of creating space for separating from patterns of conditioning. It is within that space that lies the path of wisdom.

THE BUDDHA, SPIRITUALITY, AND SEEING

My first efforts to explore Buddhism were not very productive. It was 1971, and as I was preparing to spend a year of college in Japan, I would be asked whether I was planning to study Zen. While I was generally aware of the writings on Zen coming out of Japan during the 1960s, my interest in Japan sprang from family connections and I had little interest in Buddhism. Nevertheless, I thought I would at least explore the question behind the questions. I struggled through Alan Watts's (1957) *The Way of Zen*—and remember thinking that it was somewhat ridiculous to consider the "sound of one hand clapping." I also skimmed Suzuki Roshi's (1970) *Zen Mind, Beginner's Mind*, but again did not find myself becoming engaged with these concepts; I was far too much of a logical positivist, and far too invested in managing my sense of self through the rational and intellectual, to grasp the basic premise. I also dipped a toe into meditation practice, going through the initiation into Transcendental Meditation (TM); while finding it intriguing, it did not particularly help me engage with what I was reading about Buddhist meditation.

At the same time, despite this rational bent, I was also on what I now recognize as a spiritual search. I had been looking for something I had failed to find in my own upbringing. My religious experience had started in an austere New England Congregational church in Byfield Parish, Massachusetts. It continued in New Jersey with a suburban Methodist church, with its stained glass windows and large spare crosses, but the images associated with Christianity had never fully engaged me emotionally, even during mid- to- later childhood when I was quite involved with the church. When I was 16, I spent a summer at a Methodist mission site in West Virginia where my commitment to social action was deepened, but my faith—and the credibility of religion—was weakened with my exposure to more fundamentalist perspectives. This dissatisfaction with what the Protestant church offered as a belief system deepened when we then moved to Durham, North Carolina, shortly thereafter, and I witnessed the racism which, rather than being challenged by the church as was happening in New Jersey, was still being practiced and embraced.

At the same time, the complexities of social and economic factors that I observed driving the poverty of West Virginia and the race issues in North Carolina led me for the first time to reconsider my career plans to become a basic scientist. I loved the rationality of math and the mental challenge of the sciences but had not understood from my high school social science courses that there was rigorous methodology that could be used to explore social problems. This interest remained largely uncultivated through the rest of high school, but exploded and then focused during my first psychology course at Swarthmore College. Through psychology, I realized I could combine biology, sociology, care-giving, and research in one discipline.

By the time I went to Japan in 1971, I had given up trying to find a spiritual connection in the churches I knew, even though I had explored both the Quaker meeting on the Swarthmore campus and a Unitarian congregation in Philadelphia. I understood that the focus on social action I found there was an expression of Christian compassion, but there seemed to be many other paths to serving that goal. Virtually no one I knew spoke of spirituality, and even if I was still searching, I did not expect nor intend to find it in Japan. My motives in going to Japan were fairly mundane and only loosely tied to academic goals. My parents had lived in Tokyo for four years after World War II, coming back to the states only a few months before I was born, very ordinary participants in the somewhat extraordinary world of the American postwar occupation of Japan. However, they brought back with them a substantial admiration for Japanese culture and its aesthetic. As a young child, I was exposed to the material world of Japan through the keepsakes, furniture, prints, kimono, and art they had brought back, and to the cultural world and Japanese values by reading my mother's collection of books on Japan, and by contact with many Japanese visitors. However, I was not taught anything about Buddhism. In fact, the Japanese family with whom my parents maintained the strongest contacts was strongly Christian and Catholic. My trip to Japan was primarily a search for a more personal connection with these relatively tenuous roots; the interest in cross-cultural studies was secondary.

When I arrived in Tokyo, I was disappointed by the apparent Westernization and pervasive modernization. My romanticized expectations of "quaint" and exotic were not met at all by what I saw around me. Even in 1971, the billboards at the airport looked almost like the ones in the United States. Much of Tokyo was quite unattractive, filled with the unappealing concrete construction that was thrown up to replace the destruction of the U.S. fire bombings. It was full of traffic, business, crowds, and exceedingly materialistic. In other words, it was a vital, busy, modernized, commercial city, engaged with commerce, popular culture, education, and politics. The school I was attending, International Christian University, was established on an American model, with an American-style campus.

It was several weeks before I was able to get out of Tokyo. With several classmates, I went to Kamakura, the historical capitol of Japan from 1185 to 1333 A.D., and there I began to find what I was looking for. It is a very traditional city, with perhaps a dozen Buddhist temples laid out in large stately rectangles along boulevards lined with huge trees. One enters a parklike promenade—and sitting totally solid and somewhat bemused at the far end is the great Buddha, almost 40 feet high. The immensity of the space created was not only physical, as in the great cathedrals, but also psychological, a sense of total calmness, of not asking for anything, but simply offering a place of quiet, dignity, and peace.

When I began to consider how to write this chapter, this was the image, to my surprise, that kept coming to mind as the beginning of my connection with Buddhism and to something spiritual in myself. The surprise comes from recognition of something previously not realized. In preparing to write this chapter, I had to ask myself Where did I start? And the answer was, over and over, the image of the great Buddha of Kamakura—the *Daibutsu*. And then the question comes, Why would this image, from another culture, have been so compelling? I could argue that I had been "primed" by my childhood exposure, by reading, and by the increasing exposure to Buddhist thought and culture within the United States. Cultural explanations are easier than universal ones to consider, but are always partial answers. These influences have also applied to many others who have become captivated with Japanese aesthetics; but aesthetic appreciation is not the same as spiritual experience. In looking back, I am instead clear that this calm, serene face, looking both inward and onward, brings me to a connection with my own sense of peace, of understanding, of *śūnyatā*, emptiness, the opening up of a different way of responding than what has been conditioned. This created the beginning. Universal needs are expressed, and perhaps even modified, by cultural structures, but I now understand that there is something integral to my own makeup that was drawn to the quietness and gentle presence of the Buddha which, however shaped by my own cultural and psychological background, was touched in the same way that the creators of these figures were touched.

I am still asked whether I spent time studying Zen meditation or Buddhism during my first two-year stay in Japan. Despite this encounter in Kamakura, I still did not seek this out. Perhaps I was too defended—which might explain why it took 30 years to realize the impact of that encounter. But Buddhism kept presenting itself during those two years. For example, I had been systematically reading Yukio Mishima's works (in translation) while preparing a paper on a cultural analysis of his dramatic suicide in 1970 (Kristeller, 1972); while Mishima is generally linked with Japanese nationalism, and hence Shintō, his last four books, a tetralogy entitled *The Sea of Fertility*, drew heavily—and darkly—on Buddhism and concepts of reincarnation. I remember struggling to understand that work. I also began to seek out Buddhist temples, both as a tourist, and for the feelings they evoked. In Europe, as a tourist, one can hardly avoid cathedrals; in Japan, one cannot seriously explore the culture and avoid Buddhist temples and gardens. Just as the magnificence of a cathedral and the figures of the Christ and Mary might raise questions of meaning, one is continuously presented with the iconography of the Buddhist world in Japan. Gradually, I began to realize a heightened sense of well-being and peace contemplating the gardens, the spaces, and the figures of Buddha. I was slowly coming to understand something different, something that can occur in contemplative spaces. At the same time, I was uncomfortable presenting even to myself that these visits were perhaps more than sightseeing.

An experience at the end of my first year in Japan gave me some inkling that I was beginning to see through different eyes. The International Congress of Psychology was held in Tokyo in 1972. It was my first psychology conference. I had been in Japan one year, taking courses on various aspects of Japanese culture, traveling, and learning a modest amount of the language. I felt isolated from my personal interest in psychology and was very eager to hear not only the talks of the internationally known American speakers, but the number of Japanese psychologists who were there. My clearest memory of these meetings put these two traditions into sharp juxtaposition. I had been enjoying the intellectual atmosphere, the questions, the modest debates in many sessions. A symposium was given by several prominent Japanese psychologists on concepts in Japanese psychology, and one of the lectures was on *wabi, sabi,* and *shibui,* three elements of the Japanese aesthetic which are subtle and somewhat difficult to grasp (Tachibana, 1938; Koren, 1994). Tachibana (1938) refers to *sabi* as "complexity within simplicity . . . calmness in activity." I found myself becoming acutely embarrassed by the confrontive and generally antagonistic questions that were raised as soon as the talk ended. What are your definitions? Where is your control group? What are the psychometrics? Even as an undergraduate, I knew that these were valid questions—but the point of the talk had been to introduce these terms conceptually as a window into Japanese mind and culture. I was embarrassed, both because the manner of the questions was extraordinarily rude in Japanese culture, and because these members of the audience could not hear what the important points were—and, as I was realizing, I could. I was beginning to understand how to hear one hand clapping. It was not until several years later that I also realized that this was the moment when I began to let go of being a logical positivist, and to conceive of a value of understanding beyond the rational.

When I returned home to the states after a second year in Kyoto, I still had a very shallow sense of what Buddhism entailed. It was still an "other," an exotic part of my experience. On my way home, I'd traveled through Korea and Thailand, also Buddhist cultures. I also visited Borobodur in Indonesia, the extraordinary, anachronistic Buddhist *stūpa* dating from the seventh century. The appearance of the Buddhist temples changed substantially with each culture—Korea felt the most familiar, as a progenitor of the Japanese aesthetic, whereas the Buddhas in Thailand were all gold and glitter; nevertheless, the pull, the draw to the great statues remained similar. I still didn't understand, however, what I was seeing or the cosmology behind it.

My first substantive exploration of Buddhist thought came shortly after my return to the United States. Back for my senior year of college, I enrolled in a survey course on Buddhist traditions, because I was interested in gaining more of an intellectual foundation for the exposure I had had to Buddhism during my time in Asia—and because the course fit into my schedule. The professor, Don Swearer, had come to Swarthmore from Oberlin College while I was out of the country. He was already recognized on campus as a master teacher and scholar; he is also an extraordinary individual who had integrated Buddhism into his own personal life through many extended stays in Thai monasteries. Only a few weeks into the course, the juxtaposition of the Buddhist texts, Don Swearer's guidance as a teacher, and the welling up of layers of experience from Asia came together to produce something that I experienced as truly transformative—an experience that I view now as a *satori* awakening. I was reading our assigned work, reading ahead, consuming it—and what had previously seemed obscure and even ridiculous—was clear. This time, when I read Alan Watts, he made complete sense. I saw and something was awakened, and I wanted to explore it further. This was the point where I reconsidered developing and committing to a personal meditation practice.

Unfortunately, missing from our course was opportunity for actual practice. One of the books we used, *The Secret of the Lotus* (Swearer, 1971), recounted the experiences of a group of students under the tutelage of a Thai *vipassanā* meditation teacher, and a Zen priest, whom Swearer had invited to Oberlin several years earlier. I recently raised the question to him why he had not included any practice in our course at Swarthmore. He commented that he personally, despite extensive practice, felt uncomfortable teaching meditation himself—and that he was concerned that it would be deemed inappropriate by the college. At the time, he ascribed to the view, still held today, that meditation training should be undertaken only under the tutelage of recognized masters and within an appropriate religious framework. My exposure to Transcendental Meditation three years earlier, and the publications on meditation as a therapeutic technique that were coming out of the laboratories at Harvard and elsewhere, represented the beginning edge of a somewhat different perspective.

MEDITATION: THE CORE OF PRACTICE
AND A PATH TO SEEING

Even without the opportunity to engage in practice as part of that course, I still view it as the point at which I purposefully began to consider how I might develop both a personal and professional commitment to exploring meditation. One of the primary paths to seeing that I have continuously found valuable has been meditation practice. My practice has slowly evolved over about 30 years, beginning with Transcendental Meditation (TM), expanding to a broader based Yogic practice, and finally settling most solidly into vipassanā mindfulness meditation. Although my meditation practice has come to inform my spiritual growth, it has always done more than this. It has helped me connect, as it can do for anyone, to a wisdom-level of experiencing that applies to all of our modes of being, whether physical, emotional, behavioral, or spiritual. The Buddhist perspective on meditation, which encompasses a broader psychology than do other contemplative traditions, and does so more explicitly, has been particularly useful for me in understanding the potential value of meditative work therapeutically, but the Hindu traditions, with more emphasis on mind-body balance, has also informed my work as a psychologist for many years.

As noted above, a few months before I left for Japan in 1971, I had my first exposure to meditation through TM, the first mass introduction of meditation techniques to the United States (Maharishi Mahesh Yogi, 1963-1995); (Bloomfield, Cain, & Jaffe, 1975). Looking back, I am not sure why I sought out the TM training. I recall mostly that I was reading about Zen and that TM was an easier and more available option to trying something "Asian." I was also intrigued by the mind-body research data that formed part of their promotional materials. I had had a course in physiological psychology and was tremendously excited by extending these concepts into clinical application. I do remember the training as a rather brief exposure; it was not until 30 years later that I had another "formal" session during a visit to the Maharishi University of Management. Nevertheless, this training was enough to transmit the basic essentials: a simple cognitive technique, a "personal" mantra, and the induction of a momentary experience of substantial calm, well-being, and release from the constant stream of mentation that I normally entertained and clung to. In fact, the experience gained credibility with me then because it induced a state similar to a "trick" I had used in boring high school classes a few years before. I had discovered that I could self-induce a mild trancelike state while remaining enough aware of the stream of the class to "come back" when needed. The TM experience was less trancelike and more relaxing because this was a true first window into "seeing" rather than simply a "tuning out" or disengagement. Intuitively, I think I understood this at the time and also understood that there was something special behind the hype and the Hindu rituals; this was neither simply a "relaxation" technique nor a recreational drug-type experience.

I do not remember how long I practiced the recommended 20 minutes, two times per day of TM. Perhaps for a week or less before the impracticalities of doing this while living in a dorm with a roommate interfered. In my usual skeptical way, I also remember immediately questioning the necessity for such consistent practice, as I was experiencing useful effects from relatively brief and more intermittent use, and as there was a lack of adequate explanation for the necessity for such discipline. In addition, while I valued and was intrigued by the empirical evidence for TM effects, however limited it was at the time, I was very uncomfortable with the traditional Hindu/Vedāntic trappings that surrounded the "transmission"—flowers, prayers, and so on—not only because they were inconsistent within the scientific rationale that I found more interesting, but also because they were even less personally relevant than the rituals of the Protestant church I was leaving behind.

I continued, however, to use the TM practice intermittently over the next four years, two years while in Japan and two years back in the States. In an indirect way, this TM training and practice was probably essential to the spiritual growth I would experience in Japan and immediately after, through my exposure to Buddhism. Having the personal positive experience with meditation made me more receptive to other contemplative aspects of Asian religion. Paradoxically, however, it may have interfered with seeking out practice experiences with Zen meditation while I was there, in that TM was clearly much easier than the rigorous discipline that I knew was required in the training temples in Kyoto.

The introduction to TM also made me aware of a different paradigm of mind-body functioning and of the nascent beginnings of this research area. While in Japan, I received encouragement to explore this further from a mentor, Dr. Takeo Umemoto, at Kyoto University. On returning to Swarthmore to finish my degree in psychology, I began to read whatever was available, and to consider pursuing this type of research in graduate school. I had gone to Japan intending to become a social psychologist—and came back looking more broadly. The early meditation and biofeedback research was coming out, both from Benson's group (Wallace, Benson, & Wilson, 1971; Wallace & Benson, 1972) and from a few others (Schwartz, 1975; Green, Green, & Walters, 1970), and gaining scholarly and popular attention (Schwartz, 1974). Human psychophysiology research, which had begun in the late 1800s examining the effects of psychological manipulations on basic autonomic nervous system functioning, was to serve as one of the bases for the development of more contemporary mind-body research and health psychology, which did not emerge as a defined area until the late 1970s. It seemed to offer the framework to pursue two directions of increasing interest: physiological bases of behavior and clinical application; this led to a decision, for my graduate work, of pursuing a degree in clinical psychology. In 1974, one had to choose a graduate program in clinical psychology very carefully by the dominant "school" of thought represented: psychodynamic, humanistic, or behavioral. Only within behaviorally oriented clinical programs was there a strong commitment to research and establishing the empirical basis of the practice. The psychology department at the University of Wisconsin had this commitment and was one of only a few to provide training in human psychophysiology within a clinical psychology program.

When I began graduate school at Wisconsin in 1975, I was searching for ways to reestablish a meditation practice. Because I still found the perspectives of Buddhism more compelling than those of Hinduism, I again explored Zen practice, attending a workshop with Phillip Kapleau Roshi (Kapleau, 1967) in Madison; unfortunately, my concerns about Zen practice were reinforced, as I found the day draining and punishing. I was not convinced by the Zen perspective that meditating on pain was a desirable path to "breaking" through to enlightenment; I found the gentler "relaxation response" model proposed by TM and Benson (Benson, 1975) far more appealing and consistent with my own personal goals. I really was not looking for an enlightenment experience or for profoundly changing my worldview. These goals seemed too distant and the discipline too intense, almost like working out with a group of marathoners simply to gain basic physical conditioning. The next opportunity that presented itself in Madison was with, ironically, another Hindu-based yogic meditation program, one founded by

Swami Rama, through the Himalayan Institute. The Madison group was being run by his associate, Swami Ajaya, née Allen Weinstock, who was at UW finishing postdoctoral work in counseling psychology and actively trying to integrate Western and Hindu psychology (Rama, Ballentine, & Ajaya, 1976). This group also provided the opportunity to begin some yoga work and to go to regular sittings. I was reinitiated by Swami Ajaya and received another, more truly personal mantra and began a more regular practice of concentrative meditation. He was also very encouraging of my research work (Kristeller, 1977). However, my meditation practice and spiritual growth continued to be somewhat disjointed; I still found the religious aspects of Hinduism unappealing, but I had not found any good way to link my experiences with Buddhism to practice.

FROM PRACTICE TO THE LABORATORY

Of as much significance in Wisconsin was my first opportunity to integrate my personal practice with work in psychology. The field—and my own interest—was still very much focused on demonstrating the physiological distinctiveness of meditation effects. Peter Lang, the head of the psychophysiology laboratory, was engaged in cutting-edge research on the relationships among physiology, treatment of clinical disorders, and parameters of biofeedback control of heart rate (Lang, Troyer, Twentyman, & Gatchel, 1975). I became part of a research team that began comparing biofeedback and meditation, using Benson's relaxation response approach (Benson, 1975). There were a number of assumptions we (and others) were making: that it was viable to study these effects in nonclinical participants (college undergraduates) who were novice meditators, and that the Benson variation on meditation (repeating the word *one*) was an adequate substitute for traditional approaches. In a series of four studies, various aspects of heart rate training were manipulated: whether subjects received summary feedback, when they received it, and finally, the quality of the interaction between the experimenter and the subject, which, we suspected, was accounting for some differences in effects in the earlier studies. What we found was exciting (Cuthbert, Kristeller, Simons, & Lang, 1981): while biofeedback produced modest results relative to baseline, the largest and most consistent results were with meditation, after only three sessions of brief training. Of as much interest, the effects depended on the social context of the training. When the trainer/experimenter was highly interactive, acting more like a "coach," the biofeedback training produced the larger effects. When the experimenter was more detached in interacting with the subject and a minimum of information was provided, the meditation subjects lowered their heart rate more, by over eight beats per minute, a very large amount for this experimental paradigm. While these results were consistent with meditation as a "relaxation" technique, they also highlight how sensitive the therapeutic effects can be to "set" and self-expectations.

Disturbing the fundamental process of meditative disengagement by introducing social expectations interfered with the value of the meditative state.

Although I appreciated the opportunity to pursue this research, the general tone of the psychology program at Wisconsin was reductionistic, and there seemed to be little appreciation for exploring the meaning or "wisdom" behind what we were doing. I wanted to move to a program where a wider range of theoretical perspectives was being considered. I continued my graduate work at Yale with Gary Schwartz, who had gone there from Harvard where he had conducted studies on the effects of meditation and emotion with his doctoral students Daniel Goleman (Goleman & Schwartz, 1976) and Richard Davidson (Davidson, Goleman, & Schwartz, 1976). At the time, and in retrospect, the most important influence on my thinking was Schwartz's theoretical work on self-regulatory processes—particularly his perspective on the "brain as a health care system" (Schwartz, 1979). He posited that much of the dysfunction that was, at the time, still being referred to as "psychosomatic," came about because subtle physical cues were being ignored or disregarded, creating a state of "disregulation." The corollary of this disregulation principle is that the brain-mind inherently carries in it the ability to move toward a healthier state if appropriate awareness is given to the salient cues and if there is a disengagement of competing cues. Schwartz viewed awareness as a key element in modulating health, and posited this as the critical ingredient linking biofeedback and meditation. The disregulation/self-regulation model of meditation effects was a powerful extension of, or alternative to, the "relaxation response" model of meditation.

At Yale I had my first opportunity to work with a clinical use of meditation in the general population, with Steven Warrenburg (Warrenburg, Pagano, & Woods, 1977), who as a postdoctoral fellow was studying behavioral treatment of hypertension in a local industrial plant, using both dietary modification and several types of relaxation training. Because of the aura of the "esoteric" that hovered around meditation in the 1970s, we had anticipated that the groups comprised of management personnel would be more receptive to the meditation component of the relaxation training than would the groups comprised of the factory workers. The opposite was true, however, encouraging me to consider to use of meditation in the therapeutic environment with the general public.

I also had the opportunity to begin work in the area of food intake regulation under the influence of Judith Rodin (Kristeller & Rodin, 1989), and I began to explore how to translate some of Gary Schwartz's self-regulatory concepts into the treatment of eating disorders. Rodin's (1981) work on the apparent oversensitivity of obese individuals to external cues provided the background for this work, but I was also strongly influenced by Marlatt's research (Marlatt & Rohsenow, 1980) on alcohol intake and by Herman and Polivy's work (Herman & Polivy, 1975) with re-strained eaters. These findings illustrated the degree to which cognitive and emo-tional experiences can override biological needs or physiological pressures. Such a "disconnection" then engenders a sense of being out of control. From a clinical per-spective, Susie Orbach's (1978; 1990) *Fat as a Feminist Issue* provided compelling de-scriptions of the experience of hunger for the compulsive eater struggling with the confusion engendered when excessive dieting disrupts normal use of physiological signals of hunger and satiation, and as eating occurs more and more in response to emotional needs. These patterns develop a synchrony with each other, further dis-connecting the behavior of eating from the physical need for food. The feedback cues exist, but are neither entering awareness nor being attended to. Individuals be-come caught within a net of competing conditioned responses, each triggering off a dysfunctional cycle that is self-sustaining but ultimately disregulatory and self-destructive. I began to explore, in the clinical setting, how meditation might facili-tate a retraining of sensitivity to internal experience that could then reregulate attention to normal internal signals of hunger and satiety, and might thereby pro-vide an alternative to standard cognitive-behavioral interventions.

While on my clinical internship at Brown, I began to experiment with inte-grating meditation training into treatment for compulsive eaters, first introducing it as a "relaxation" method and then as part of a self-regulation process. I found that the compulsive eaters I was working with were very receptive and responsive to using meditation in this way. My own background in mantra meditation, how-ever, seemed inadequate to this undertaking. In 1983, I moved to the Boston area and began to work with a wider range of meditation approaches including vipas-sanā, first at the Cambridge Hospital with Dan Brown as we were developing the behavioral medicine services there, and then at the University of Massachusetts Medical Center (UMMC) in Worcester in preventive and behavioral medicine. Dan Brown had an impressive ability to integrate complex conceptual perspectives drawn from a very deep knowledge of original Buddhist texts with contemporary cognitive-behavioral and humanistic psychological principles (cf., Brown & Engler, 1980; Fromm & Brown, 1987). At UMMC, Jon Kabat-Zinn had recently estab-lished his Stress Reduction and Relaxation Program (SRRP), the basis of which is mindfulness meditation supplemented with Yoga practice, group discussion, and some cognitive techniques (Kabat-Zinn, 1990). The 10-week program (now referred to as the Mindfulness-based Stress Reduction Program), using groups comprised of about 30 people with a widely diverse set of presenting problems, has shown ef-fectiveness for managing chronic pain (Kabat-Zinn, Lipworth, & Burney, 1985) and anxiety disorders (Kabat-Zinn et al., 1992), and for persons suffering from problems such as AIDS, cancer, and depression.

Although I was not teaching in the SRRP program, I had the opportunity to participate in the program, and then to collaborate on research. Jon Kabat-Zinn's ability to adapt traditional techniques to a contemporary medical environment was compelling. He was able to work with people from a wide range of backgrounds who were not necessarily seeking meditation as a personal spiritual practice, but rather for relief from their symptoms. His flexibility, in the context of his own extensive orthodox training in meditation practice, was profoundly influential in supporting my own perspective that this type of adaptation was both possible and appropriate. I began to integrate meditation into both my individual work with clients in the UMMC behavioral medicine clinic, which primarily provided services within traditional cognitive-behavioral and counseling modalities, and within treatment services that I was developing for individuals with binge eating disorder. While I would continue to use concentrative/mantra-based meditation approaches with many clients, I began to focus my own work on the importance of cultivating "bare attention" to the physical and emotional experiences that arise. Another key aspect of mindfulness meditation is the importance placed on explicit integration of meditative practice into all aspects of daily life. This emphasis also fits better than does TM, I believe, with developing a meditation-based approach to treating a syndrome such as compulsive binge eating disorder.

However, common to both the TM literature and to the growing body of research utilizing mindfulness techniques, is an attempt to disengage meditation practice from both the esoteric and from the spiritual—to demystify and secularize the use of meditation. Even with relatively little practice, meditation appears to produce self-regulatory effects relatively quickly and easily. By documenting that meditation can produce these meaningful effects across a wide range of functioning, with relatively little practice, meditation is reframed as a psychological *process*, rather than as an esoteric discipline. Meditation is thereby inherently valuable at virtually any level of practice or capacity, rather than something limited to the adept or the natural contemplative.

From a therapeutic perspective, both mindfulness and mantra-based meditation approaches have something to offer. Insight or mindfulness meditation has the distinction of more actively engaging the individual in a transformative way with the nature of salient issues than does mantra meditation. In my experience clinically, there is a more rapid movement with mindfulness meditation than with mantra-based meditation toward what I would call "wisdom functioning"—drawing on those higher levels of choice and possibility that are within our capabilities but are often blocked out by more powerful and immediate conditioning effects or survival needs. In contrast, I find that mantra meditation can be more useful for individuals in need of basic relaxation effects, who find a mantra particularly valuable in disengaging from a stream of incessant thought content. Furthermore, it is apparent that TM can also produce behavioral effects (Gelderloos, Walton, Orme-Johnson, & Alexander, 1991), and that the "space" opened up by skillful use of the mantra can also be very powerful in accessing higher levels of functioning. To date, however, no adequate direct empirical comparisons of these two distinct approaches to meditation have been carried out.

After leaving UMMC in 1991 and moving back into an academic position in the doctoral program in clinical psychology at Indiana State University, I continued the meditation work in two directions: clinical research and teaching. One of our doctoral students, Brendan Hallett, had a background in meditation practice, and we adapted the meditation-based treatment program for compulsive eaters that I had been using at UMMC, developing a seven-session program for obese women with binge eating disorder (BED) (Kristeller & Hallett, 1999). Although we did not view this as a comprehensive approach to treating all aspects of BED, we were interested in evaluating the effectiveness and acceptability of such an approach for these women who had no previous exposure to meditation. The first group was not successful—we had a very high drop-out rate because we had not taken enough time to orient the participants, individually, to the underlying rationale of using meditation. Once we did so, our participants stayed with the groups, and we found almost immediate benefits: within six weeks, binge eating dropped markedly in both frequency and intensity, depression improved, and most important, the women reported an increased sense of inner control, decreased "struggle" around food, and a new capacity to "let go" of much of the inner turmoil about their relationship to food—and their relationships to others. The program follows the general principles of Kabat-Zinn's approach: use of mindfulness, taped meditation exercises, and group discussion of experiences. In the SRRP there is an early experience referred to as the "raisin meditation" in which a single raisin is eaten as slowly and mindfully as possible. We expand that experience to a range of foods and eating experiences, focusing explicitly on developing a mindful relationship to food and the experience of eating: each session is structured around one aspect of the eating experience, such as awareness of emotional triggers, awareness of hunger and satiation cues, and awareness of anger at self and others. The key goals are heightening awareness, decreasing negative self-judgment, and heightening a sense of inner control. When the participants begin to experience these changes—and begin to let go of the endless cycle of obsessing, self-loathing, and attraction to and disgust with food, they experience a sense of freedom. This is the release from the burden of suffering described in the Buddhist literature as the wheel of *samsara*. This research is being continued as an 8-week program that we are evaluating further in a randomized clinical trial funded by the NIH.

At Indiana State I was also allowed the freedom and opportunity to develop and teach a seminar on the psychology of meditation and self-regulation at the advanced undergraduate/graduate level. The first syllabus covered meditation as a relaxation technique, the differences between concentrative and mindfulness meditation, the experimental literature on TM and other modalities, the thera-peutic effects from Kabat-Zinn's work, and so forth, in addition to covering other techniques such as progressive muscle relaxation and issues of self-regulation, such as addictive processes. I planned to touch briefly on the religious context of meditation, but my intention was primarily to demystify and, in fact, secularize, meditative approaches as much as possible for the purpose of framing it in terms of psychological and psychotherapeutic processes. But on the first day of class, one of the graduate students asked me whether I was going to address the spiritual ef-fects of meditation. Giving relatively little consideration to his question at the time, I responded that I did not see that as appropriate because spirituality was not an empirically supported psychological construct. To my surprise, he dropped the course, but his question did not drop. This single question, in fact, became the catalyst for a new stage of growth and work, both personally and professionally.

INTEGRATING THE WORK OF MEDITATION AND SPIRITUALITY

After moving to Terre Haute to teach at Indiana State University, although still identifying myself as a "Buddhist" with a small b, I rejoined the Methodist church, partly because I had found no accessible spiritual group in the local community, and partly because I met my husband, and this was a background we shared. For about four years, I worked at it. I joined the choir and rediscovered a joy in singing. Although I still attended meditation workshops and retreats elsewhere, I tried to reengage with the Christian theology and cosmology, keeping in mind the Dalai Lama's suggestion to seek within one's own tradition, and searching for a spiritual space for myself in the church.

As I began to teach on the psychology of meditation, I was also beginning to explore this question of the meaning of spirituality from a psychological perspec-tive. I began to look at what was available on spirituality, both within the psychol-ogy of meditation literature and within the psychology of religion literature. I was immersing myself in some of the substantial material on meditation as a spiritual path by Kornfield and his associates (Kornfield, 1993; Levine, 1979), by Thich Nhat Hanh (1995), and by others. I rediscovered Huxley's *The Perennial Philosophy* (Hux-ley, 1970), and my husband and I taught from it in a study group at church. There was more than I could possibly have time to read, but there was very little empirical work on the spiritual effects of meditation. Looking further, I soon realized that this mirrored, in 1996, the lack of much substantial work on spirituality in the psychol-ogy of religion. Even a major textbook on the psychology of religion, such as Wulff's (Wulff, 1991), had minimal references in the 1991 edition explicitly to spirituality, though it certainly dealt with related aspects, such as altered states, peak experiences, and religious conversion. Furthermore, in 1996 the research that existed tended to be tied almost exclusively to Christian expressions of spiritual experience, without considering how that might relate to identification of universal principles. However, interest in the area of the psychology of spirituality was growing rapidly, and shortly thereafter, I began to develop a line of research looking at spirituality as an element in adjustment to cancer; in particular, I was influenced by work coming out of a large research group in Chicago, headed by David Cella, that had been developing comprehensive measures of quality of life (QOL). This group was in the process of adding a scale that tapped into two important dimensions of spiritual well-being, meaning and peace, and faith, to their other measures of QOL in cancer patients. They had succeeded in creating items that could be responded to by individuals of virtually any faith—or even by atheists. The results of one of their studies suggested that a high level of meaning and peace (more so than faith) contributed substantially to overall well-being in adjustment to cancer, regardless of other distressing symptoms such as fatigue or pain, and independent of measures of depression (Brady, Peterman, Fitchett, Mo, & Cella, 1999). In pursuing this area of research, I found myself reading more broadly into the underlying elements of what is meant by spiritual experience, and in particular, to be impressed with how potent even "modest" levels of such experience is for most individuals.

When I taught the meditation seminar again, I had no question that I would address spirituality as one of the core domains of effects of meditation. That course then formed a basis for a teaching fellowship from the Fetzer Institute and the Nathan Cummings Foundation on Contemplative Practice, expanding further my exposure to other ways of "seeing" and "seeking wisdom," as I met with other recipients of the fellowships. Out of this teaching I also began to grapple with developing a model of meditation effects that incorporates all aspects of change (from the physical to the spiritual), rather than looking at them one by one, as much of the literature has tended to do (Marlatt & Kristeller, 2000; Kristeller, 2001).

In the process of this rather intellectual exploration, I then also had to face more immediately my relationship to my own spiritual side and to acknowledge that my efforts to move back into the Methodist church were not proving satisfying. I found that my time in church kept bringing me up against an edge of "No," rather than "Yes." The contemplative side seemed unsupported or even missing. Furthermore, the dogmatism and lack of acknowledgment of the validity of other ways to seek spiritual grace were insulting to my respect for Buddhism and other world religious views. As I continued exploring how to validate the importance of the spiritual needs of others, I also had to acknowledge the validity of my own needs—and that these were not being met. I found a spirituality group at the Unitarian Universalist congregation and an informal sitting group to join. As I found better ways to meet these spiritual needs, attending the Methodist church services became increasingly painful. Finally I left, to join the community—a *sangha*—that I was finding within the Unitarian Universalists. I had discovered a place where I could openly say that I was more Buddhist than Christian, but a spiritual being before either, aware of many paths and able to use those that opened up seeing for myself. In this context and others, I can now look for wisdom in the doctrines and the teachings of many of the masters. I can recognize the place that they come from as being universal in their essence, and all of them involving the seeing with the third eye.

As I began teaching and working therapeutically with meditation, I also began to explore some of the issues that arose for me in my own practice, because they were ones that also arose with my students and my patients. One of the issues that I have grappled with repeatedly is the question of amount and dedication to practice. I have always experienced a struggle with what I perceived as the expectations (from others and myself) that I must be more engaged, do more long retreats, maintain a daily practice, and so on, particularly if I had any aspirations to teach or write about meditation practice. Yet the practice I have done has been extraordinarily valuable, and I have come to terms with the truth that I am *not* a "natural contemplative," such as is described in the medieval Christian text *The Cloud of Unknowing* (Progoff, 1983), but rather a "person of action." The person of action also benefits from contemplative prayer and intermittent practice, but then returns back to daily activities. This tradition also exists in Buddhism—for example, the expectation that all young Thai men engage in an extended retreat experience, regardless of their vocational intent. But possibly this dichotomy—between the contemplative and the person of action—is false. This way of seeing is, in truth, a universal human capacity, and meditation is a tool. While more practice may bring with it better ability to access the contemplative side of being, there is a danger in imposing expectations better suited to those seeking a particular state of "enlightenment" or level of mastery. Considering a parallel to training ourselves in other aspects of human endeavor, such as music or athletics, is helpful. We now realize that maintaining physical fitness is a process, the effects of which can be best understood as lying along a continuum, rather than in a dichotomy of the "unfit" versus the star athlete. Even elderly individuals in nursing homes are now known to benefit remarkably from mild exercise. A less dramatic contrast can be considered with musical training. Few would argue that virtually everyone has some ability to appreciate and understand music—and that such understanding is improved with even modest training. We do not mistake the skills needed to provide such training to schoolchildren with the discipline and skill needed to become a professional classical musician, nor do we minimize or disparage the value to the individual of whatever level of musical experience someone wishes to seek out.

My personal identification with Buddhism has been much more experiential and spiritual than doctrinal, yet to the degree that it has informed my work as a psychologist, it has also been intellectual. Probably the earliest influence was being exposed to the Buddhist repudiation of the Cartesian separation of mind-soul from body. The second aspect of Buddhist psychology that began to insinuate itself into my thinking was a questioning of rationality as the hallmark and pinnacle of the human thought processes—and later questioning the Cartesian principle of "cogito ergo sum," realizing there is both more—and less—to who I am than conscious thoughts reveal. Third was the recognition that Buddhism and learning theory overlap in identifying conditioning, particularly operant conditioning, as one of the most powerful motivating factors in human behavior—and one of the primary sources of attachment and suffering. Coming more slowly, and unfolding with my own journey of self-exploration, has been the understanding that the search for the spiritual/enlightenment/transformation of the self is valid as a fundamental psychological process, rather than to be either accepted or discounted as a supernatural process. Much of that process has to do with disengagement of our more usual modes of being: satisfying needs and urges; relating to the world as a source of pain or pleasure; use of our usual analytic thought processes; grasping onto the self that these create as if it were all that we are.

There are many paths to accessing our higher levels of wisdom, but meditation practice may be among the most powerful because it provides the means by which one can train the mind to disengage those patterns of conditioning systematically and purposefully, opening up the possibility of bringing other ways of relating to a situation. Meditation practice is one means toward cultivating wisdom, defined as the ability to make optimal use of our internal resources (whether spiritual or other) that lie beyond basic survival and adaptive functioning; engaging in meditation practice is one aspect of growth, of learning to see. Perhaps it is because the effects of meditation for me are more subtle, like those I experience playing music or being physically active, that I feel as comfortable integrating it into all aspects of life. There have been few points of exaltation, no altered states that were compelling, no engagement with a guru. Yet it is there—and it is uniquely powerful—and that is what I want to communicate and bring to my students and to my patients.

So where does this path of seeing lead?

- It keeps me from thinking too much.

- It provides an inner core of calmness and balance.

- It helps me recognize my patterns of conditioning—and to experience some choice in joyfully staying with these patterns or disengaging from them.

- It helps me recognize when I overreact—and helps me rebalance.

- It provides me a powerful tool to offer some—although not all—of my patients.

- It helps me listen—to my patients, my colleagues, my friends, and my students.

- It helps me be aware of how hard it can be to listen sometimes.

- It helps me to cultivate a sense of inner peace and a sense of connectedness with all things.

- It provides a physical calmness and sense of body.

- It helps me to much more completely enjoy the pleasures—of food, music, art, and nature.

- It helps me experience the spiritual process—however limited my own abilities may be.

- It helps me see.

In the last few years I have reengaged with Buddhism, with my own contemplative practice, and with the purpose and value of meditation as a powerful tool for growth. Through reengaging the contemplative process, I have finally come back to a richer understanding and grasp of the meaning and value of spiritual experience. I can see the peace in the eyes of the Buddha. And beyond that peace I can see more. Coming back and embracing the practice more intellectually, in balance with practice, has been proving to be the right path for me. Writing and teaching more about practice, reading what my colleagues write—and what our predecessors have written—has created the better space for my own practice. This has been an intellectual and personal journey that has now linked with the spiritual. I have been finding the self—and catching glimmers of the not-self.

REFERENCES

Benson, H. (1975). *The relaxation response.* New York: William Morrow.

Bloomfield, H. H., Cain, M. P., & Jaffe, D. T. (1975). TM. *Discovering inner energy and overcoming stress.* New York: Delacorte Press.

Brady, M. J., Peterman, A. H., Fitchett, G., Mo, M., & Cella, D. (1999). A case for including spirituality in quality of life measurement in oncology. *Psycho-Oncology, 8,* 417–428.

Brown, D. P., & Engler, J. (1980). The stages of mindfulness meditation: A validation study. *Journal of Transpersonal Psychology, 12,* 143–192.

Brown, D. P., & Fromm, E. (1987). *Hypnosis and behavioral medicine*. Erlbaum Associates; Hillsdale, NJ.

Cuthbert, B., Kristeller, J. L., Simons, R., & Lang, P. J. (1981). Strategies of arousal control: Biofeedback, meditation, and motivation. *Journal of Experimental Psychology: General, 110,* 518–546.

Davidson, R. J., Goleman, D. J., & Schwartz, G. E. (1976). Attentional and affective concomitants of meditation: A cross-sectional study. *Journal of Abnormal Psychology, 85,* 235–238.

Gelderloos, P., Walton, D., Orme-Johnson, D., & Alexander, C. (1991). Effectiveness of the Transcendental Meditation program in preventing and treating substance misuse: A review. *International Journal of the Addictions, 26,* 293–325.

Goleman, D. J., & Schwartz, G. E. (1976). Meditation as an intervention in stress reactivity. *Journal of Consulting and Clinical Psychology, 44,* 456–466.

Green, E. E., Green, A. M., & Walters, E. D. (1970). Voluntary control of internal states: Psychological and physiological. *Journal of Transpersonal Psychology, 11,* 1–26.

Greenwald, J. (1996). *Shopping for Buddhas*. Oakland, CA: Lonely Planet Publishers.

Herman, C. P., & Polivy, J. (1975). Anxiety, restraint, and eating behavior. *Journal of Abnormal Psychology, 84,* 666–672.

Huxley, A. (1970). *The perennial philosophy*. New York: Harper and Row.

Kabat-Zinn, J. (1990). *Full catastrophe living*. New York: Delacorte Press.

Kabat-Zinn, J., Lipworth, L., & Burney, R. (1985). The clinical use of mindfulness meditation for the self-regulation of chronic pain: Treatment outcomes and compliance. *Journal of Behavioral Medicine, 8,* 163–190.

Kabat-Zinn, J., Massion, A. O., Kristeller, J. L., Peterson, L. G., Fletcher, K. E. P. L., Lenderking, W. R., & Santorelli, S. (1992). Effectiveness of a meditation-based stress reduction program in the treatment of anxiety disorders. *American Journal of Psychiatry, 149,* 936–943.

Kapleau, P. (1967). *The three pillars of Zen*. Boston: Beacon Press.

Koren, L. (1994). *Wabi-sabi for artists, designers, poets and philosophers*. Berkeley, CA: Stone Bridge Press.

Kornfield, J. (1993). *A path with heart*. New York: Bantam Books.

Kristeller, J. L. (1972). Mishima's suicide: A psycho-cultural analysis. *Psychologia, 16,* 50–59.

Kristeller, J. L. (1977). Meditation and biofeedback in the regulation of internal states. In Swami Ajaya (Ed.), *Meditational Therapy*. Glenview, IL: Himalayan International Institute Press.

Kristeller, J. L. (2001). Meditation: Multiple effects, a single mechanism? Paper presented at *Neuroscience, Religious Experience and the Self* (a CTNS Science & Religion Course). Montreal.

Kristeller, J. L., & Hallett, B. (1999). Effects of a meditation-based intervention in the treatment of binge eating. *Journal of Health Psychology, 4,* 357–363.

Kristeller, J. L., & Rodin, J. (1989). Identifying eating patterns in male and female undergraduates using cluster analysis. *Addictive Behaviors, 14,* 631–642.

Lang, P. J., Troyer, W. G., Twentyman, C. T., & Gatchel, R. J. (1975). Differential effects of heart rate modification training on college students, older males and patients with ischemic heart disease. *Psychosomatic Medicine, 37,* 429–446.

Levine, S. (1979). *A gradual awakening*. New York: Doubleday.

Maharishi Mahesh Yogi. (1963–1995). *Science of being and art of living: Transcendental Meditation.* New York: Penguin.

Marlatt, G. A., & Kristeller, J. L. (2000). Mindfulness and meditation. In W. Miller (Ed.). *Integrating spirituality in treatment* (pp. 67–84). Washington, DC: American Psychological Association.

Marlatt, G. A., & Rohsenow, D. R. (1980). Cognitive processes in alcohol use: Expectancy and the balanced placebo design. In N. K. Mello (Ed.), *Advances in substance abuse* (Vol. 1, pp. 159–199). Greenwich, CT: JAI Press.

Mishima, Y. (1956–1994). *The temple of the golden pavilion.* New York: Vintage Press.

Nhat Hanh, T. (1995). *Living Buddha, living Christ.* New York: The Berkeley Publishing Group.

Orbach, S. (1978; 1990). *Fat is a feminist issue.* New York: Berkeley Press.

Progoff, I. (1983). *The cloud of unknowing.* New York: Dell Books.

Rama, S., Ballentine, R., & Ajaya, S. (1976). *Yoga and psychotherapy: The evolution of consciousness.* Glenview, IL: Himalayan Institute.

Rodin, J. (1981). The current state of the internal-external hypothesis: What went wrong? *American Psychologist, 36,* 361–372.

Schwartz, G. E. (1974). The facts on Transcendental Meditation: TM relaxes some people and makes them feel better. *Psychology Today, 7*(11), 39–44.

Schwartz, G. E. (1975). Biofeedback, self-regulation, and the patterning of physiological processes. *American Scientist, 63,* 314–324.

Schwartz, G. E. (1979). The brain as a health care system: A psychobiological framework for biofeedback and health psychology. In G. Stone, N. Adler, & F. Cohen (Eds.), *Health psychology.* San Francisco: Jossey-Bass.

Suzuki, S. (1970). *Zen mind, beginner's mind.* New York: Weatherhill.

Swearer, D. K. (Editor). (1971). *Secrets of the lotus.* New York: Macmillan Company.

Tachibana, K. (1938). The psychological structure of *sabi. Japanese Journal of Psychology, 13,* 451–463.

Wallace, R. K., & Benson, H. (1972). The physiology of meditation. *Scientific American, 226,* 84–90.

Wallace, R. K., Benson, H., & Wilson, A. F. (1971). A wakeful hypometabolic state. *American Journal of Physiology, 221,* 795–799.

Warrenburg, S., Pagano, R., & Woods, M., et al. (1977). Oxygen consumption, HR, EMG, and EEG during progressive muscle relaxation (PMR) and Transcendental Meditation. *Biofeedback and Self-Regulation, 2,* 321.

Watts, A. (1957). *The way of Zen.* London: Penguin.

Wulff, D. M. (1991). *The psychology of religion.* New York: John Wiley & Son.

CHAPTER 6

Awakening from the Spell of Reality
Lessons from Nāgārjuna

Kaisa Puhakka

Neither from itself nor from another,
Nor from both,
Nor without a cause,
Does anything whatever, anywhere arise.
—*Mūlamadhyamakakārikā*

These opening lines of Nāgārjuna's (1995, p. 3) famous text leave little to stand on. And it gets worse with the stanzas that follow: every foothold on reality that a philosophically agile mind could conceive of is shattered by the merciless sword of his dialectic. Nāgārjuna, who lived in the second-century A.D. in India, was my intellectual hero in the days of my graduate studies in philosophy. He is generally recognized as having laid the philosophical foundations for all the Mahāyāna Schools of Buddhism that flourished in China, Tibet, Mongolia, Japan, Korea, Vietnam, and most recently in the West. To talk of him as "laying foundations," however, is ironical, for it was his mission to dispel the belief that there are any "foundations" on which any views of reality can rest.

My first encounter with Nāgārjuna was in a graduate seminar devoted entirely to his teachings. This seminar was not part of the regular curriculum of the philosophy department in which I was a student, but it was offered at the request of a few brave souls among the graduate students interested in Indian philosophy. In the weeks that the seminar was conducted, I witnessed some of my fellow students fall into deep existential depression and others find themselves in profound perplexity as the ground on which they had stood and established the intelligibility and livability of their worlds crumbled, with no new ground being offered in its place.

I, too, found myself being stripped of everything by which I would have affirmed my identity and worth. Yet, at the brink of nihilistic despair, I also took delight in the increased transparency of the mind and the freedom from thinking that Nāgārjuna's relentless analyses promised. Liberation seemed to be just on the other side of these analyses.

Alas, the subsequent years did not deliver the promised liberation. Quite the contrary, I encountered seemingly endless psychological depths at which thinking, in the form of unconscious egoic identifications, held its grip on the mind. In the decades that followed, I discovered that the journey from the kind of intellectual insights I enjoyed in that philosophy seminar to a real taste of liberation was indeed a long and convoluted one. I suspect that the convolutions, and the length, of this journey are highly individual, and so this chapter, will inevitably reflect the idiosyncrasies of my journey. Along this journey I believe that most people experience, as I have, certain shifts in thinking and consciousness that seem to correspond to the progression through the four "positions" in Nāgārjuna's four-cornered negation (*catuskoti*) toward "no position" which, in my understanding, is the culmination of Nāgārjuna's dialectic. Nāgārjuna does not claim or hold forth as a "position" that the dialectic produces or brings about liberation as a result—doing so would contradict his teaching. Yet, paradoxically, his teaching seems permeated with the possibility that when nothing is affirmed or denied, nothing reached for or held onto, liberation into the fullness of what is naturally occurs.

THE DIALECTIC OF THE MIDDLE WAY

According to tradition, Nāgārjuna's teachings are presented in a terse, logical language of deconstruction, and commentaries and discussions of these teachings by both traditional and contemporary scholars are often rather technical (Kalupahana, 1986; Murti, 1955; Streng, 1967; Wood, 1994). Because of this, they can easily be dismissed as idle mind games or just as easily embraced as weapons of intellectual warfare. I must confess that the latter held fascination for me in the early years. I liked the clarity of mind that came with the understanding of the forms of the dialectic and, yes, the power that came with wielding Nāgārjuna's sword to cut down beliefs however dearly held.

In contrast to the dialectic of Hegel and Marx which leads from a contradiction to a new synthesis, Nāgārjuna's dialectic aims not at a synthesis but at liberating the mind from attachment to any new view or position. Because his approach is to neither affirm nor deny anything, it is called the dialectic of the Middle Way. But what does it mean to "neither affirm nor deny" any views and how is this different from rejecting all views? The difference is crucial, and how one comports oneself toward an openness that neither affirms nor denies anything is what we shall explore in this chapter.

The form of the dialectic is captured in four statements that are mutually exhaustive of all possibilities—the so-called four-cornered negation (catuskoti).

Letting *P* stand for any proposition and not-*P* for its opposite or contradiction, the four statements that comprise the four-cornered negation are as follows:

1. *P*

2. not-*P*

3. both *P* and not-*P*

4. neither *P* nor not-*P*

We can readily fit the first stanza of the Mūlamadhyamakakārikā into this fourfold formula as follows:

1. Things are caused from themselves (*P*)

2. Things are caused from another (not-*P*)

3. Things are caused from themselves and another (both *P* and not-*P*)

4. Things are caused from neither themselves nor from another (neither *P* nor not *P*)

In Buddhist literature, starting with Nāgārjuna and continuing with his disciples such as Chandrakīrti (Rabten, 1983), the propositions to which the dialectic was applied were typically derived from questions that were put to the Buddha and to which he responded by remaining silent. Examples of such statements are "The world is infinite," and "The *Tathāgata* (the liberated one, the Buddha) exists after death." Nāgārjuna shows that every one of the four possibilities is untenable or self-contradictory, and thus one is left with nothing to assert, no ground to stand on.

NĀGĀRJUNA THE MAGICIAN

As my understanding of Nāgārjuna deepened over the years, I came to see that he was no mere logician or show-off of mental gymnastics. He was revered by his students and subsequent generations of Buddhists as a great spiritual teacher whose ultimate concern was with liberation. I did not really appreciate the transformative power of Nāgārjuna's teachings until I was willing to leave behind (only temporarily to be sure and for very short periods at first) the clarity of the mind as well as the confidence it had bestowed on me and to enter the nether domains of darkness and confusion that lie just below that clarity. Here I encountered the domain of psychological dynamics and the attachments to various beliefs—the spells that bind—which had been largely unaffected by the sword of the dialectic I had so arduously applied to my own and others' beliefs in philosophical discourse and argument. I came to see that the transformative power of Nāgārjuna's teachings was not in its logic, but in its potential for dispelling the spells that bind us—that Nāgārjuna's intent was not merely to be a logician, but to be a magician. Indeed, in Tibet he is revered by many as a great magician (Lindtner, 1997).

I came to appreciate that the psychological domain is the doorway to Nāgārjuna's magic. Psychological insights have an ontological "edge," that is, they reveal something about the nature of reality. This ontological edge is the doorway. Let me illustrate this by an example. A woman has been unhappily married for seven years to a husband who complains constantly. In a psychotherapy session, she has an insight into how, for all her life, she has been being her mother without realizing it. It was as if a veil she never knew had covered her eyes suddenly dropped. She could now exercise, for the first time, the freedom not to be her mother, which in turn can bring about a significant improvement in her marriage. The psychological content in this example refers to the woman's experience of her mother and introjection of her as well. The ontological edge has to do with the shift in the woman's experience of reality: it is as if she has just awakened from a spell. Many of us have been graced by such blessed moments of awakening when the spell breaks and reality shines forth afresh.

Nāgārjuna differs from psychotherapists and other, more traditional magicians in that he was not interested in liberation from particular spells; the aim of his teachings was to push the ontological edge until there is liberation from any and all spells. Psychological insights of the sort described above typically liberate from particular spells. This means that the awakening from a particular spell is almost simultaneously an awakening to what is now taken to be real. But neither the Buddha nor Nāgārjuna talked about what it is that we presumably awaken to. They were concerned with awakening, period. The Buddha strongly discouraged any metaphysical speculation about it, and Nāgārjuna offered his dialectic as a systematic way of quelling the mind's insistence on such speculations. Both thus challenged the very tendency, deeply ingrained in us as it is, to take things as real.

We are typically not aware of ourselves as taking something (P) as real. Rather, its reality "takes us," or already has us in its spell as soon as we become aware of its identity (P). Furthermore, it's impossible to take something (P) to be real without, at least momentarily, ignoring or denying that which it is not (not-P). Thus the act of taking something as real necessarily involves some degree of unconsciousness or lack of awareness. This is true even in the simple act of perception when we see a figure that we become aware of as "something." As the

German gestalt psychologists demonstrated, for each figure perceived, there is a background of which we remain relatively unaware. We can extend this to texts or spoken communications. For every text we understand there is a context we are not fully cognizant of. Thus, with every figure noticed or reality affirmed, there is, inevitably, unawareness. Is this not how a spell works? It takes us unawares.

An objection might be raised that it is only the background we are unaware of, not the figure or the thing whose reality is affirmed. A Nāgārjunian answer to this might be that our ability to affirm this reality requires our relative unawareness of the background.

This raises the question, Where do realities arise from, how are they produced? It is no accident that the opening stanza of the Mūlamadhyamakakārikā addresses the issue of production or "cause." When we take something to be real, we implicitly assume that it has a cause (in the broadest sense that includes "context"). Whether we think in terms of mechanical causes or in terms of cultural, linguistic, and geographical context, the absence of cause or context is tantamount to unreality. For example, if, on the one hand, a white rabbit suddenly materialized in the middle of the room, seemingly "out of the blue" (i.e., without cause or context), we would be inclined to think of it as an apparition rather than as real. On the other hand, if someone supplied us with a believable "story" of how the rabbit got to be there, we would be more likely to think of it as real. In the stream of everyday consciousness, the causes or context of what we take to be real tend to be implicit and largely unconscious. The point of Nāgārjuna's dialectic is to show that these unconscious contextual notions necessarily contain the opposite or contradictory of what one consciously affirms as "real." Once the context and the contradiction are brought into full awareness, the mind is liberated from the spell of the real. The uncovering of the contextual notions that are buried in the background of our awareness is not merely a logical affair, but calls for a deep psychological and cultural inquiry.

THE SPELL OF REALITY IN CONTEMPORARY CULTURE: DECONSTRUCTIVISM AND TRANSPERSONALISM

We might apply Nāgārjuna's four positions to the broad shifts that have swept through Western culture in the past century. Modernity, with its confidence in the capability of science to reveal the "real" and in its "metanarratives" or overarching views of what the real is, exemplifies the type of consciousness that operates with truths it takes to be absolute. The consciousness of modernity thus reflects the first of Nāgārjuna's four positions. Interestingly, we also saw its opposite, "not-P," manifested in the revolutionary movements and ideological polarizations that have characterized cultures on a global scale during modernity.

Contemporary culture in the West, and to a lesser extent elsewhere, is now characterized as "postmodern." The foundational beliefs of modernity, for example, the belief in the "objectivity" of science and in the evolutionary progress of humankind, have been deconstructed and relativized to their psychological, cultural, and social contexts. The notion that there can be absolute truths that are independent of the viewpoints and contexts (the unconscious habits, beliefs, and presuppositions) of those who speak them has fallen by the wayside. Most intellectuals and academics today would put quotation marks around "truth" and consider it more like a figure of speech that can only be understood and appreciated in the context in which it is spoken (or written). Not only truth (P) but, equally, its opposite (not-P) are relativized and dissolve into their contexts in postmodern deconstructive analyses. Thus postmodernity has arrived at Nāgārjuna's fourth position, neither P nor not-P.

Postmodern consciousness promises to do (and to some extent has done) away with the oppressive and marginalizing social and political structures of modernity. It celebrates diversity and difference; it is vast, open, and free compared to the consciousness of modernity. Yet its problems also are vaster: relativized truth that is just one perspective among others cannot really provide the perspective we look for, the orientation we need, the sense of proportion we crave. Instead, we are called to sort through contexts within contexts indefinitely, wading through a fragmented, chaotic world where cynicism and despair lurk just below the surface. Nāgārjuna referred to the fourth position as "nihilistic," and for him, nihilism, or the position that rejects all views, is just as absolutistic as the first and second positions. The oft-described "postmodern malaise" has much to do with the absolute truths that we cling to and nostalgically harken back to, even as we deny that we can ever have such truths. The very meaning of "relative" depends on that of "absolute." Similarly, the meaning of "context" depends on that of "text," and of "truth" on that of "non-truth" or "falsehood." According to Nāgārjuna, the nihilistic consciousness is still spellbound by polarities such as these.

The logic of this argument stirs the surface of consciousness, and gives rise to questions that probe deeper: What do the absolute/relative and truth/nontruth dichotomies really mean? What is consciousness like when it is free of these dichotomies? Notice how each of these questions presupposes a dichotomy, the first that of the "real" (as opposed to "not-real") meaning, and the second that of a consciousness that is "free" (as opposed to "not-free"). The postmodern consciousness, sophisticated and perhaps more awake than before, does not miss the paradox and the impasse here, hence the depth of its cynicism and despair. Nāgārjuna offers no solution, no "way out" of the impasse. He only reminds us to not affirm anything, not even the impasse, as a position. Perhaps we could say that the way out is a way through, and that there is a cultural consciousness in the West today that hovers somewhere in the middle phase of this way. Will it bolt from the pain and move back to some form of positive absolutism thus affirming a new *P*? Will it remain stuck in absolutizing relativism? Or will it embrace and move through the anxiety and despair of there being nothing at all to hold onto—no objective absolutes or substantial realities out there, and no subjective absolutes in here?

A way out of this postmodern impasse is sought by many who embrace any of the varieties of spiritual worldviews, beliefs, and practices that are available today. Transpersonal developmental theories, grounded in what are taken to be universal principles of perennial philosophy, offer a vision of evolution that is flexible and open-ended, yet has direction. Unlike the grand views of modernity, these theories emphasize wholeness and an inclusivity that leaves nothing out. The consciousness associated with these theories, and in general with contemporary spirituality, seeks to affirm both sides of any dichotomy. The oneness of seeming opposites is emphasized in what transpersonalists call "both/and" thinking. With this thinking, many old and seemingly unsolvable metaphysical questions seem to resolve themselves. For example, reality is no longer thought of as being "either one or many," but viewed as being (somehow) "both." The "both/and" thinking contrasts with the exclusive "either/or" thinking that characterizes modern rational discourse. It embraces Nāgārjuna's third position: both *P* and not-*P*.

Certainly, the transpersonal "both/and" thinking is much broader, more flexible, more inclusive, and softer than the "either/or" assertions associated with modern science or religion. Yet its softness tends to be more foggy than fluid. The all-inclusive holism that characterizes much of transpersonal theorizing today tends toward a grand synthesis of a new *P* as absolute as any before, though more vague, more changeable, less precise, and less literally formulated than the absolutisms of modernity. The inscrutability of the *nirguna Brahman* (nirguna = devoid of qualities or attributes) of Hinduism or the śūnyatā (voidness, emptiness) of Buddhism has more intellectual appeal than does the more personal, more definite Judeo-Christian God. The "both/and" thinking can "eat its cake and have it too" by objectifying what it knows to be not an object ("Reality," "Consciousness," the "One," etc.). Such thinking is comforting because it reassures us that there is a Ground, even if it cannot be described, that even as we let go of everything, we can have all. Letting go of everything without the reassurance of having anything might take us back to the brink of a nihilism far deeper than the Existentialists' abyss that New Age thinking and much transpersonal theorizing promised to both transcend and include. David Loy (1999) has offered a rich and provocative analysis of how individuals and culture in the 20th century have attempted to avoid, as much as to come to terms with, the suspicion that behind what we take ourselves to be there may be nothing at all. Thus individually and collectively, we cycle through Nāgārjuna's four positions. At the present time in our Western culture, we are inclined to eschew the hard absolutisms of the first and second positions, but find the foothold in the more sophisticated third and fourth positions to be precarious.

MOVING THROUGH NĀGĀRJUNA'S POSITIONS IN SPIRITUAL PRACTICE: A CASE ILLUSTRATION

The process of shifting through the four positions can be especially transparent in the context of spiritual practice. This is because serious spiritual practitioners tend to be strongly attached to their spiritual practice. For many such practitioners, their sense of identity, meaning, and purpose is tied up with their practice, which tends to be seen as a means to enlightenment with liberation as the end. The feeling that "I am not doing well in my practice," or "as well as I should," or that "I am making progress" all imply that the practice is a means to some end. The means-ends dualism is another version of the cause-effect dualism that empowers the spell of reality. The stronger the investment in causes that presumably bring about the effects or results, the more solidly real the effects or results seem to be. Thus when one works especially hard at spiritual practice, the liberation to which the practice aims seems powerfully real. Is there a serious practitioner who does not feel that enlightenment or liberation, however out of reach, is very real? (Contrariwise, those not engaged in serious practice seem not to be caught up in the spell of this reality!)

This mind-set seems innocent enough, yet betrays an extremism or absolutism that still lurks even among sophisticated Mahāyāna practitioners despite the admonitions against such a mind-set by many of the great Mahāyāna teachers such as Bodhidharma (1989), Dōgen (Okumura & Leighton, 1997), and more recently Thich Nhat Hanh (1987). The spell of spiritual practice is often too strong to allow these admonitions to have much effect until the practitioner has moved through the four positions to "no position," in which the means-end dualism dissolves.

Paradoxically, a very rigorous spiritual practice can sometimes help dissolve the means-end dualism. I would like to illustrate this by my own experience with the Zen training I undertook in a traditional *Rinzai* monastic setting, only slightly modified to accommodate American and European practitioners (Puhakka, 1998). The seven-day intensives (*Dai-sesshin*) followed a strict protocol, called "the Form" by the practitioners. The Form meticulously prescribed the manner in which every move and nonmove, including the positions of eyes and hands, had to conform at all times; there was no room for individual expression or choice (other than to leave the sesshin, which was available as a choice at any time). Much of the time was spent in sitting meditation (*zazen*), punctuated by fast walking (*kinhin*) or private meetings with the Zen Master (*sanzen*), all of which activity conformed strictly to the Form.

The Form was there to take the place of the ego and its functions; surrendering to the Form was to surrender the ego and its will. Yet it took an enormous effort of will, not just once but each moment, to stay with the Form and to put oneself fully into it. The novices' and even experienced practitioners' efforts at this were only partially successful at best. And what was the purpose of so much will and effort? To deliver the practitioner into the spontaneous, creative, formless, and will-less activity of reality which in Mahāyāna traditions is called śūnyatā (void, emptiness). The paradox inherent in this situation was blatant enough, and the discipline that forced the practitioner to face it moment by moment tough enough, to occasionally activate a process in which the dualism of means and ends, of practice and nonpractice, began to dissolve.

As with any very difficult and demanding undertaking, those who participated in this Zen training tended to have a strong commitment to it (*P*). In my own case, this practice represented the culmination of 25 years of meditation practice. Many other participants also had decades of practice behind them. The glimpses of heavenly bliss that soon grace the long hours of sitting in the *zendo* tend to reinforce one's commitment to the practice. It certainly seemed to me that this was *the* practice! At this point, I was affirming Nāgārjuna's first position.

As any practitioner knows, with prolonged sitting, "stuff" (*samskāras* in Buddhist terminology) inevitably comes up, like clouds rolling in and covering the initial clearing, hardening into bewildering, jarring emotions, body sensations, and images. One then finds oneself falling into a veritable Zen Hell from which there seems to be no escape by means of any amount of will or effort. I found myself in such a Hell and eventually gave up, exhausted and demoralized, not minding the Form anymore, not practicing and not caring. I had arrived at Nāgārjuna's second position, not-*P*.

At this point, many practitioners leave, disillusioned with this particular practice or perhaps with any practice. They may then remain, for a time being at least, stuck in not-*P*. But those who stay, which I did, find themselves undergoing a further shift: the Hell loosens its grip, inexplicably and effortlessly, and one may awaken to a new lightness of being, much calmer, saner, and more mature than the initial glimpses of heavenly bliss had been. Anything that happens now, whether Heaven or Hell, seems to be just more grist for the practice mill. One is ready to embrace Nāgārjuna's third position, both *P* and not-*P*. (In reality however, at least in my case, the sense of well-being that came with this new clarity generated a sense of gratitude for—and renewed attachment to—this particular form

of practice that I found myself going back to embrace P, and to cycle through
Heaven and Hell, and Nāgārjuna's first and second positions, several more times.)
Once a measure of equanimity with Heaven and Hell is reached, however, the ups
and downs of the practice smoothen out into an easy, effortless ride. At this point,
the end of the practice seemed near to me.

This last thought, however, can throw one into a Hell of an altogether different order. It did do that to me. This new Hell made its appearance with the realization that my questing after liberation and any practice (or no practice) that
served the end of liberation were egoic agendas. This practice and any other practice, even no formal practice, were all a self-defeating quest of the ego to liberate itself from itself! Far from being at the pinnacle of my practice, I crashed, this time
into a bottomless abyss. My will to practice was suddenly gone, not to a noble surrender in final liberation as I had imagined the end point of practice to be, but dis-
solved into sheer futility. The "reality" of this profound pointlessness held me in
a spell more powerful than anything before. At the heart of this spell is, of course,
the affirmation of Nāgārjuna's fourth position, "neither P nor not-P." St. John of
the Cross has described it in the context of Christian mysticism as the "dark night
of the soul," the loss of faith and of the feeling of connection with God. In my
case, the only game in town—liberation—was blown, my life project turned to
sham. My sense of identity and purpose that had been grounded in this project
were shattered. Years ago in the philosophy class I had tasted the intellectual discomfort of Nāgārjuna's fourth position, but what I now experienced ripped away
my heart and soul.

How the spell of this most convincing and most pernicious reality eventually eases its grip I do not know. But a factor that played no small part in my own
case was remembering what I had learned years ago from Nāgārjuna, namely, that
my profound nihilism and disdain for everything was no more defensible than
any of the other three positions. Curiously, the same teachings that in the earlier
years had led to a display of intellectual prowess on my part now cut away at the
root of the pride and arrogance that had motivated that prowess. Eventually, the
dichotomy (of enlightened/unenlightened, liberated/unliberated) on which both
the intelligibility and the gripping reality of my nihilism rested began to melt, and
with it, the paralysis of my Dark Night slowly thawed.

When movement returned to my heart, mind, and limbs, the steps that
began to take form were (and still are) like those of a newborn learning to walk—
much too small, erratic, and hesitant to be those of a liberated person as one
might imagine such a person. The steps are unique to each person. But when one
no longer walks toward liberation but just walks, each step gives birth to the
ground beneath it and the world comes into being with the walk.

REFERENCES

Bodhidharma (1987). *The Zen teachings of Bodhidharma* (R. Pine, Trans.). Berkeley, CA: North Point Press.

Hahn, Thich Nhat (1987). *The miracle of mindfulness: A manual of meditation.* Berkeley, CA: Parallax Press.

Kalupahana, D. J. (1986). *Nāgārjuna: The philosophy of the middle way.* Albany, NY: State University of New York Press.

Lindtner, C. (1997). *Master of wisdom: Writings of the Buddhist master Nāgārjuna.* Berkeley, CA: Dharma Publishing.

Loy, D. (1999). *Lack and transcendence: the problem of death and life in psychotherapy, existentialism, and Buddhism.* Amherst, NY: Humanity Books.

Murti, T. R. V. (1955). *The central philosophy of Buddhism.* London, England: Allen & Unwin.

Nāgārjuna (1995). *The fundamental wisdom of the middle way: Nāgārjuna's Mūlamadhyamakakārikā* (J. L. Garfield, Trans.). New York: Oxford University Press.

Okumura, S. and Leighton, T. D. (Trans.). (1997). *The wholehearted way: A translation of Eihei Dōgen's Bendōwa with Commentary by Kōshō Uchiyama Roshi.* Boston: Tuttle Publishing.

Puhakka, K. (1998). Dissolving the self: Rinzai Zen training at an American monastery. *The Journal of Transpersonal Psychology, 30*(2), 135–160.

Rabten, G. (1983). *Echoes of voidness.* London, England: Wisdom Publications.

Streng, F. (1967). *Emptiness: A study in religious meaning.* Nashville, TN: Abdingdon Press.

Wood, T. (1994). Nāgārjunian disputations: A philosophical journey through an Indian looking-glass. *Monographs of the Society for Asian and Comparative Philosophy,* Honolulu, HI: University of Hawaii Press.

CHAPTER 7
Reflections on Mirroring

Robert Rosenbaum

Great Master Seppō Shingaku once said to his disciples: "To experience our real selves is the same as facing the Eternal Mirror. Whatever appears is reflected."[1]

1

Psychology is based on self-knowledge. Buddhism is based on truth. When self-knowledge meets truth, a mirror appears.

These words may not mean what they appear to signify. Words are tricky. Buddhism knows that truth lies beyond words. Psychology acknowledges there are preverbal and nonverbal ways of knowing. Words, however, also are a form of experience.

This chapter may appear bound by words. Sometimes words are used to explain thoughts, or feelings, or sensations, or consciousness. Are words, then, reflections of these? Or are words mirrors? When words expound on words, what do words reflect, and where do such reflections appear? When you read this here, are you the words, or are you the mirror?

When you read this, you are facing the Eternal Mirror, and experiencing your real self.

2

In psychology, when we talk about mirroring we often think of the psychoanalytic formulations of self-psychology. In this view, mirroring is classed as one of the "noninterpretive interventions." Prior to the rise of intersubjective approaches, psychoanalysis relied on an atmosphere of neutrality to provide a holding environment; it was thought this provided an opportunity for clients to see themselves through the medium of the analyst's interpretations. This was a concept of the therapist as a kind of mirror: one which was objective, clear, and so could (at the proper time) cut through the patient's defensive self-deceits and present core unconscious knowledge—knowledge that had previously been hidden—to the patient.

In contrast, self-psychology views experiential understanding as different from knowledge "about" something. An understanding phase precedes an explanatory or interpretive phase, and "understanding" here means not knowing, but feeling. The patient must *feel* understood by the analyst before he or she can take in the necessary information—often painful—about his or her wishes, frustrations, and defenses and how they influence behavior and experience.

This sense of being understood relies on a kind of "empathic immersion" rooted in core, often preverbal, experiences of self and other. Before there were words, there was a sense of having another person who was responsive to the feelings and needs of the infant, and who helped regulate those emotional states. Later, there came a sense of attunement between self and other, and gradually a process of validation and shaping through actions and, eventually, words. Psychoanalysis has made the valuable observation that many people have a subjective sense of doubt about their own experience; the mirroring process is an attempt to bring the patient back to his or her experience through the holding and responsivity of another person (Kohut, 1971; Bacal and Newman, 1990; Ornstein & Ornstein, 1985; Goldberg, 1988; Stern, 1985; Holinger, 1999).

There seems to be some connection between mirroring and experiencing one's self. Interestingly, psychologists often attempt to study the emergence of self-recognition by examining how human infants or our primate cousins react to seeing themselves in mirrors (e.g., Povinelli et al., 1993). Within the clinical realm, empathic attunement and experiencing are central to the practice of humanistic psychotherapies (Bohart & Rosenbaum, 1995). Once we concentrate on attunement, though, we start to become aware that being attuned to something "out there" is a different experience from a sense of attuned *connectedness* and participating in a *shared* experience. How can we be "optimally empathic" if we are ultimately separate from the object of our reflections? Along with the humanistic psychologists, both constructivist (e.g., Lax, 1996) and intersubjective theorists (e.g., Jordan et al., 1991) have attempted to resolve this conundrum by insisting self always arises in—and is therefore inseparable from—relationship.

Without an object, there is no mirror; without a mirror, there is no object. Let me give a concrete experience of this.

When I was a young man, I spent my senior year of college in Japan. Shortly after arriving, I was sitting in the living room of the Japanese family I was staying with, and I happened to sneeze. Nobody reacted.

In United States culture, and even more so in the Jewish culture in which I'd grown up, it is common to react to a sneeze with a "God bless you" or "Gesundheit!," so unconsciously I was expecting something of the sort to follow my sneeze. I didn't know it at the time, but sneezing is considered impolite in Japan, and it is even more impolite to draw attention to someone sneezing. The Japanese, having lived in close quarters with each other for many hundreds of years, have become skilled at the art of not reacting to small "improper" disturbances. When I sneezed, nobody glanced at me or even blinked. Conversation continued uninterrupted.

I experienced something rather odd, though, when nobody reacted. Failing to receive the mirroring of my experience I was accustomed to, for a moment, *I was not sure whether I had, in fact, sneezed. The lack of a reaction made me doubt my own experience of myself.* None of this was mediated by conscious thought or expectation, and all of this took no more than a second or two of clock time. Yet immediately after my sneeze, for a moment "I"—Bob-who-sneezed—was called into question, and my sense of myself, and the world associated with it, rocked subtly.

3

Buddhism has grappled with the problem of the mirror for several thousand years. Sitting in zazen meditation, facing a wall, is facing the mirror. Psychotherapy, being much younger, has only begun to face the mirror. While we talk of "mirroring" or "reflecting" the client, we rarely talk about the nature of the mirror itself. Although it is hard to conceive of "mirroring" existing without a mirror, we tend to take the existence of the mirror for granted and do not question it much.

What is the mirror in the psychotherapy process? The immediate answer seems to be: "The therapist is the mirror for the client." Let us examine this a bit. What makes it possible for a therapist to be a mirror?

As noted above, one hundred years ago the idea was that the therapist's neutrality provided the basis for the mirror. The twentieth century, though, involved a lengthy process where social and physical sciences, as well as the humanities, began to come to terms with the myth of the neutral observer. This is not the place to go into that history, but most people today would agree that the observer is neither a blank slate nor separate from the observed: the observer is somehow tied to—influenced by and influencing in turn—the object under scrutiny. All observation is participant observation. Furthermore, that which is being observed is not a static entity, but has its own life in time. If I, as observing subject, deny that the object of observation (my client) is also a subject, I turn a person into a thing. If I try to become "objective" by objectifying the other, in the process of reifying the person I am working with, I turn myself-as-subject into an object.

Thus, many therapists find themselves in a bind. It seems impossible to both *engage* with a client and remain "objective" about the client. Therapists feel they "should" be a good mirror to their clients, but realize that they are influenced both by the client and by their own personal reactions. If they hold on to the idea of an ideal mirror as being a clear object, they may struggle somewhat guiltily with a sense that they are *imperfect* mirrors.

Dōgen's fascicle on the Eternal Mirror helps clarify this dilemma. It begins with a story:

The 18th Patriarch, Venerable Kayashata, was from Matai in Central Asia. . . . since his birth, a clear and bright round mirror had naturally been living with him . . . it appeared at the moment of his birth in front of him, as if it were a natural accessory. The nature of this round mirror was extraordinary. When he moved forward, it was as if he were holding up the round mirror before him with both hands, yet it did not cover his face. When one saw him from behind, the round mirror seemed to be on his back, but it did not hide his body . . . it followed all of his movements. What is more . . . all problems and issues of the heavens above and the human world came cloudlessly to the surface of the round mirror. It was clearer to look in this round mirror to understand the past and present than to read the sutras. Nevertheless, once he left home, became a monk, and received the precepts, the round mirror never appeared before him again.

This first part of the story has a counterintuitive twist. Kayashata is born with a mirror, but when he becomes a monk and dedicates himself to helping others, *the mirror disappears.* We usually think that becoming a monk—which involves pledging one's self for the benefit of all beings—is a step toward sanctity: Wouldn't it make more sense for the mirror to appear when the adult commits himself to the practice of the sacred? At the very least, shouldn't the mirror remain as an aid to the monk? It seems almost unfair to be deprived of this helpful mirror just as one begins to tread the path of serving others.

Yet a similar thing happens to the psychotherapist. Most beginning psychotherapists have a kind of innocent purity. They come into the field wanting to help people, and usually have a naive belief that they will learn techniques that will provide healing. They tend to have a basic trust that the work is "good," as are the people performing it. In my opinion, it is this innocence and faith that allows beginning therapists to be especially helpful to their clients, even in the midst of egregious errors of "technique."

Rather quickly, though, we lose our innocence as therapists. We learn a technique and attempt to adhere to the "rules" in applying it, and our clients do not respond as the books say they should. We encounter a teacher or a supervisor who is difficult to work with, or whose personality quirks lead us to question the purity of his or her motives. We go into therapy ourselves, and discover its limitations along with its helpfulness.

At such times, we are in the same position as Kayashata. Our intentions and actions become complicated in learning the systems of psychotherapy theory and practice, just as Kayashata's would have become complicated in learning the rules of monastic life and the theories of Buddhism. We appear to have lost our "clear mirror."

This is why the precepts—the moral guidelines—play such a central role in Buddhist practice; they define and create the means for practice. The precepts are not specific rules so much as overarching pathways; they are the touchstone by which we distinguish whether a particular action is in harmony with our basic intention. The precepts are *kōans*, existential problems that must be solved with our whole being moment by moment.

The mirror disappeared when Kayashata took the precepts because in taking the precepts, Kayashata devoted himself to become the living embodiment of the precepts. This does not mean Kayashata became "pure." Rather, it means that he devoted the rest of his life to *realizing* the precepts: putting them into play in the rough and tumble of everyday life, where the details of their application are full of errors, mis-steps, and doubts. It is the *practice* of the precepts that takes them from some abstract ideal and expresses them in actual forms.

In becoming the living of the precepts, Kayashata became the mirror. How, then, could the mirror appear as anything other than Kayashata himself?

Similarly in psychotherapy, beginning therapists have a great deal of theoretical knowledge and images of how psychotherapy "should" proceed. As they enter day-to-day clinical work, though, they have to make many modifications which do not match the "pure" ideals which may have motivated them to enter the field. Psychotherapists have a more difficult job of it than monks, though, in that the precepts of psychotherapy are not clearly spelled out. We have some basic guidelines about maintaining confidentiality, and some laws which mandate certain actions, but there is very little else that we *explicitly* commit to as psychotherapists in the same way that a monk commits to the precepts. Most of us make an implicit commitment within our moral and ethical code, but without a clear statement of principles we may often be unsure of our anchoring principles when faced with clinical conundrums. Such clinical problems occur not only in obvious instances of ethical dilemmas, but in the constant, momentary ebb and flow of our interactions with each client.

Consider the first three Zen Buddhist precepts:[2]

I vow to refrain from all evil.
I vow to do all that is good: to make every effort to live in enlightenment.
I vow to live and be lived for the benefit of all beings.

The issue here is not the content of these precepts: there will always be disagreements about how these are put into effect in concrete actions. The issue here is being clear about one's *intent*. Buddhism presumes that proper intent is itself the mirror, that it arises from an absolute reality which is not tainted by personal or relative concerns (though it can never be expressed outside of the personal and the relative). It is important to recognize, though, that intention is not the same as wishing, or having amorphous benevolent aims and a vague desire to "do good." Intention must be cultivated, honed, and practiced. By cultivating our intent we use the mirror to become the mirror.

Most therapists would have no problems agreeing with the idea that we should do no harm. How do we reconcile this, though, with the research findings that a significant proportion of psychotherapies have negative effects (Strupp and Hadley, 1995)? How do we balance the harm we do by causing transitory emotional hurt—say, in confronting a person's egocentrism—against the possible (but by no means inevitable) growth that may occur? Different therapists, even those sharing a common theoretical base, will disagree about whether a particular intervention was or was not appropriate. Furthermore, how do we reconcile the vow to refrain from all evil with the knowledge that, as human beings, some of our motives in becoming therapists are less than "pure," and some of our interventions are influenced by our own personal concerns and blind spots?

The second precept gets even a bit more difficult: What does it mean to do *all* that is good? This raises issues about the boundaries of a therapeutic relationship. If a patient is in distress, is it all right to hold the patient's hand (Kohut, 1979)? These questions become even more acute when we come to the third precept: a therapist might want to *help* all beings, but that is rather different from "to live and *be lived*" for the benefit of all beings. We are probably reluctant to give out our home phone numbers to clients. Does this mean we hold back from doing all that is good, and dedicating our life to the benefit of all beings? Yet if we do extend ourselves and open up our house to our clients (either figuratively or literally) doesn't that cross some important boundary of who "I" am and who "you" are?

The continuation of Dōgen's fascicle addresses these concerns.

4

One day, when he [Kayashata] was walking around the country, he met Honorable Sōgya Nandai [the 17th Patriarch] and stood before him. Sōgya Nandai asked him, "What do you have in your hands?"
Kayashata answered:
"The great round mirror of the buddhas.
It has no flaws or blurs, within or without.
You and I can see it:
the eye of our mind is the same."

The Mirror is unclouded inside and out: this neither describes an inside that depends on an outside, nor an outside blurred by an inside. There being no face or back, two individuals are able to see the same. Everything that appears around us is one, and is the same inside and out. It is not ourself, nor other than self, but is

mutually one and the same. Our self is the same as other than self; other than self is
the same as our self. Such is the meeting of two human beings.

The key phrase here is *"the meeting of two human beings."* All of our vows, all our intentions and interventions, are enacted within meeting fields. The practice of doing
all that is good, of refraining from evil, of living and being lived, occurs not within
my mind's eye but within the eye of *our* mind, where we are inextricably joined.

When we meet each other we touch each other. Touch itself, though, is self-
reflexive. When we touch the other, we feel not only the other, but also ourselves.
As Merleau-Ponty (1964) puts it, we touch ourselves touching. We can only experience the other through ourselves touching; we can only experience ourselves
touching through the other. We need something outside ourselves to develop our
inner experience. Thus individuality arises from interdependency; interdependency arises from individuality. Acknowledgment of the interdependency of all
beings is crucial to both Buddhism and all fields of psychotherapy that adopt an
intersubjective stance. However, Buddhism goes a bit further.

So far we have talked about a meeting between two separate people; there is
self and other, inside and outside. But Dōgen points to a Mirror where inside does
not depend on outside, self does *not* depend on other. When there is "no face or
back" we have gone from two-dimensional differentiation to the empty unidi-
mensionality of a single point.

It is not possible to understand Buddhism without understanding emptiness, but emptiness cannot be captured in words or thought. We tend to think of
the unidimensional as "smaller" than the two-dimensional, but this is a two-
dimensional view. The unidimensional has no length, no breadth, no height, no
before, and no after: it is infinite in its emptiness. As soon as we think about
emptiness, we tend to give it qualities: perhaps it is black, or a hole, or a feel of gap-
ing absence. None of these is what Buddhism means by emptiness.

Dōgen invokes the experience of emptiness through the image of the Mirror, "unclouded inside and out." Emptiness is Clarity. Sometimes it is referred to
as the ground of existence. It is what experience springs from, while inseparable
from the experience itself. There is no self nor other in emptiness, yet it does not
hinder self and other.

What is this emptiness in everyday life? When we shake hands with a
client, at the moment our hands touch, there is an *instantaneous* meeting. We
often shake hands as a kind of empty ritual, but if we pay close attention, we will
find so much is conveyed in that moment: it is an opportunity to convey empathy and caring, to discover whether a client responds to contact with hesitancy
or eagerness. As we touch each other, our whole being-in-relationship rests in

that touch. We can subsequently reflect on what we felt during the handshake, but at the moment of touching, the experience is beyond thought, beyond history, beyond sensation. Thinking about it is dizzying: touching ourselves touching the other we experience being touched by someone else touching herself touching us. Our conceptions cannot contain our experience. We can count on the fact, though, that when our hands touch, they *touch concretely and completely.* This touching, then, is our entire life in its totality that moment. In touching, I-see-you. This is how our mind sees. It is not the same as relying on what we conventionally think of as vision. It is this eyeless vision—the eye of the Mind— which is the Mirror.

Dōgen (1233/1985) puts it this way:

> The whole moon and the entire sky are reflected in dewdrops on the grass, or even in one drop of water . . .
> The depth of the drop is the height of the moon. Each reflection, however long or short its duration, manifests the vastness of the dewdrop, and realizes the limitlessness of the moonlight in the sky.

Or, in a more mundane example, there is an old riddle (Tolkien, 1966, p. 85):

> An eye in a blue face saw an eye in a green face.
> "That eye, is like to this eye" said the first eye,
> "But in low place not in high place."

The riddle's answer? Sun on the daisies. This is our meeting in psychotherapy, the mirror of our practice and the practice of our mirror: the sun on the daisies.

5

What a Buddhist practitioner offers in mirroring is somewhat different than what a therapist offers in mirroring. This is due to the Buddhist practitioner's familiarity with, and reliance on, emptiness. Most people who have been involved in both psychotherapy and Buddhist practice can attest to the different "feel" that exists in one-on-one interactions in the two practices. An interview between a Zen Buddhist teacher and student (*dokusan*) feels different than the meeting that occurs in one-on-one psychotherapy. This can be made clearer by contrasting aspects of mirroring in Buddhism versus mirroring in psychotherapy: in the following, the perspective of psychotherapy is in plain text while that of Buddhism is in italics:

In psychotherapy, merging is both a basic fear (in which self is lost and annihilated) and a basic need (to merge with the other, which provides self-regulation, validation, and love).

In Buddhism, merging is auspicious.

In psychotherapy, mirroring "adds" self, "confirms" and "validates" self.

In mirroring nothing is added, nothing is taken away, nothing is gained, nothing is lost.

In psychotherapy, mirroring is connected to an (early) developmental stage. Because the view is developmental, there is a "self" that is born in "ignorance" (i.e., without certain attributes it needs to acquire); the self matures, usually with certain structural "flaws" that lead to suffering. There may be further maturation but eventually the self dies. Psychotherapy is thus part of the cycle of birth and death.

All aspects of existence (including the illusion of having a "self") are empty. In emptiness, no ignorance and also no extinction of it; no old-age-and-death and also no extinction of it; no suffering, no origination, no stopping, no path; no cognition, also no attainment.

In psychotherapy, self and other exist as separate, distinct (though interacting) entities.

Self and other are but different expressions of the same reality.

In psychotherapy, mirroring provides empathy, which is generally warm and kindly; however, there are inevitable failures of empathy.

Mirroring provides constant, ongoing reflection of what actually is: what appears is what is reflected. In a sense, this reflecting is merciless in the completeness of its acceptance.

In psychotherapy, the mirror leans toward being approving; the client basks in the "twinkle in the parent's (therapist's) eye" to take in a positive sense of self. The interaction revolves around hope, desire, gratification, and the defenses against these wishes: their frustration and gratification. However, in the act of being approving, the possibility of disapproval inevitably arises, since the basic framework is dualistic. Attainment is tied to loss; anticipation is tied to both satisfaction and disappointment.

The mirror not only does not judge, in the sense of suspending judgment: it is beyond judgment. Rocks and trees do not judge; our mirror mind is a constantly flowing stream of mountains and rivers. Nondualistic, the mirror is neither approving nor disapproving nor "neutral." Interactions revolve around "thusness," the basic ground of being, the experiencing of experience. Since each moment is complete, there is nothing to attain, nothing to push away, and there is no hindrance.

When teacher and student meet in dokusan, a mirror appears which is neither "in" the other person, "in" the self, "between" the two people, nor "underlying" their efforts. Nonetheless, it is always present; each person, the interview process, and the room itself are expressions of the mirror. The teacher and student *rely* on this mirror. In psychotherapy, the therapist attempts to take on the function of mirroring. What does the therapist rely on?

The problem in psychotherapy is its unwillingness to identify the Absolute on which it rests. This is like taking refuge in a boat without acknowledging the role water plays in buoying it up. When psychotherapy relies on analysis of the Relative without sufficient attention to the Absolute, it falls into a one-sided view. The Absolute is that Self which rests on and is coextensive with the entire universe of all space and all time: it is form and emptiness, not emptiness and not form, neither form/emptiness nor not-form/emptiness, totally beyond and totally within form and emptiness. It is the basis of all existence and nonexistence, and of their interplay.

> Dew in the moonlight
> A river of stars
> Snow on the pines
> Clouds enveloping the peak.[3]

Words here can only point to truth, but are not truth itself. Since from the Absolute's point of view there is no thing that can be grasped, truth cannot be grasped. This ungraspable, inescapable truth of our existence presents itself to us moment by moment and cannot be held hostage to our ideas, wishes, or dreams. This being so, from a Buddhist point of view in psychological suffering there is no ultimate "core conflict" at the bottom of a problem; there is no "core fault" creating a hollowness in a self; there is no personal "self" other than the mirror its-self.

How can we reconcile this Buddhist sense of no-self with the core individualistic sense of "I'm *me?*" As the bumper sticker on my daughter's car says, "Always remember you're unique, just like everybody else." Buddhism does not deny the existence of a personal, relativistic ego, but it does deny it any permanent, static qualities.

We tend to think of ourselves as accumulations of experience: I am the person who was yelled at by my teachers, loved by my parents, played a wrong note in a concert performance, painted a beautiful painting. When we do this, each experience we have added to our store of "I ams" becomes both a part of our definition of ourselves *and* a limitation, an injunction to "be that way." In fact, though, we are much larger than the sum of our experience: when we touch the Absolute as the basis of our true self, we can experience a sense of freedom.[4]

I was seeing a woman who recently had become overwhelmed with childhood memories, previously suppressed, of being used as a sexual object by her parents and her parents' friends. She was filled with self-loathing; she felt soiled and dirtied by these experiences, and disgusted with herself. The more memories she recovered, the worse she felt. Over a number of sessions of psychotherapy neither empathy, reassurance, interpretation, cognitive processing, nor structured relaxation did anything to help; she kept spiraling into further self-abhorrence.

I looked for some way to both acknowledge her terrible experiences and free her from them, and said,

"You know, when you take a mirror, and hold it up to a piece of shit, it looks like the shit is in the mirror. Imagine how awful it would be if you were a mirror, and you made the mistake of believing you were everything you reflected. But that's the mistake you're making here. You look at yourself, and see the shit in the mirror, and think you're the shit. You fail to see that *you are the mirror, and the mirror isn't stained.*"

She had an immediate response. She stopped her litany of self-recrimination and disgust and sat quietly for a few seconds. Then a change seemed to pass over her; her body relaxed and her face took on a look of wonder and excitement.

"I'm *me* . . ." she stated, amazed. "I'm not what *happened* to me."

When this patient saw herself as the mirror, when she saw herself as *"me,"* who was looking at whom? The Mirror was looking at the mirror. When we realize "I'm *me*," we see ourselves as the mirror: we identify with the *basis* of our existence, the Absolute, rather than the relative particulars of our history or our desires. It is important, when we do this, not to mistake our Absolute basis as a kind of self-aggrandizement. Tōzan Ryōkai (c. 850/1980), after seeing himself reflected in a stream (once again, a mirroring experience) said, "I am not It; It actually is me." My small personal ego is not the Absolute; rather, the Absolute forms the wonderfully limitless, empty heart of my existence.

I am not It; It actually is me. I am not here; rather, here is what I am. At the moment the bird sings and fills my hearing before "I" stop to hear it, the birdsong is my life. I owe my life to birdsong; I am its servant. When a client visits me, she is not my client; I serve her as her therapist. My life and hers are inextricably intertwined, each realizing the other, each making what is real, real.

> Smiles and a grimace
> A sparkle of eyes
> Morning fog mind
> Hurts developing hearts' truth.

6

Just as psychotherapy tends to ignore the Absolute and concentrate on the vicissitudes of personal experience, there is a parallel problem in Buddhist teaching: the frequent lack of acknowledgment of the self (with a small *s*: that is, the vagaries of the personal ego). Dōgen's fascicle relates a kōan which addresses this:

Great Master Seppō Shingaku once said to his disciples: "To experience our real selves is the same as facing the Eternal Mirror. Whatever appears is reflected."
Then Gensha asked him: "If all of a sudden a clear Mirror appears, what happens?"
The master answered: "Whatever is there will be hidden."
Gensha said: "I doubt that."
Seppō asked: "What is your view?"
Gensha said: "Please, ask me the question."
Seppō asked him: "If all of a sudden a clear Mirror appears, what happens?"
Gensha said: "It will break into hundreds of pieces."

Gensha's "It will break into hundreds of pieces," means it smashes into a hundred thousand myriad pieces. In other words, when the clear Mirror suddenly emerges, it breaks into pieces. Studying these pieces is itself the clear Mirror.
If we try to grab the clear Mirror, it will certainly break into pieces. Breaking into pieces is in itself the clear Mirror. Do not take the narrow view that formerly there was a moment of not yet being smashed to bits and pieces and that latterly there may be a moment of no longer being smashed to bits and pieces: it simply breaks. These pieces are nothing but pieces: a solitary, steep unity. We must ask, what is the nature of these pieces? Eternal blue depths; the moon in a vast and endless sky.

We must study the "pieces" that are our fragmented selves. When our small selves are not acknowledged, they are not known; when they are not known, they run the show from off stage. There is, unfortunately, a long history of teachers (and students) acting in ways which are harmful to self or other; this seems to happen more frequently when there is a naive reliance on enlightenment as a once-and-for-all removal of the flailings and failings of the ego. The ego is always with us. Knowing that the ego is itself the mirror lets us look at the ego. When Buddhism relies on the Absolute without sufficient attention to the Relative, it falls into a one-sided view.

The mirror has two faces. Absolute and Relative are different sides of the same coin. "What happens when a Clear Mirror comes?" is the same as asking What happens when a mirror faces a mirror? It breaks into a thousand pieces, each of which is the Mirror.

In the early years of my zazen practice, I encountered many disturbing childhood memories. I gradually learned neither to push them away nor to be caught by them. Sometimes, if I were in particular distress, I would endeavor to open my sitting, expand it to hold the memories, and let the empty mirror reflect them calmly.
I thought I had come to terms with such experiences, but some years later, when I was seeing a therapist (Robin Fine) about a different matter, the childhood experiences resurfaced. To my surprise, I found it difficult to discuss them with my

therapist. I felt ashamed and fearful. It was one thing to acknowledge these feelings to myself, quite another to acknowledge them to a witness.

During one therapy session I was feeling deeply understood by Robin: "mirrored" in the best psychological sense of the word. I expressed my gratitude to her for this, but in a way which tended to place me in a "one-down" position. Robin picked up on this and commented:

"You know, Bob, when I bring something up in a way that helps you feel understood, but you express your appreciation to me in a way that emphasizes how understanding I am, then your experience turns into being about me; it stops being about you."

At first I insisted the gratitude I had expressed to her was not about her or me but from the Absolute which makes intimacy possibly. But her comment helped me realize this was a defense; I didn't want to look at the "pieces" of myself which felt submissive or vulnerable. At such times, it is hard to see that experience is itself the mirror.

I wanted to flee to something "bigger" than myself. By attempting to contain rejected aspects of my experience "in" the mirror, I was separating myself from these experiences and, in the process, separating myself from the mirror. It was as if a part of me were saying: "Okay, the mirror *stops right here!*"

If "I" hold "the mirror," then the mirror is "there" and I am "here," separate from the experience. Once that split comes in, I separate myself both from myself and from others. This tends to happen whenever we clutch our experiences to ourselves by keeping them private.

When experience is shared, however, the dynamic shifts. We can no longer maintain this separation. Denial melts in the compassionate witnessing of another person. Unlike the clarity of zazen, our messy interpersonal interactions impart a different form and a different quality to our experience. Paradoxically, to attain clarity in these relationships, to touch Self to Self absolutely, we must experience our fragmentation, acknowledging and cherishing every little piece of our small selves.

We are all constantly breaking into hundreds of thousands of pieces. Studying the pieces of the mirror is the mirror. When we study ourselves, we become the mirror facing the mirror. When we study ourselves in the presence of another person, two mirrors face themselves and face each other: we meet in mirroring. Each fragment of our experience is a clear mirror, is our entire life. Each piece is a whole; *that* whole is no different, in its wholeness, from *this* whole. This is complete realization.

7

Because each fragment is complete in itself, the Mirror need not add or subtract anything to reveal the truth. Each fragment appears fully, and thus expresses fullness (emptiness). "Whatever appears will be reflected." This means

that if a foreigner comes, he will be reflected, and if a Chinaman comes, a Chinaman will be reflected. . . . Because the present Chinaman is not 'a Chinaman' the
Chinaman appears. By "Chinese" is meant not only Chinese, but . . . the realm of
enlightenment.

Another way of saying this: when there is nothing extra, truth manifests itself in whatever form is currently present. The Mirror is completely accepting; it
has no "self" that colors or distorts reality. Usually, when we see a person with
Chinese or other ethnic physiognomy, we form a certain impression of him or her
based on our experience and preconceptions. We do the same if a person is short,
or tall, or slender, or obese, or "average." Our mind *compares* the person before us
to other persons. This is relative understanding.

In truth, the person who is four feet six inches is neither short nor tall; they
are simply four feet six inches. In fact, they are not even four feet six inches; their
height is changing constantly during the day, so that in the evening, after being
pulled by gravity all day, they have a little less height, and in the morning, after
stretching out in sleep, they gain another fraction of an inch. The person who is
four feet six inches is tall in some countries and historical epochs, short in others.
But the Mirror does not make these comparisons; it simply reflects what is actually there, moment by moment.

When whatever appears is reflected, the Chinaman is not "a Chinaman"—
an example of a type or category of people—but rather *the Chinaman appears*. The
person appears in actuality, in absolute terms as complete life. Enlightenment is
simply an unburdening of all the accretions of thought, of preconceptions, of
sense distortions, of preferential feelings that obscure reality; enlightenment is
simply the manifestation of that which is.

8

This is the stance the therapist orients to: complete acceptance of that which is,
not in the sense of approval, but in the sense of truth. If a person comes to us
who has beaten his or her child, the first step is to simply *see* that person. It is
not easy to see people who have beaten their child without adding something
to the meeting: even a stifling of disapproval and an artificial neutrality and
pseudo-acceptance is not a true mirror. But child beaters cannot see themselves; they usually fend off full awareness of their selves by either denial or
guilt. It is as if they cannot metabolize an action they are ashamed of, and instead approach it as something outside the self, "not-me." So long as they are
alienated from this aspect of their experience, they cannot make fundamental changes.

For this reason, the therapist, if he or she is to provide a true mirror, must recognize and accept how the therapist is also a child beater. The therapist must reflect the horror and the misplaced love, the hurt and the shame, the lack of awareness and the self-recriminations, until enlightenment is revealed as a child beater. Then the client can see him- or herself completely as a child beater at that moment. Only having seen the self in complete fullness, including all the split-off and rejected aspects, can the client see him- or herself as someone truly different the next moment. When child beater meets child beater, a mirror meets a mirror, and we break into millions of pieces. This is freedom.

I was meeting with a 45-year-old man who had struggled all his life with a sense of being gifted, while simultaneously feeling an inadequate fraud. This struggle had led him through much suffering. For example, in his youth he had been a gifted musician, almost a child prodigy. Then one day he heard a recording of Miles Davis and was overwhelmed. He said to himself: "That guy is really gifted, a genius . . . the only way I could get that good would be if I really practiced a lot. But if I have to practice a lot, obviously I'm not that good, I'm not a real genius." Thinking this, he stopped playing music, and lived with his regrets.

From the time Jay was 6 until about 12 his father, whom he loved, had become more and more inept and pathetic as he succumbed more and more to his alcoholism. His parents divorced and his father died as a street person. Jay had always felt he'd never received the fathering he needed to be a successful man.

After many years of substance abuse and recovery, he eventually forced himself to complete an advanced degree. I originally saw him when he was in his first post-graduate job, and had difficulties doing the kinds of writing the job demanded; he would be paralyzed by the thought that his efforts would not be up to his own exacting standards and would be plunged into despair from being disappointed in himself. By not writing, though, he was filled with self-disgust.

After some psychotherapy he was able to get over his writing block, and went on to become a successful professional. Some years later I saw him again, this time because he felt there was some block in his ability to be comfortably intimate with his wife. He also felt he was not able to be comfortably intimate with himself; he had felt compulsively driven his entire life.

One day he was talking to me about his conflicts about ambition. He felt that just being successful at his job wasn't sufficient. He would work long hours of overtime on his projects; however much he accomplished, though, never felt like enough. At the same time, he felt his compulsive overwork was detracting from his relationship with his wife and children.

I said to him: "Jay, let's face it. You want to be famous. Not just well-known; famous, Nobel Prize caliber. Part of you is sure that's the "real" you. In fact, to be honest, you won't feel like you're really fulfilling your potential unless you're up in the ranks of an Einstein or Freud, a household name."

He hesitated for a moment, made as if to deny it, then paused. Rather sheepishly, with a small smile, he said: "Well, yes."

I said: "But you know you're just not that gifted. You're smart, you're talented, but you know you're never going to be in that class."

He began to protest: he knew that, of course, but that didn't mean he shouldn't work as hard as he could, that he shouldn't keep his high goals for himself. . . .

I interrupted him: "And you fear that if you let go of being Einstein, you'll turn into the total inept, disgusting slob another part of you is sure that's the "real" you."

His body language changed. He sat back quietly. "Yes. I've always feared that."

I said: "So who, then, is the Jay that's here right now?"

There was some silence, and watching Jay's facial expression, it was as if the various conflicting self-images of his life story were chasing themselves across his features. After a bit, it looked like he "pulled himself together." He sat more solidly, and looked at me directly.

"Yes," he said.

We were out of time for that session. The next time he came back, he described a feeling as if he'd let go of something; that something had shifted, as if a split in himself which had seemed a giant rift turned out to be a knitted seam. He felt freer, less compulsive, more open to choices in his life. He was puzzled about himself, rather than conflicted; curious instead of tortured.

There was nothing special about my intervention with Jay. It simply described how he was appearing to me. It was presenting the obvious truth of himself to himself, a truth he'd always known but never quite discussed openly with somebody else.

For my part, though I had understood this dynamic in Jay's life since early on in my meetings with him, I'd never been able to put it so baldly. I had carried some conceptualizations of him as having "narcissistic features" along with "Oedipal conflicts." These had gotten in the way of my seeing Jay directly. I was afraid that Jay would not be able to tolerate it if I called attention too bluntly to both his grandiosity and his inability to live up to these aspirations.

However, in the time since I first saw Jay, he had matured. He'd held down a job, had two children, played and argued with his wife. Just as important, perhaps, was that I had matured over the years. My own conflicts about ambition, grandiosity, and inadequacy had played themselves out until I was no longer sensitive in this area. I could see myself clearly in Jay without having to "compensate" therapeutically for "countertransference." It no longer being an issue for me, I was able to reflect him clearly, without any judgment of good or bad, should or should not.

When I was talking to him in the above interchange, it did not feel there was any blurring of boundaries, but just "what appears is reflected." This interpersonal experience is the stuff of our everyday encounters, very ordinary, nothing special. Therein lies its opening to freedom. Rather than striving to be somebody special (whether gifted or flawed), we have an open invitation to experience our uniqueness whenever we meet another person directly. As one of the first clients I ever saw said to me, in words I have always remembered:

> When you can see yourself in others' eyes . . . that sure beats a mirror.

9

When we see ourselves in each others' eyes, we are the pieces of the mirror reflecting the Mirror. The truth of our existence is the completeness of each fragment, and the fragmentation of all completeness. Practice involves moving freely back and forth through this dance, until even these reflections disappear and are forgotten in the pure flow of experience.

This has long been expressed in Buddhism in multivarious forms. We say, when a person meditates, that the Fire God has come to seek for fire. We do not meditate in order to become enlightened; we meditate as an expression of that enlightenment that already exists and is not limited by our birth or death.

Psychotherapy has only recently begun to voice similar realizations. More and more schools of therapy are emphasizing that it is the health of the client that brings them to therapy (Rosenbaum, 1997, 1999; de Shazer, 1985; O'Hanlon & Weiner-Davis, 1989; Walter & Pellier, 1992). Whatever it is that leads someone to pick up a phone and call to make an appointment is already moving them along; they have already changed in the act of making the phone call. Some therapists routinely ask what changes clients have made between making the appointment and attending the first session; other therapists offer powerful arguments and cite research indicating it is the client who makes therapy work (Bohart & Tallman, 1999). Many therapists look to an unconscious drive for integration and emotional wholeness, and virtually all therapists ally themselves with the healthy parts of the client.

If this health is preexisting, though, why do we need psychotherapy? If we are already enlightened, why meditate? Dōgen addresses this toward the end of his fascicle on the Eternal Mirror.

> One day Nangaku visited Baso's hut. Baso stood and greeted him.
> Nangaku asked: "What are you doing these days?"
> Baso replied: "I do nothing but sit in zazen."
> Then Nangaku asked: "Why do you continually sit in zazen?"
> Baso answered: "I sit in zazen in order to become Buddha."
> Then Nangaku picked up a tile and started to polish it using a rock he found
>   by the side of Baso's hut.
> Baso, on seeing this, asked: "Master, what are you doing?"

> Nangaku answered: "I am polishing this tile."
> Baso asked: "Why are you polishing the tile?"
> Nangaku answered: "To make it into a mirror."
> Baso said: "How can polishing a tile make it into a mirror?"
> Nangaku said: "How can sitting in Zazen make you into a Buddha?"

Clearly, in truth, when polishing a tile becomes a mirror, Baso becomes Buddha. When Baso becomes Buddha, Baso directly becomes Baso . . . Polishing the tile to make the Mirror is the bones and marrow of eternal Buddhas. Accordingly, the Eternal Mirror is [always] made from a tile. Though we polish the Mirror, it has never been tainted. Tiles are not dirty; we just polish a tile as a tile, for its own sake. In this, the virtue of becoming the Mirror is realized . . .

If polishing a tile does not make a mirror, polishing a mirror cannot make a mirror either . . . In the action itself [polishing] is the realization of Buddha and the actualization of the Mirror. If we doubt this, are we not when we polish the Mirror mistakenly polishing it as a tile?

Now polishing a tile. Now beyond knowing. Thus . . . polishing the tile in itself makes the Mirror . . .

Who knows that when a tile comes, a tile appears, and there is a Mirror to reflect it! And who can recognize when a Mirror appears, there is a Mirror to reflect it?

In psychotherapy, we polish ourselves, we polish each other, and are polished by our polishing. The client is polishing herself, the therapist is polishing herself. Do not think that the client's polishing is separate from the therapist's, nor are they the same. When the tile is being polished, it is exercising the person who is exerting effort. At the same time, the tile's activity remains that of a tile. Because of that, the tile is always shining.

Psychotherapy cannot make persons into anyone other than they are. Psychotherapy cannot even make people be more like themselves; each person is completely him- or herself, each moment. Because of this, when we can show ourselves without artifice, when we can see others without blurs, within or without, something opens up. Truth and self meet: a mirror appears, and we appear fully.

Most of the time, though, we fail to see this. We miss others, and we miss ourselves, and thus are always yearning. Our yearning, and our cultural conditioning for accomplishment, makes us think we need to earn our selfdom. We think we must uncover something, or suffer something, or learn something, to be ourselves. We think we need psychotherapy, or at least that our clients need psychotherapy.

In fact, psychotherapy needs us, as surely as fields need grasses and grazers, as surely as songs need singers. Mind calls to mind. There is something about being human that calls us to examine ourselves and to meet each other in the process. We are inherently reflecting beings, and thus intrinsically luminous. We get together in psychotherapy, not to become something else, but because it is a natural human activity. The act of meeting is the act of realization.

We converse with each other: sometimes with people, sometimes with trees. Sometimes we lose sight of what we are doing, of the pure act of inter-acting. Then sometimes we treat people as if they were sticks of wood; sometimes we treat sticks of wood as if they were people. When we do psychotherapy to cure something, we mistakenly treat clients as diagnoses: we see not people, but borderlines and obsessionals. We polish the mirror and think we are polishing a tile. Then we treat our psychotherapeutic work as if it also were a thing, a tile. We become alienated from our activity: we feel divided in our selves, and distant from the people we touch and are touched by.

When in touching each other we are introducing truth to truth and self to self, we make that Mirror that is never *there*, always *here*. When our crazy, flawed selves refract dizzily, the Mirror reflects it and the Mirror appears. When the Mirror appears, the Mirror reflects the Mirror and breaks into a universe of pieces.

In that case, how could Dōgen's Eternal Mirror not be reflecting psychotherapy? How could psychotherapy not reflect the Eternal Mirror? Or, to put it another way:

> You are a mirror of the universe;
>   the universe is a mirror of you.
> You are a mirror for the universe;
>   the universe is a mirror for you.
> Being mirroring, a Mirroring Being!
> Reading these lines,
> you are realized completely
> mirroring is realized completely

NOTES

1. This quotation, and all subsequent quotations of Buddhist text, except where noted, is from Eihei Dōgen's fascicle "Kokyō," translated as "The Eternal Mirror." The fascicle is part of Dogen's Shōbōgenzō, "The Eye and Treasury of the True Law," written in 1243. Dōgen is difficult to translate, to the point where sometimes different translations provide somewhat different meanings. As part of my effort to convey what I take to be Dōgen's Zen, throughout this chapter I am using a compilation I have made from two translations of the Shōbōgenzō: one by G. W. Nishijima and C. Cross (London: Windbell Publications, 1994) and the other by K. Nishiyama (Tokyo: Nakayama Shobō, Overseas Distributor: San Francisco, CA, Elmsford, NY, and Tokyo: Japan Publications Trading Company, 1983).

2. Different schools of Buddhism have slightly different versions of the precepts. These variations are more marked between Mahāyāna and Theravāda Buddhism, but

translations and phrasings vary even within a single school. The ones quoted here are the ones we use in the Berkeley Zen Center.

    3. This poem appears on the back of a *rakusu* which was given to me. I have not been able to locate the source.

    4. Other versions of this case vignette appear in Rosenbaum, R. (1999) and in Rosenbaum, & Dyckman (1997).

REFERENCES

Bacal, H. A. and Newman, K. M. (1990). *Theories of object relations: Bridges to self psychology.* New York: Columbia University Press.

Bohart, A. and Rosenbaum, R. (1995). The dance of empathy: Empathy, diversity, and technical eclecticism. *The Person-Centered Journal, 2*(1), 5–29.

Bohart, A. & Tallman, K. (1999). *How clients make therapy work: The process of active self-healing.* Washington, DC: American Psychological Association Press.

de Shazer, S. (1985). *Keys to solution in brief therapy.* New York: Norton.

Dōgen (1243/1983). *A complete English translation of Dōgen Zenji's Shōbōgenzō (The eye and treasury of the true law)* (K. Nishiyama, Trans.) (Vol. 3, pp. 45–59). Tokyo: Nakayama Shobō. (Overseas Distributor: Japan Publications Trading Company, San Francisco, CA, Elmsford, NY, and Tokyo).

Dōgen, E. (R. Aitken & K. Tanahashi, Trans.). (1233/1985). Genjo-koan. In K. Tanahashi, (Ed.), *Moon in a dewdrop: Writings of Zen Master Dogen* (pp. 69–73). San Francisco: North Point Press.

Dōgen, E. (1243/1994). "The eternal mirror." In G. W. Nishijima and C. Cross (Trans.), *Shōbōgenzō, The eye and treasury of the true law* (pp. 240–259). London: Windbell Publications.

Goldberg, A. (1988). Some notes on the mirror. In A. Goldberg (Ed.), *A fresh look at psychoanalysis* (pp. 217–228). Hillsdale, NJ: Analytic Press.

Holinger, P. C. (1999). Noninterpretive interventions in psychoanalysis and psychotherapy: A developmental perspective. *Psychoanalytic Psychology, 16,* 233–253.

Jordan, J., Miller, J., Stiver, I. and Surrey, J. (Eds.), *Women's growth in connection: Writing from the Stone Center.* New York: Guilford Press.

Kohut, H. (1971). *The analysis of the self.* New York: International Universities Press.

Kohut, H. (1979). The two analyses of Mr. Z. *International Journal of Psychoanalysis, 60,* 3–27.

Lax, W. (1996). Narrative, social constructionism, and Buddhism. In H. Rosen and K. T. Kuehlwein (Eds.), Constructing realities: Meaning-making perspectives for psychotherapists (pp. 195–220). San Francisco: Jossey-Bass.

Merleau-Ponty, M. (1964). *Signs* (R. McCleary, Trans.). Evanston, IL: Northwestern University Press.

O'Hanlon, W. & Weiner-Davis, M. (1989). *In search of solutions: A new direction in psychotherapy.* New York: Norton.

Ornstein, P. H. and Ornstein, A. (1984). Clinical understanding and explaining: The empathic vantage point. In A. Goldberg (Ed.), *Progress in self psychology* (Vol. 1, pp. 43–61). New York: Guilford Press.

Povinelli, D., Rulf, A., Landau, K., and Bierschwale, D. (1993). Self-recognition in chimpanzees (Pan troglodytes): Distribution, ontogeny, and patterns of emergence. *Journal of Comparative Psychology, 107*(4), 347–372.

Ryōkai, T. (c. 850/1980). Hōkyō zamnai: Song of the jewel mirror samadhi. In T. Cleary, (Trans.), *Timeless spring* (pp. 39–41). New York: Weatherhill.

Rosenbaum, R. (1997). Form, formlessness and formulation. *Journal of Psychotherapy Integration, 6*(2), 107–117.

Rosenbaum, R. (1999). *Zen and the heart of psychotherapy.* Philadelphia: Brunner/Mazel.

Rosenbaum, R. & Dyckman, J. (1997). "No self? No problem?," in M. Hoyt (Ed.), *Constructive Therapies* (Vol. II, pp. 238–274). New York: Guilford.

Stern, D. (1985). *The interpersonal world of the infant.* New York: Basic Books.

Strupp, H. & Hadley, S. (1995). *When things get worse: The problem of negative effects in psychotherapy.* New York: Jason Aronson.

Tolkien, J. (1966). *The hobbit.* Boston: Houghton Mifflin.

Walter, J. and Pellier, J. (1992). *Becoming solution-focused in brief therapy.* New York: Brunner/Mazel.

CHAPTER 8

Psychotherapy Practice as Buddhist Practice

Seth Robert Segall

INTRODUCTION

Over the past half-century, Western Psychology has become increasingly aware of the relevance of Buddhist theory and practice to Western psychopathology and psychotherapy (Watts, 1961; Suzuki, Fromm, & De Martino, 1963; Kornfield, 1993; Epstein, 1995). The Buddha said he taught "suffering and the cessation of suffering" (Alagaddūpama Sutta, 1995, p. 234), and Buddhism can be viewed as a diagnosis and prescription for the relief of certain types of psychological distress. As an approach to the alleviation of human suffering, Buddhism developed prior to and independently from the Western psychotherapeutic tradition, and as such, it provides an external vantage point from which one can illuminate, supplement, or critique Western psychological approaches.

The degree to which Buddhist theory and practice parallel certain aspects of the theory and practice of both the cognitive-behavioral and experiential psychotherapies is truly remarkable. For example, the process of attention to somatosensory and affective processes in *vipassanā* (insight) meditation (Gunaratana, 1991) bears remarkable resemblance to Perls, Hefferline, and Goodman's (1951) continuum of awareness technique in Gestalt Therapy, and to Gendlin's (1996) analysis of "focusing." The monitoring and labeling of cognitive and affective processes in vipassanā meditation also seems to parallel the kinds of standard recommendations one finds as part of behavioral and cognitive-behavioral self-control strategies. Similarly, the Buddha's recommendations for ridding oneself of psychologically unskillful thoughts in the Vitakkasanthāna Sutta (1995) bear a significant resemblance to the thought stopping, distraction, and disputation techniques of contemporary cognitive-behavioral

165

therapy. In addition, the encouragement within Buddhist practice to loosen one's identification with egocentric and narcissistic forms of thought is similar to Ellis's (1962) process of challenging the irrational demands human beings make on the universe.

      Western Psychology has also recently begun to recognize the potential value of the Buddhist concept of *mindfulness*, and the Buddhist techniques designed to foster it, as a way to supplement and enhance cognitive-behavioral treatments. This trend is most evident in new developments such as Mindfulness-Based Stress Reduction (Kabat-Zinn, 1991), Dialectical Behavioral Therapy (Linehan, 1993), Mindfulness-Based Cognitive Therapy (Segal, Williams, & Teasdale, 2002), Marlatt's (2002) application of mindfulness in treating addictions, and Roemer and Orsillo's (2002) recommendations for the treatment of generalized anxiety disorder. We might also briefly note the emergence of newer psychotherapies that have been influenced in other ways by Buddhism including Acceptance and Commitment Therapy (Hayes, Wilson, & Strosahl, 1999) and psychotherapies that have originated in Asia, such as Morita Therapy (Morita, 1998).

      As much as it has become clear that there are ways that Buddhism either parallels or can enhance Western psychotherapies, it has also become increasingly clear that there are ways in which Buddhist theory and practice diverge from the theory and practice of the Western psychotherapies. The Western concepts of "adult development" and "personal growth" provide a rich domain for exploring these divergences. While Buddhism supports personal growth in terms of moral development, the development of a strong sense of personal responsibility for one's thoughts and actions, the development and stabilization of awareness, and the development of mental states such as equanimity and compassion, it is silent on other kinds of personal growth that are prominent in Western psychotherapy. Classical Buddhism, for example, is relatively silent on such matters as enhancing intimacy or commitment in romantic and sexual relationships, promoting integration of disowned aspects of one's personality, or learning to value and make appropriate use of what Epstein (1994) calls the "experiential" processing system.

      Western psychotherapies also tend to stress the development of a strong sense of an autonomous personal identity and may encourage varying degrees of social and material achievement. These goals seem to depart in meaningful ways from the Buddhist understanding of the quasi-illusory nature of a separate sense of Self, and the inherent unsatisfactoriness of material and interpersonal goals. It is not entirely clear, however, what the relation of the Self in Buddhist discourse is to Western psychological notions of Self. Western psychotherapists who have struggled to understand, for example, the relationship between the Freudian Ego and the Kohutian Self may understand how hard it might be to appreciate the parallels and differences between contemporary Western conceptions of Self, and those conceptions embedded in the Pāli language within a 2,500-year-old non-Western culture.

Western Psychology has also begun to show some interest in how the process and experience of being a psychotherapist might be affected by the psychotherapist's own personal Buddhist practice (Rubin, 1996; Rosenbaum, 1999). Here the emphasis is not so much on how clients might be understood or helped, but on how the person of the therapist might be transformed. Over the past six years, I have had a chance to observe how my own personal commitment to Buddhist practice has informed the way I conduct psychotherapy and the way in which I am with the client and myself during the therapy hour. This chapter grows out of my interest in delineating the subtle but seemingly important nature of those changes, and what the implications of those changes might be for therapist training and personal growth. *Changes that come as a psychotherapy*

THERAVĀDA BUDDHISM

My knowledge of Buddhism has been largely acquired though an acquaintance with the teachings of Buddhists who have been at least partly trained within the *Theravāda* tradition, such as Joseph Goldstein and Jack Kornfield (1987), Ayya Khema (1987), Henepola Gunaratana (1991), Sharon Salzberg (1995), Ruth Denison (1996), and Larry Rosenberg (1998). It has also been deeply informed by the radical "nonmethod" of meditative inquiry practiced by Toni Packer (1995), who was trained within the *Rinzai* Zen tradition of *Mahāyāna* Buddhism. Theravāda is one of the three main branches of Asian Buddhism and is practiced primarily in Southeast Asia. Theravāda differs from Mahāyāna and *Vajrayāna* (Tantric) Buddhism on a number of dimensions. Most important to this author are its relative focus on the Buddha as a human teacher rather than as an archetypal transcendent being, and its focus on the texts of the *Pāli* cannon with their realistic settings and psychological emphases, as opposed to the magical, esoteric, and paradoxical aspects of the later Mahāyāna and Vajrayāna texts. These differences are relative rather than absolute, but are discernable to the casual reader. In fact, it is possible to strip almost all the "religious" trappings from Theravāda Buddhism, as Shinzen Young (Tart, 1990) has done, and still have it recognizably Theravāda. These approaches have appealed to me because of my own pragmatic, scientific, and agnostic bent. They have made it easier for me to assimilate Buddhism to the value and knowledge structures I acquired in my training as a psychologist. Readers should be aware that this is only one possible "take" on Buddhism, however, and that other Buddhists have different views. The Buddhist community is as

A) all human existence marked by 1) ultimate unsatisfactoriness of all experiences & achievements by 2) impermanence of material + psychol worlds + by 3) delusional nature of the sense of a separate, enduring self.

Human Suffering → comes from one's attempts to control one's own experiencing by 1) holding onto pleasures + 2) avoiding unpleasant events.

multifaceted as is the Christian community in which Catholics, Pentecostals, Unitarians, Jehovah's Witnesses, Quakers, and Mormons all retain their unique voices, and have differences that are as important as their similarities.

THE FOUR NOBLE TRUTHS AND THE
EIGHTFOLD NOBLE PATH

Central to all forms of Buddhism are the Buddha's teachings of the *Four Noble Truths* and the *Eightfold Noble Path*. These teachings posit that human existence is marked by the ultimate unsatisfactoriness of all experiences and achievements, by the impermanence of the material and psychological worlds, and by the delusional nature of the sense of a separate, enduring self. In this schema, human suffering derives from one's attempts to control one's own experiencing by holding onto pleasures and avoiding unpleasant events. The route to freedom from suffering is through following the Eightfold Noble Path marked by moral action, meditation, and philosophical wisdom. The ultimate achievement of *enlightenment* is marked, in part, by a decentration of the self, a profound acceptance of existence, a sharpened attentiveness to all of one's mental and physical activities, a freedom from identification with states of greed, hatred, and delusion, and a deep compassion for one's fellow beings.

The moral component of the Eightfold Noble Path includes the concepts of "right action," "right speech," and "right livelihood." The moral precepts nurture the development of one's potential to make one's words and actions be part of an agenda for compassionate and caring engagement with others and with the world. Buddhists are encouraged to find professions that are ethical in nature and to avoid uses of language that harm other people. The doctrine of "right speech" encourages Buddhists to use the right word in the right situation to the right person at the right time. One is urged to practice honesty, except in situations when honesty would subject others to greater suffering than an untruth would. One may also withhold the truth when it would only hurt someone without, in the long run, being of benefit. Truthful speech must also be skillfully worded so that it is effective in its intended beneficial consequences.

therapy

PSYCHOTHERAPY AS BUDDHIST PRACTICE

At its best, practicing psychotherapy can be conceived of as a form of right livelihood that depends, to a great extent, on right speech. As such, every encounter with a client becomes a spiritual encounter for the therapist. The therapist's tasks are to (1) maintain mindfulness, (2) avoid ensnarement in transient states of desire and aversion that might divert the therapeutic endeavor, and (3) skillfully employ compassionate and discerning speech with the intent of relieving the client's

My tasks
1) maintain mindfulness
2) avoid ensnarement in transient states of desire & aversion that might divert therapeutic endeavor
3) skillfully employ compassionate & discerning speech w. intent of relieving client's suffering

suffering. This kind of moment-to-moment attentiveness and compassionate nonegoistic focus is consistent with all forms of psychotherapy, but raising the commitment from one that is "only" professional to one that is also spiritual raises the seriousness of the therapeutic enterprise another notch. Being fully present with the client in this way is not only a means to earning a living or fulfilling a moral imperative, but is also part of the path to the practitioner's own spiritual development. Every client encounter becomes part of the therapist's own learning process, not just learning in terms of becoming a better therapist, but in terms of becoming more fully human. Every therapeutic encounter becomes a sacred opportunity to make every word and moment count. *??.*

In exploring psychotherapy as a practice conducted within the context of the Eightfold Noble Path, it is useful to examine several key Buddhist concepts to discover how they might illuminate the psychotherapist's craft. The concepts are concepts of *sīla* (or virtue), *samādhi* (or concentration), and *paññā* (or wisdom). *Virtue, concentration, wisdom.*

Sīla (Virtue)

For lay Buddhists, sīla consists of the attempted practice of the *Five Precepts*. These five precepts involve (1) desisting from killing other beings, (2) not taking what is not freely given, (3) not harming others through acts of speech, (4) refraining from sexual immorality, and (5) abstaining from intoxicating substances. For therapists, making sure that intoxicating substances do not cloud the therapist's mind (Precept 5) and guarding against sexual boundary violations (Precept 4) are part of the minimum standard of care. The duty to prevent suicide and homicide on the part of one's clients (Precept 1) is also part of the therapist's standard of care. The ethical precept against "not taking what is not freely given" (Precept 2) is part of the therapist's practice when it comes to fair billing practices and ethical dealings with both clients and insurance companies. The ethical injunction against harmful speech (Precept 4), however, is perhaps the most subtle, complex, and fertile ground for practice.

What did the Buddha mean by harmful or wrong speech? In the Mahācat-tārīsaka Sutta (1995, p. 936) the Buddha identified wrong speech as "false speech, malicious speech, harsh speech, and gossip." Similarly, In the Kakacūpama Sutta (1995, p. 221), the Buddha states that speech can be "timely or untimely, true or untrue, gentle or harsh, connected with good or with harm, and spoken with loving-kindness or inner hate." In therapy, then, the therapist's words should be spoken out of loving-kindness, and the words should be gentle, timely, true, and spoken with the intent of being helpful to the client. Following this precept requires an enormous amount of mindfulness on the part of the therapist, who is continually monitoring his or her own mood states, intentions, tone of voice,

Wrong speech - "false - malicious, harsh - gossip
Speech - timely or untimely, true or untrue
gentle or harsh, connected w. good or w. harm
spoken w. lovingkindness or inner hate":

[handwritten: most precious gift we can give any one is the quality of our attention. no other purpose than to be fully present]

verbal content, and nonverbal communication to attend to countertransferential feelings, and to guard against the acting out of angry, flirtatious, ingratiating, narcissistic, controlling, self-righteous, distancing, or other antitherapeutic behaviors.

Samādhi (Concentration) *[handwritten: rt. concent a, rt - mindfulness; rt. effort -]*

The Samādhi component of the eightfold path emphasizes "right concentration," "right mindfulness," and "right effort." Rubin (1996) has commented on the similarity between the Buddhist idea of "mindfulness" and Freud's concept of "evenly-hovering attention" as a technical aspect of the psychoanalytic method. The most precious gift we can give anyone is the quality of our attention. Those moments we have had with others that seem most meaningful to us have been moments when others have freely and genuinely given us their full attention. In existentially based psychotherapies, such attention is given with no other purpose than to be fully present. This means, to the extent that it is humanly possible, leaving all private concerns at the office door; letting go of all concerns for the previous client at the start of the new therapy hour; letting one's attention be "bare attention," rather than analytic attention; listening with one's body rather than with just one's ears. The goal, over and over, is to attend to *this* client-therapist interactive field in *this* moment, just as in meditation the goal is to attend to *this* breath in *this* moment, over and over. In meditation, the meditator quickly discovers how easily attention slips off of the breath and wanders, and learns to keep bringing attention back to the breath without judgment. Similarly, in psychotherapy the therapist quickly learns how easily attention wanders from bare attention to the client-therapist field, and learns to keep bringing attention back to the client-therapist field without judgment. Mindful concentration is an essential ingredient to forming a positive therapeutic alliance and to the kind of deep listening that, within the Rogerian paradigm (Rogers, 1951), creates the interpersonal space where transformation and healing occurs. It is also essential within *any* paradigm; whatever theory we operate within, our very next intervention, our very next interpretation, our very next action, is going to proceed from the depth of our understanding of this very moment in this particular client-therapist interactive field.

One is also mindful of one's tendency to identify with or distance oneself from the client in each passing moment of the therapy session. If unwatched, one's tendency is to take what is being said and what is happening personally, rather than just hearing it openly and freshly, with curiosity and wonder. If the client is critical or resists the therapist's interventions, the therapist can be angry and defensive; if the client is compliant and friendly, the therapist can be co-opted or seduced. Therapists can think/feel that the client is "one of us" or "one of

[handwritten: hear it as. curiosity & wonder - openly & freely]

them." The therapist's sense of self can become inflated as a client improves, or deflated as a client's illness festers despite the therapist's best efforts. Mindfulness listens to and watches all of this impartially: the contracting and expanding, the distancing and merging, the openness and the defensiveness, the criticism and the appreciation. It is for or against none of it. It does not get ensnared and entangled, or if it does, it notices the ensnarement and entanglement with equanimity and compassion. *a friendly attitude toward*

As one listens, one strives to maintain a friendly attitude toward the client, toward oneself, and toward one's own experience, an attitude marked by *mettā* (loving-kindness), *karuna* (compassion), and *upekkhā* (equanimity). The term "loving-kindness" within the Buddhist tradition does not have sentimental or erotic overtones (Salzberg, 1995). It is neither soft-minded nor sappy. It implies an openness, receptivity, and willingness to accept oneself just as one is and others just as they are, with equanimity, and without needing to distance oneself. The idea is to not be ensnared by states of aversion that separate oneself emotionally from the phenomena one is observing.

Rogers (1951) stressed the importance of unconditional positive regard, in addition to accurate empathy, as a necessary condition for therapeutic improvement. It seems a mistake to separate out empathy and unconditional regard as two separate factors, however. Accurate empathy *requires* unconditional positive regard; one cannot accurately understand the client's stance and viewpoint if one emotionally distances oneself from the client, feels separate from or superior to the client, or condemns or feels disgusted by the client. This does not mean one approves of all the actions of the client; on the contrary, one clearly recognizes those actions on the client's part that lead to his or her own misery, and the misery of others around him or her. One understands, however, the conditions out of which these undesirable actions arise, and how the therapist him- or herself, faced with similar causes and conditions, might act no better. One also understands how one's condemnation and disgust can engender states of humiliation, shame, and rage in the client, closing the client off behind a wall of defensiveness, and making the client less able to comprehend the consequences of his or her own actions and take responsibility for them. Words of instruction are called for here, spoken from a compassionate heart and, when called for, decisive action to prevent future harmful actions on the part of the client, rather than states of aversion, and revulsion.

The therapist's friendly stance toward the client and the client's experiential world is of paramount therapeutic importance in that it supports the client's eventual acceptance, toleration, and integration of thoughts, feelings, attitudes, and behaviors that have hitherto fore been objects of self-aversion. The therapist's ability to be with the client in a friendly, experience-near way is often a precondition for the client's ability to take a friendly, self-nurturing stance toward his or her own experiencing, which can eventually ripen into wholeness and appropriate self-regard and self-care. In many therapies this shift from self-loathing to appropriate self-caring is the turning point on which a successful outcome depends.

Pañña (Wisdom) *understa. of nature of suffering/unsatis fortion impermanence, nonself + emptiness/interbeing*

The Wisdom component of the Eightfold Noble Path refers to an understanding of the nature of *dukkha* (suffering/unsatisfactoriness), *anicca* (impermanence), *anattā* (nonself), and *śūnyatā* (emptiness/interbeing). It posits that all phenomena are impermanent, devoid of a solid, unchanging essence, and coexistent as aspects of the entire web of being. As a corollary, all phenomena are ineffective as permanent solutions to the existential unsatisfactoriness of the human condition.

Dukkha (Unsatisfactoriness). In understanding *dukkha*, one understands that unsatisfactoriness is not only an essential fact of the client's life, but also the therapist's. As the therapist conducts a psychotherapy, there will be many unpleasant moments for him or her. If the therapist shrinks from these unpleasant moments, or avoids them, or fails to maintain his or her awareness of them, the therapist's efficacy as therapist is reduced. The therapist needs to be able to sit with the client's pain unflinchingly and without minimization. The therapist also needs to sit with his or her own pain: the ache of the therapist's own uncertainty and insufficiency, the moments of discouragement and hopelessness, the moments of boredom and disinterest, and the therapist's own myriad personal distresses that often reverberate in sympathetic harmony with the client's problems. If the therapist withdraws emotionally or attentively, or reacts without mindful attention, breaks in the therapeutic alliance are almost inevitable at these points. If the therapist can be attentive to these states, accept them, hold them within his or her own spacious being, and tolerate them, the therapy is more likely to be successful.

Annica (Impermanence). In understanding *anicca*, the therapist understands there is no solidity to existence; existence is always in a state of transformation. Everything is always on its way to becoming something else. This is as true for the therapist's world as the client's. The therapist often gets caught up in psychological constructs which reify the client rather than seeing the client as a changing, fluid being: the client *is* a Borderline or *is* a Schizophrenic; the client's momentary symptoms become his or her essence; fluctuating ego-states can be reified as separate personalities; personality traits can be seen as fixed and unmalleable. To the extent that the therapist assumes a static and unchanging world, the therapist becomes blind to the possibilities for change within each moment.

The therapist may cling not only to reified diagnostic concepts, but also to rigidity within the therapeutic relationship. The therapist's own changing, flexible, protean self may be encrusted within a rigid conception of the therapist's role; the therapist's own ability to flow and adapt may be hidden behind an ascribed social role, or within personal character armor. The therapist thereby looses the ability to see the genuine therapeutic possibilities of *this* moment right here, right now, which may just call for something original, daring, and never-before-thought-of. In a world that is constant transformation, the possibilities inherent in *this* moment may never come again.

In understanding *anicca*, the therapist also understands that he or she is also subject to causes and conditions just like all other extant beings in the world. One moment the therapist is attentive, the next moment lost. One moment the therapist is brilliant, the next moment befuddled. One moment the therapist is compassionate, the next moment threatened and self-centered. The therapist must be at home with this, as attentive as possible to his or her own shifting mental states, accepting of change, and ever ready to seek a new state of balance. In addition, the therapist must be willing to allow the role of client to mutate and change as the client's needs shift as a consequence of either growth or deterioration.

Anattā (Nonself). Since things are in a constant state of flux, there can be no such thing as an immutable identity to things. In addition, things happen according to the laws of cause-and-effect, and there can be no entelechy standing outside of the chain of cause-and-effect directing the way things happen. In Buddhism there is no Being standing outside the flux of being, be it a god or be it an eternal soul. Buddhism is in accord with our current understanding of neuropsychology and information processing which find observations, but no observer, thoughts, but no thinker, actions, but no actor (Dennett, 1991; Epstein, 1995).

Buddhist doctrines, such as the doctrine of anattā, are often misunderstood as being primarily ontological statements, when in actuality they serve the pragmatic purpose of helping to liberate us from our selfish preoccupations. The more the therapist understands anattā, the less the likelihood that the therapy will be about the selfhood of the therapist. Why should the therapist work so hard to protect an identity that has only a quasi-existence? The therapist does not need to cling as tightly to an image of him- or herself as smarter than the client, healthier than the client, more knowledgeable than the client, or more right than the client. If the client is angry with the therapist, the therapist need not get caught up in an identity narrative about being the aggrieved helper: "How can you be angry with *me* after all *I've* done for you?" The therapist does not need to conduct the therapy so that he or she will be approved of by the client. If the client improves, the value of the self of the therapist does not have to go up ten points, nor does his or her stock need to decline when the therapy fails. The client does not need to get better for the therapist, or stay sick for the therapist. With less of a sense of self to protect, the therapist is freer to hear the client and open to the client. Self is always defined in opposition to Other, and as such, serves to cut one off from intimacy with others. When the identification with self loosens, a natural connectedness to and caring for the suffering of others manifests itself freely. That connectedness and care is impeded in everyday life by the need to protect oneself and one's possessions, and flows when attention to "me" and "mine" abates.

Śūnyatā (Emptiness/Interbeing). Although the concept that the Sanskrit noun śūnyatā points to is not completely foreign to Theravāda Buddhism, which has its own cognate *Pāli* noun *suññata,* it is a term that only comes into full flower in Mahāyāna Buddhism. It is usually translated as "emptiness," although Thich Nhat Hahn's (1993) term *interbeing* seems a more felicitous and creative translation. Interbeing is a natural consequence of impermanence and nonself: it points to the interconnectedness and interdependence of all phenomena. Nothing exists except in interrelationship with everything else. Its implications for therapy are readily discernable: the client does not exist as an entity separate from the family and social system of which he or she is an integral part; the client and the clinical phenomena that he or she exhibits in the therapy room do not exist separate from the client-therapist interaction; the therapist is different when with this client than when with any other client; transference and countertransference are two sides of the same coin. Phenomena do not exist by themselves, but only as part of a field, and the arrow of causality within a field is always multidirectional.

These insights are not new: Anthony Barton (1974) wrote over a quarter-century ago about how clients and their pathology are different with different therapists; similarly, Robert Langs (1976) eloquently articulated how therapist and client are both integral parts of a bipersonal field; family therapists have long applied von Bertalanffy's (1968) general system theory to understanding interpersonal relations within families.

While these insights are not new, it is hard to make perceiving the world in this way seem like second nature. Guisinger and Blatt (1994) have pointed out how Western psychology has had a historical bias in favor of emphasizing independence, autonomy, and identity in self-development over interpersonal relatedness. Our cultural and personal biases cause us to continually lapse into unbalanced and simplistic modes of thought that fail to take interbeing into consideration. It is often hard to see how client and therapist cocreate phenomena during the complex and often intense emotional pushes and pulls the therapist experiences within the therapeutic relationship. Buddhist practice is one way to help therapists ground themselves in an appreciation of interbeing even within the most emotionally charged of therapeutic interchanges.

IMPLICATIONS FOR TRAINING

Psychotherapists are supposed to know how to monitor their own emotional processes, to see complex interpersonal transactions with a minimum of defensiveness, and to use this monitoring and seeing in service of maintaining a therapeutic relationship that is focused on relief of the client's suffering. These *expectations* are taught in graduate school, but the emotional skills required to achieve them rarely are. All too often, training in psychotherapy has to do with the acquisition of skills that can be externally measured and quantified, for example, the mastery of a body of facts and theories, the development of specific communication skills, and adherence to a manualized protocol. Buddhist practice may be an important vehicle for developing emotional skills that are vital for the practice of psychotherapy, but are harder to teach: openness, receptivity, awareness of internal process, equanimity, compassion, and an enhanced sensitivity to interrelatedness. There is already a small amount of empirical evidence in support of this contention: Shapiro, Schwartz, & Bonner (1998) have shown that a course in mindfulness meditation can improve empathy levels in medical and premedical students. Whether Buddhist practices can, in fact, meaningfully enhance therapist performance is an empirical question that is amenable to research.

As an aside, we might note that the Buddha would probably have appreciated the use of the experimental method to test his ideas. He urged those he taught to apply empirical tests to the doctrines they were taught. As he told the villagers from the Kalama clan:

> It is proper for you . . . to doubt, to be uncertain. . . . Do not go upon what has been acquired by repeated hearing; nor upon tradition; nor upon rumor; nor upon what is in a scripture; nor upon surmise; nor upon an axiom; nor upon specious reasoning; nor upon a bias toward a notion that has been pondered over; nor upon another's seeming ability; nor upon the consideration, "The monk is our teacher." (The Instructions to the Kalamas, 1981/1994, para. 4)

The Buddha was a firm believer in "come and see for yourself." Every aspect of his teaching was intended to be tested rather than to simply be believed.

CONCLUSION

In the last half-century there has been a growing appreciation for the relevance of many of Buddhism's core concepts and practices to the practice of psychotherapy.

Many Buddhist ideas parallel and extend concepts that already exist in the Western psychotherapies, and in addition, newer therapies have recently emerged which have imported Buddhist themes and practices directly into their content. These concepts and practices include practices that emphasize the development of ethical behavior, mindfulness and concentration, and compassionate wisdom that grows out of an understanding of the nature of unsatisfactoriness, impermanence, non-self, and interbeing.

Practicing psychotherapy within this frame alters the existential nature of the psychotherapeutic endeavor from a set of interactions that are purely professional in nature to a set of interactions that are also part of the therapist's path of spiritual growth. Whether one views this alteration as a positive or negative development no doubt depends on one's beliefs about the relationship between the spiritual and secular domains. This is a kind of spirituality, however, that asks nothing of and makes no demands on the client. It is the therapist alone who is challenged to meet a new standard of commitment.

A commitment to such practices can possibly improve therapists' abilities to: (a) self-monitor emotional states, (b) decrease self-preoccupation and defensiveness, (c) experience caring and empathy for self and client, (d) maintain an awareness of the ongoing therapist-client relationship without getting lost in proliferation of thought and reification of personality traits and dynamics, and (e) understand therapist-client interactions within field terms. Psychology supervisors universally desire these behaviors in their trainees, but often struggle to find effective pedagogical methods to nurture them. Future research can help clarify whether the adaptation of a Buddhist frame for psychotherapy practice, and extended practice with Buddhist meditative and training techniques, can help develop and enhance these behaviors.

REFERENCES

Alagaddūpama Sutta (1995). In B. Ñānamoli and B. Bodhi (Trans.), *The middle length discourses of the Buddha: A new translation of the Majjhima Nikāya* (pp. 224–236). Boston, Wisdom.

Barton, A. (1974). *Three worlds of therapy: Freud, Jung and Rogers.* Palo Alto, CA: Mayfield Publishing.

Dennett, D. C. (1991). *Consciousness explained.* Boston: Little Brown and Company.

Denison, R. (1997). Bowing to life deeply: An interview with Ruth Denison. In *Insight: A Joint Newsletter of the Insight Meditation Society and the Barre Center for Buddhist studies,* Spring 1997, 3–5.

Ellis, A. (1962). *Reason and emotion in psychotherapy.* New York: Lyle Stuart.

Epstein, M. (1995). *Thoughts without a thinker.* New York: BasicBooks.

Epstein, S. (1994). Integration of the cognitive and psychodynamic unconscious. *American Psychologist, 49,* 709–724.

Gendlin, E. T. (1996). *Focusing-oriented psychotherapy: A manual of the experiential method.* New York: Guilford Press.

Goldstein, J., and Kornfield, J. (1987). *Seeking the heart of wisdom.* Boston: Shambhala.

Guisinger, S., and Blatt, S. J. (1994). Individuality and relatedness: Evolution of a fundamental dialectic. *American Psychologist, 49,* 704–711.

Gunaratana, H. (1991). *Mindfulness in plain English.* Boston: Wisdom.

Hahn, T. N. (1993). *Interbeing: Fourteen guidelines for engaged Buddhism* (F. Eppsteiner, Ed.). Berkeley, CA: Parallax Press.

Hayes, S. C., Wilson, K. G., and Strosahl, K. D. (1999). *Acceptance and commitment therapy: An experiential approach to behavior change.* New York: Guilford Press.

Kabat-Zinn, J. (1991). *Full catastrophe living: Using the wisdom of your body and mind to face stress, pain, and illness.* New York: Delta.

Kakacūpama Sutta (1995). In B. Ñānamoli & B. Bodhi (Trans.), *The middle length discourses of the Buddha: A new translation of the Majjhima Nikāya* (pp. 217–223). Boston: Wisdom.

Khema, A. (1987). *Being nobody going nowhere: Meditations on the Buddhist path.* Boston: Wisdom Publications.

Kornfield, J. (1993). *A path with heart.* New York: Bantam.

Langs, R. (1976). *The bipersonal field.* New York: Jason Aronson.

Linehan, M. (1993). *Cognitive-behavioral therapy of borderline personality disorder.* New York: Guilford Press.

Mahācattārīsaka Sutta (1995). In B. Ñānamoli & B. Bodhi (Trans.), *The middle length discourses of the Buddha: A new translation of the Majjhima Nikāya* (pp. 934–941). Boston: Wisdom.

Marlatt, G. A. (2002). Buddhist philosophy and the treatment of addictive disorder. *Cognitive and Behavioral Practice, 9,* 44–50.

Morita, M. (1998). *Morita therapy and the true nature of anxiety based disorders (Shinkeishitsu).* (Peg LeVine, Ed.). (Akihisa Kondo, Trans.). Albany, New York: State University of New York Press.

Packer, T. (1995). *The work of this moment.* Rutland, VT: Charles Tuttle.

Perls, F., Hefferline, R. F., and Goodman, P. (1951). *Gestalt therapy: Excitement and growth in the human personality.* New York: Delta.

Rogers, C. R. (1951). *Client-centered therapy: Its current practice, implications, and theory.* Boston: Houghton Mifflin.

Roemer, L. and Orsillo, S. M. (2002). Expanding our conceptualization of and treatment for generalized anxiety disorder: Integrating mindfulness/acceptance-based approaches with existing cognitive behavioral models. *Clinical Psychology: Science and Practice, 9,* 54–68.

Rosenbaum, R. (1999). *Zen and the heart of psychotherapy.* Philadelphia, PA: Brunner/Mazel.

Rosenberg, L. (1998). *Breath by breath.* Boston: Shambhala.

Rubin, J. (1996). *Psychotherapy and Buddhism: Towards an integration.* New York: Plenum Press.

Salzberg, S. (1995). *Lovingkindness: The revolutionary art of happiness.* Boston: Shambhala.

Segal, Z. V., Williams, J. M. G., and Teasdale, J. D. (2002). *Mindfulness-based cognitive therapy for depression: A new approach to preventing relapse.* New York: Guilford Press.

Shapiro, S. L., Schwartz, G. E., and Bonner, G. (1998). Effects of mindfulness-based stress reduction on medical and premedical students. *Journal of Behavioral Medicine, 21,* 581–599.

Suzuzki, D. T., Fromm, E., and De Martino, R. (1963). *Zen Buddhism and psychoanalysis.* New York: Grove Press.

Tart, C. T. (1990). Adapting eastern spiritual teachings to western culture: A discussion with Shinzen Young. *Journal of Transpersonal Psychology, 22,* 149–165.

The instructions to the Kalamas in *The Kalama Sutta: The Buddha's Charter of Free Inquiry.* (1994). (S. Thera, Trans.). DharmaNet Edition. Retrieved January 14, 2001 from the World Wide Web: http://watthai.net/talon/Wheel/wheel8.htm. Republished from *The Kalama Sutta: The Buddha's Charter of Free Inquiry.* (1981). (S. Thera, Trans.). The Wheel Publication Number 8, Kandy, Sri Lanka: Buddhist Publication Society.

Vitakkasanthāna Sutta (1995). In B. Ñānamoli & B. Bodhi (Trans.), *The middle length discourses of the Buddha: A new translation of the Majjhima Nikāya* (pp. 211–214). Boston: Wisdom.

Von Bertalanffy, L. (1968). *General system theory: Foundations, development, applications* (Rev. ed.). New York: George Braziller.

Watts, A. (1961). *Psychotherapy, east and west.* New York: Pantheon Books.

CHAPTER 9

Buddhism and Western Psychology
An Intellectual Memoir

Eugene Taylor

The large canvas on which I wish to paint my view of Buddhism and Western psychology begins with the Prabhavananda and Manchester translation of the *Upanishads* (1957), stolen from my sister's library when I was age 12. Later, I devoured the book, which appeared to be filled with enigmatic pronouncements about the nature of the individual self and its relation to Supreme or Universal Consciousness (Ātman). As a teenager, these were precisely the same questions I was asking: Who am I? What is the nature of the self? What is its relation to a Higher Consciousness? What about the experience of the Void? Is there a path to an awakened intelligence? Can I ever know what the nature of the Ultimate is all about? What is this mystery that is my existence? I felt all this, even as I could not find words to express these questions at that time. Although this was a Hindu text translated by a Vedantic Swami, it was a good introduction to Buddhism, as the Buddhists also read this text and raised the same questions but answered them in a radically different way.

After my excursion with that book, nothing happened for a number of years. I worked my way into college at Southern Methodist University, simultaneously as the drummer in a dance band and as an advanced biology major. I started as a laboratory assistant and worked my way up to Assistant Curator of the Biology Collections, where I worked rescuing the university's rare bird collection, integrating it into the other collections between the insects and reptiles. I then took a leave of absence for a year in 1967, when I was 21, and joined the music community in San Francisco for a year.

While on this *wunderjahr* from college halfway into my junior year, I was traveling in Northern California and happened to spend the day in Muir

Woods with a former Bally shoe salesman, Steve Gaskin, who later held the charismatic Monday Night Class at San Francisco State University (Gaskin, 1970) and still later led a band of 20 Volkswagen buses from California to Tennessee, where they established a large commune. On that day in Muir Woods, I was sitting out on a high and wide promontory, under a large shady tree, surveying a 50-mile horizon of the Pacific Ocean against the setting afternoon sun, when Steve climbed up the hill leading from the house to the tree. When he got under the big, wide, overhanging branches, he handed me a copy of W. Y. Evans-Wentz's (1954) *Tibetan Book of the Great Liberation* (with a psychological commentary by Carl Jung), opened to a particular page that he wanted me to read. This is a companion of sorts to the *Tibetan Book of the Dead* (Evans-Wentz, 1957).[1] Both works are texts of the Tibetan Vajrayāna Buddhist tradition, heavily influenced by the indigenous religion of *bön-po*, both books then recently the rage in the American psychotherapeutic counterculture. I contemplated the complexities of that page for the rest of the day, between long meditative moments gazing out into the vast expanse of the sea, but afterward did not think much about it.

Then, possibly a year or so later, I stumbled onto Hubert Benoit's (1955) *The Supreme Doctrine: Psychological Studies in Zen Thought*. The link between Western existentialism and Zen was obvious. I remember in it the story of the man standing on the top of the hill alone by himself, looking out into the distance. A long way off two men saw him and began arguing about what that man must be doing alone out there on the hill. One man said, "He must have had difficulties in his relationship with a women who loves him and there has been some misunderstanding, so he has come up there, isolated and morose." The other said, "No, the man is surely a fugitive and is running away. Otherwise why would he be all the way out here on the hill off a lonely road, away from people?" They continued to argue all the way up to the top of the hill. When they got there, as they passed they stopped and asked the man why he was standing there. "You've been unrequited in love," one asserted. "You're on the run," the other said. "Neither," said the man. "Then what are you doing here?" they demanded. He shrugged his shoulders and said, "Nothing. I'm just standing."

So do we always ask too many questions? Do we always prejudge the answer? When is it all right to just do nothing? Do we always need a motive? Can the mind be perfectly clear, the surface completely calm, the depth profound, yet consciousness still be called Empty?

Afterwards I found D. T. Suzuki, and was led into his discussions about the sound of the thundering silence in Zen meditation; *satori*, the moment of just awakening—of just coming to; and the expression of No-mind (*wu*, *wu-wei*, *wu-nien*) (Suzuki, 1949, 1958, 1963). I was impressed with the positive affirmation of what I later found Tillich had called "the Abyss" and that in these systems, intuition and insight transcended mere rationality and sense attachment.

When I returned to Southern Methodist University from my year on the West Coast, I changed my major from biology to psychology and Asian studies, focusing on Hindu and Buddhist materials. I did this because of two pivotal experiences.

First, I went to the Chairman's Office in the Biology Department to see Dr. Stallcup, the professor with whom I had taken genetics. I was thinking about changing my major. I had a blank changing slip with me, but I still did not know what I was going to do and was not completely sure I was doing the right thing anyway. I had to design some quick litmus test to push me one way or the other as I stood there and he asked me what I wanted. So I asked him if, as a biologist, he ever went and just sat out in the woods. He said no, but gave no further explanation, except to suggest that the real scientific work always happens in the laboratory. He also seemed kind of puzzled that I would ask a question like that. I took that as a negation of my quest, not an affirmation, and without making any judgment about him personally, immediately asked him to sign the slip changing my major to psychology. He readily obliged.

The other event was my first class with the late Frederick J. Streng. Thinking back to the *Upanishads* and the *Tibetan Book of the Great Liberation*, at registration I had blindly signed up for "An Introduction to Eastern Religions," not actually knowing what to expect. On the first day, I sat in the back of the classroom, which was completely packed with students. A tall, massive man walked in with a large head, hair pushed back, and a serious demeanor. He made some preliminary remarks about the University of Chicago tradition in comparative religions and then began to lecture on the spiritual traditions of Asia. I was transfixed by both his attitude and the depth of his erudition. Moreover, he was talking about an interior psychological language and about awakening to a higher state of consciousness. I knew this language, but intuitively and not academically and intellectually, as he was describing it.

Unknown to me at the time, this was Frederick Streng, internationally known Buddhist scholar in the Indian Mahāyāna tradition of Nāgārjuna. A Lutheran minister interested in Buddhist-Christian dialogue, he was also a friend and colleague of Paul Tillich. Streng had met Tillich somewhere between the University of Chicago and Harvard when he was just finishing his doctoral dissertation in 1961 under Mircea Eliade, the Romanian scholar and pioneer in comparative religions, who, with Joachim Wach and Joseph Kitagawa, represented the University of Chicago tradition in comparative religions. Streng, himself, had done a translation of Nāgārjuna's *Mūlamadyamakakārikās* and the *Vigrahavyāvartanī* for his dissertation, later published as *Emptiness: A Study in Religious Meaning* (1967).

On that first day, everything he said, it seemed to me, required further comment, so I interrupted him continuously with questions. This then became the pattern of the class. He would begin the lecture, I would interrupt him with a few questions, and he would spend the rest of the class answering them. There were three or four texts for the course and 3,000 pages of outside reading. Finally, he called me into his office after a few classes and told me I could not ask any more questions in class unless I had read the outside materials. I said, 'no problem,' and stayed late in the library at night for the rest of the semester reading everything, including all that he had put on reserve. This was his way of introducing me to a vast secondary scholarly literature on Asian thought.

After that, I took a course in Hinduism with him, but he said I could not stay in the course unless I got past the secondary literature and started to look at the English translations of the available Hindu and Buddhist texts. Later, after taking more courses from him, he said I could not go on unless I got into the original languages, so I studied Hindi and Urdu at the University of Rochester and took a tutorial in Sanskrit with the late Indologist Harvey Alper. After I earned a BA in general/experimental psychology, I went on for the MA in psychology at SMU, but at the same time began studying advanced Indian Mahāyāna Buddhism with Streng as a graduate student at Perkins School of Theology, the Divinity School attached to SMU.

From the beginning, Streng maintained the position of the Indian Mahāyāna Buddhists and I took up the *Sāmkhya* metaphysics, the philosophical and psychological frame of reference adopted by Patañjali in codifying the great *Yoga Sūtras* (Woods, 1914). Sāmkhya was non-Vedic in that, as one of the heterodox schools, it ultimately did not derive its final authority from the Vedas; it was dualistic, not a monistic system, and it opposed the unitary teachings of Vedānta, the tradition of Hinduism most like Christianity and the most well-known of the Hindu schools in the West.

Meanwhile, my declared major remained general/experimental psychology. My courses were filled with statistics, computer programming, experimental learning theory, advanced experimental designs, and so on. Religion was down the hall from psychology, and the School of Arts and Sciences, which housed both of them, was up the Hill from the Divinity School. For eight years I traversed between the great but radically different epistemologies of Eastern and Western thought, seeking to build bridges between science and religion, religion and psychology, Western experimental psychology, and what I came to call Classical Eastern Psychology, focusing on the various pan-Asiatic expressions of Buddhism.

The Psychology Department, however, had become dominated by a younger generation of eager experimental learning theorists and psychophysicists. The "self" and the "ego" were terms not allowed to be mentioned in the introductory psychology class. Statistics and experimental design were requirements, and students were encouraged to elect only the advanced courses in experimental psychology like psychophysics, learning theory, and sensation and perception.

Fortunately, however, there was a level of more liberal, learned, and senior tenured faculty, who sheltered my broader interests. Among them were Richard Hunt, the University's ace statistician, a Methodist minister and a Rogerian therapist, who also ran the Student Counseling Center; William Tedford, the senior psychophysicist who chaired my master's thesis; the late Virginia Chancey, a renowned child psychologist, who had sung her way through college with the Big Bands and, from one musician to another, used to write me personal checks when I was at low water. There was also an old friend of Virginia's, Jack Roy Strange, who was a professor of abnormal psychology and taught the history of psychology course as well. It was Professor Strange who first introduced me to personality theory, to his large collection of old books in the history of psychology, and to the life and work of William James. His wife Sally was also my freshman English teacher, and on purchasing a new typewriter, she bequeathed her old one to me, the first I ever owned, which essentially launched me on my writing career.

During the eight years I spent with these professors in both psychology and religion, I sought to investigate concepts of personality and consciousness as well as methods that might be comparable to related constructs in Western psychology. At the same time, I was completing all the courses in experimental psychology, statistics, tests and measurements, computer programming, and advanced learning theory that were required of a psychology major at both the bachelor's and the master's level.[2]

My first publication drawing these two areas together was "An Annotated Bibliography in Classical Eastern Psychology," a guide to readily accessible translations of some primary texts from the classical periods of India, China, Tibet, and Japan (Taylor, 1973). The texts I focused on included the four *Vedas*, especially the *Upanishads*, various translations of the *Gītā* and *Mahābhārata*, the *Yoga Sūtras*, the *Sāmkhya-kārikās*, the *Vedāntasāra Samgraha*, Śankara's *Crest Jewel of Discrimination*, the *Sat Cakra Nirūpana*, the *Tripitaka*, especially the *Dhammapada*, the *Jātaka Tales*, Nāgārjuna's *Madhyamikakārikās*, the *Prajñāpāramitā Sūtras*, the *Vimalakīrtinirdeśa Sūtra*, *The Saddharma Pundarīka Sūtra*, *The Awakening of Faith*, Śantideva's *Bodhicaryāvatāra*, The Five Confucian Classics, *Tsongkapa's Six Yogas of Naropa*, the *Tao-tê-Ching*, The Sūtra of Hui Neng, and the *Lankāvatāra Sūtra*.[3]

Specifically, I was looking for linguistic concepts of personality and consciousness in a variety of Asian languages that I thought could be related to growth-oriented definitions of mental health in the West. While the Vedantists focused on the *jivanmukta*, one who is liberated while still in the body, and the classical yoga tradition on the *kaivalyan*, one who had separated consciousness from lifeless inert matter, the Confucians looked at character development and idealized such concepts as *chün-tzu*, "gentlemanliness based on strength of character, rather than on hereditary, feudal acquisition," *Jên*, "true human-heartedness based on fellow feeling," and *Li*, "reciprocity." There is also the concept of *wu* in philosophical Taoism, the action of nondoing, or no-thought. The conceptualization of the liberated personality in the Chinese tradition might be epitomized by the texts on the *Lohan*, a marvelous combination of Buddhist and Taoist beings.

Buddhism, however, probably had the most well-developed conceptualizations of a liberated personality, because it was a pan-Asiatic movement. The early Buddhist texts developed concepts of the *Arahant*, one who has attained the farther shore by achieving a "burning out of the flame of desire (*nibbāna*)." The later Mahāyāna schools transformed this idea into the *bodhisattva*, one who has attained enlightenment through experiencing the emptiness of the Void (*śūnyatā*) and who has escaped from the world of suffering, but who has turned back to aid all sentient beings down to the last living blade of grass, helping them to pass over first, before completing his own liberation.

There is also the Tantric tradition of the 84 *Siddhas*, 84 liberated personalities largely from the Tibetan Vajrayāna Buddhist tradition. There is also the generalized concept of *hamsa*, meaning, "swan," or "wild geese," referring symbolically to personalities in whose lives spiritual liberation is unconnected with any specific religious tradition.

We have no equivalents for these conceptualizations in Western psychology, except the theory of a growth-oriented dimension of personality appearing in the early history of personality theory in psychology. Such theories began to appear after 1882, corresponding to the Sanskrit revival and subsequent English language translations of Hindu and Buddhist texts initiated by the Theosophical Society and the early translations of the Pali Text Society, and University efforts, such as the Sacred Books of the East series, edited by F. Max Mueller.

In psychology, we can point to the works of F. W. H. Myers, Theodore Flournoy, and William James, initiated by their joint studies of multiple personality (Taylor, 1983); there are also contributions from depth psychology, such as the Swiss psychiatrist, C. G. Jung's concept of individuation, referring to the interaction and integration of the opposites as well as their transcendence (Jung, 1915). At the same time, expanded human potential is a persistent theme in existential-humanistic and transpersonal psychology, such as the concept of the self-actualizing personality of Abraham Maslow (1954), or the idea of the Higher Self in Roberto Assagioli's (1965) system. Within the domain of the cognitivists, positive psychology points in this direction, but Seligman's epistemology is too unsophisticated to be able to handle the iconography of the transcendent. His colleague Csikszentmihalyi comes somewhat closer (Taylor, 2001).

A survey of psychologists and psychiatrists knowledgeable about Asian thought in general and Buddhism in particular, or who were interpreters of Buddhism to Western psychology whose works were available in the 1960s and early 1970s, comprised a very short list. Aldous Huxley and Gerald Herd had championed Vedānta to the American public starting in the 1940s (Jackson, 1994). Alan Watts sponsored D. T. Suzuki's return to the United States in 1951, after which Suzuki became a nationally recognized figure interpreting Zen to the Beat generation. John Cage and Erich Fromm attended his lectures at Columbia, and Suzuki escorted the aging Karen Horney on an extended trip to the religious shrines of Japan. She planned to write on Buddhism and psychoanalysis, but died within a few months after her return.

Suzuki's various works on Mahāyāna Buddhism and Zen, which originally appeared to an uncaring world, were now all republished to great acclaim. His student, Alan Watts (1961), followed with *Psychotherapy East and West*, possibly one of the most influential texts of the American psychotherapeutic counterculture. Jung was already known for his psychological commentary to Wilhelm's translation of the *T'ai-i Chin-hua Tsung-chi*, his forward to Wilhelm's translation of the *I Ching*, and for his introduction to Evans-Wentz's *Tibetan Book of the Great Liberation* (Coward, 1985). In the 1950s, the clinical psychologist at Napa State Hospital, Wilson van Dusen, was publishing on the psychological use of the Void when doing psychotherapy with schizophrenics; the journal *Psychologia*, which boasted psychologists such as the Harvard personality-social theorist Gordon Allport on its board, and which represented itself as an international journal of the Orient, started in the late 1940s and published numerous articles on Buddhism and western psychology. Then in 1968, Gardner and Lois Murphy produced their pioneering text, *Asian Psychology*, the first formal work by recognized psychologists to inoculate Western psychology with Hindu and Buddhist epistemology.

Meanwhile, I was immersing myself in these materials at Southern Methodist University while I was also working for a Presbyterian social agency counseling with runaway teenagers. Through these church connections, I met Ryuchi Shinagawa, a Japanese businessman who convened a meditation group at a Methodist youth center called, appropriately, Satori House. There, we would meet once a week and sit to reach for Emptiness. I also became a student of

Kumar Pallana, a local Hindu yoga teacher originally from Poona, India, and took nadi yoga (nerve and joint yoga) from him for two-and-a-half years.

Then one day, I was walking past the flagpole on the SMU campus with Professor Richard Hunt, who suddenly turned to me and said, "You know, you are the only one here at the University into all these subjects. But there is a group of similar minded people whom you should probably get in touch with—they are the humanistic psychologists." I told him I did not know any, so we decided I should write to Gardner Murphy, who was then a visiting professor at George Washington University.

Murphy's letter was cordial and to the point. He introduced me to Anthony Sutich, close colleague of Abraham Maslow and founding editor of both the *Journal of Humanistic Psychology* and the *Journal of Transpersonal Psychology*. Sutich, in turn, introduced me to James Fadiman, an organizational consulting psychologist, and Robert Frager, founder of the transpersonal psychology Ph.D. program (The California Institute of Transpersonal Psychology, now called the Institute for Transpersonal Psychology, or ITP). Both were Harvard trained, but transplanted to the West Coast. They later authored *Personality and Personal Growth* (1976), now in its fifth edition (2002), which was the first personality theory textbook in the West to incorporate chapters on Hindu, Buddhist, and Sufi psychology, along with the Skinnerians, the Freudians, the humanistic psychologists, and others.

Frager had done his Ph.D. at Harvard on Japanese conformity in the Social Relations Department, and while in Japan doing research began instruction in the Japanese martial art of Aikido, under its aging founder, Morei Ueshiba. Aikido, a nonviolent martial art with a goal of universal disarmament and world peace, grew out of Kendo, Judo, and Aikijutsu. While it has deep roots in Shintō, the indigenous shamanic religion of Japan, at certain periods it has been significantly influenced by Japanese Buddhism.

Frager drew me into this art, but while he taught in California as part of the ITP Ph.D. program in Palo Alto (aikido is taught in California as a form of psychology), I remained where I had been in Dallas, Texas and began training under William Sosa in a Ki Society dojo over in Oak Cliff. Eventually I earned four black belts in Hombu style and have been teaching as the Chief Instructor of the Harvard University Aikido Club for the past 20 years.

Of all the teachers I have trained with, including Roy Suanaka, Rod Kobayashi, Robert Nadeau, John Takagi, Koichi Tohei, and Yosamitsu Yamada and Matsunari Kanai, only Fumio Toyoda most explicitly taught aikido from the point of view of Zen. I met him when he was a 26-year-old fifth degree black belt under Koichi Tohei. Tohei had sent him to a Zen monastery to study for two years as part of his aikido training, and Toyoda filled his classes with Zen sitting, Zen chants, and a general Buddhist point of view. While Mr. Ueshiba was apparently very clear that aikido was not a Buddhist art, nevertheless, the Buddhist element has crept in, in part because of the historical and epistemological affinities between Buddhism and Shintō.

For my master's thesis, I carried out a study on meditation, entitled "Psychological Suspended Animation: Heart Rate, Blood Pressure, Time Estimation, and Introspective Reports from an Anechoic Environment," trying to simulate the experience of Buddhist emptiness. Through my professor in psychophysics I had exclusive access to an anechoic sound chamber, a completely dark, echo-proof, sound-deadened chamber normally used to test microphones. I kept this room essentially intact for its original purposes, except that I turned it into a meditation chamber by adding a large oriental-American rug, draped over a large set of suspended springs, on which the subjects sat. Eventually, over a two-and-a-half year period, I took almost 250 people in different combinations through a sitting experience lasting on the average of a half-hour. From various cohorts of subjects I extracted heart rate, blood pressure, time estimation, and introspective reports. A phenomenological analysis of the introspective reports indicated the consistent elicitation of a series of transitional states of consciousness leading to a profound state of quiet relaxation, which we called "psychological suspended animation" (Taylor, 1973).

The physiological measures taken were consistent with those reported by Wallace and Benson (1972). That is, heart rate and blood pressure decreased with a pleasant experience. There was also a trend toward wildly over and underestimating the time spent in the chamber when the experience was judged more emotionally positive, as compared to consistent time underestimation with most sensory deprivation studies when subjects just had a so-so experience.

The transitional states leading to psychological suspended animation we defined in the following way:

1. *Exploratory Awareness of External Stimuli.* Here, consciousness stays with an awareness of purely external events—sights and sounds in the environment, particular smells, perception of movement, and so on.

2. *External Bodily Awareness.* Awareness of stimuli in the immediate external environment gives way to attention to the physical body, particularly the placements of hands and feet in the complete darkness, feeling the placement of the facial muscles, comfort of the sitting position, air against the skin, and so forth.

3. *Internal Bodily Awareness.* Attention soon shifts to such activities as the flow of air in and out of the nostrils, swallowing, sounds emanating

from the digestive tract, ringing in the ears, feeling of the heart beat, concentration on the expansion and contraction of the chest cavity.

4. *Internal Cognitive and Emotional Awareness.* Awareness suddenly shifts to the cognitive flow of thoughts and the rise and fall of accompanying emotions.

5. *Visual Translation and Projection.* Consciousness of the flow of thoughts and feelings becomes visible to the mind's eye in the form of mental images, oftentimes colorful and in three dimensions, as in the experience of a waking dream. Sometimes the subject experiences this like watching an animated cartoon sequence. Other times the projection of mental images out onto the darkness may be experienced as a stream of insights. What usually emerges from the stream of visualizations is the identification with some deep symbol, or mythic image reflecting aspects of both personal and collective destiny.

6. *Awareness of Transitive and Substantive Alteration of the Stream of Consciousness.* Here, consciousness splits and two halves share the field. One is an intuitive mode, where the subject becomes increasingly aware of longer and longer periods of no mental and emotional activity. The other, which is interspersed in between, is a rational, analytic mode, made up of long chains of thought with accompanying images and feelings.

7. *Psychological Suspended Animation.* Here, by ignoring the flow of thought and seeking out only the longer and longer periods of quiet, consciousness reaches a resting state where the subject merely witnesses that nothing is happening. Prolonged immersion in this quiet condition was often reported. The subjects told us of extreme relaxation, profound stillness, the complete absence of cognitive thinking, the feeling of great serenity and peacefulness, and a secure sense of well-being.

Finally, there was an eighth stage, the return to waking reality. There were many ways in which the subjects psychically decompressed from their inner subjective experiences and made a successful transition back to the waking material condition. Two phases occurred; one was the immediate experience of return on coming out of the anechoic chamber. The other was what might traditionally be called long-term follow-up, or an analysis of the effect of the isolation experience on subsequent functioning as reported by a selected cohort of subjects, in some cases as long as a year afterward (Taylor, 1993).

These studies show that by optimally biasing the experimental, subject, and environmental variables, a state not unlike that described as emptiness in Buddhist meditation can be consistently evoked. Existentially, what each person did with the experience was different in every case.

In the spring of 1975 I took a course with Lama Anagarika Govinda at Perkins School of Theology on the Spiritual Traditions of Buddhism. This was followed by publication of "Asian Interpretations: Transcending the Stream," in Pope and Singer's *The Stream of Consciousness: Scientific Investigations into the Flow of Human Experience,* in which I made a linguistic comparison of different terms from Hinduism, Buddhism, Taoism, and Zen related to consciousness beyond the margin of everyday waking reality (Taylor, 1978).

Publication of this work gave me entry into the Harvard Divinity School, where I studied the history of Buddhist thought with Masatoshi Nagatomi, professor of East Asian Studies and son of a Shin Buddhist priest, and I took beginning Sanskrit with Daniel H. Engels, Wales Professor at Harvard. I found a place to live, first on St. Botolph in the Back Bay, and then in Jamaica Plain, through my connections to Robert Frager. Frager had given me the address of Madeline Nold, a longtime transpersonal psychotherapist into the Esalen scene who had converted her Green Street apartment in Cambridge into a Buddhist Temple, presided over by Kalu Rinpoche.

These connections at Harvard and in the community eventually led me to Charley Dusey's cross-cultural seminar on psychoanalysis at the Cambridge City Hospital, and subsequently to well-known figures involved with Buddhism and psychotherapy, such as Dan Brown, Dan Goleman, Jack Engler, and as a more momentary acquaintance, Mark Epstein. My own contributions have remained more scholarly. I have consulted with the IndoChinese Refugee Clinic serving 18,000 Cambodians, mostly Buddhists. And I have published several pieces meant to assist psychologists interpreting Asian ideas to the West (Taylor, 1978b, 1982, 1986, 1988, 1995, 1996, 1997, 1998).

In yet a separate opportunity that developed out of some consulting work I was doing, I landed an all-expense paid trip to India to go trekking in the Himalayas. We went to the little country above Darjeeling in North East India called Sikkhim. It was a Lindblad trip led by Tenzin Norgay, then in his early 70s, the man who had taken Sir Edmund Hilary to the top of Mt. Everest in 1953. We attempted to reach the base camp of Mt. Kenchenjunga, but were driven back by bad weather above 15,000 feet. As a result, we spent the extra time in the jungles visiting out of the way Sikkhimi Buddhist monasteries. We paid special attention to the plight of the Tibetan refugees in the area, the most venerated site we passed being a circle of seven *chortens* at the fork of two rivers, commemorating the lives of seven monks lost on the escape of His Holiness the Dalai Lama from Tibet in 1958, as this was the route of his descent.

Even before that, I became interested in the historical flow of Asian ideas to the West and had already begun examining the libraries of famous psychologists and psychiatrists for the sources of their reading. Through Professor Engels at Harvard I met Charles Rockwell Lanman's daughter, age 85, who had known William James as a neighbor and friend to her father. She was 11 when James died and was lifelong friends with James's children. She remembered James coming to meetings of the History of Religions Club and hearing about the latest scholarship in Buddhist studies, some of which James incorporated into his chapter on mysticism in *The Varieties of Religious Experience* (1902). Later, David Kalupahana (1987) would draw numerous comparisons between James's theory of consciousness and the early Theravāda conception of the stream of thought (*pratītya-samutpāda*).

Then in 1992, I became directly involved with the Tibetan Buddhists. Ed Bednar, a Catholic and also lay Buddhist meditator, lobbied senators and representatives alike in the U.S. Congress and drafted the wording for an amendment to the Immigration act of 1991, allowing 1,000 stateless Tibetans to enter the United States as immigrants. I joined the Mental Health Committee of the Tibet/U.S. Resettlement Project along with Connie Harris, a health psychologist who had come up to Boston from the University of Texas at Austin. She and I helped survey Tibetans already residing in the United States and Canada for their advice to the 1,000 Tibetans about to come, and 3,000 of their dependents who would follow within three years. We also wrote manuals to assist the Tibetans on the cultural transition from India to the United States.

Eventually, I became a founding member of The Tibetan Community Assistance Project and a sponsor of the Tibetan Association of Boston (TAB started with 85 members but soon grew to 350). We have been deeply involved in the religious ceremonies that are a part of their calendar, we have sponsored monks who come through to chant and teach meditation, and generally we interact closely with their families. From their group I was also able to recruit a Tibetan Buddhist chaplain for duty at the Massachusetts General Hospital. Later, in gratitude, the Tibetans introduced me to His Holiness, the Dalai Lama.

Through connections I had made in Humanistic and Transpersonal Psychology over the years, I was invited to 3 of the 8 conferences on advances in meditation research, held over the course of a decade at Esalen Institute, sponsored by the Institute of Noetic Sciences (IONS), Mike Murphy, and Marius Robinson. Out of these conferences I was invited to revise Murphy and Donovan's annotated bibliography on meditation research for IONS and to survey the current experimental literature on research involving numerous systems, including Buddhist meditation. Vipassanā, Vajrayāna, and Zen, it turns out, are the most frequently practiced forms of Buddhist meditation in the United States today. Jon Kabat-Zinn (1994), for instance, combines yoga and insight meditation in the stress-reduction program at the University of Massachusetts Medical Center, while Herbert Benson (et al., 1982) of the Mind/Body Medical Institute at Harvard, has scientifically studied *gTum-mo* yoga techniques in advanced Buddhist meditators in the Himalayas.

CONCLUSION

Of all the intuitive systems in the classical psychologies of Asia, Buddhist models of personality and consciousness appear to have had the most enduring conversation with Western science. This is to say that the inner sciences of Asian cultures may be regarded as a complement to Western, outward, and primarily behavioral approaches. The interesting problem is that the various Asian systems have no separate word for psychology, as we have in the West. The closest we come to their understanding in the West is depth psychology, which continues to have an uncertain status in scientific circles, or transpersonal psychology, which in truth has no scientific status at all in the mainstream of scientific ideas. This is simply to say that there are many definitions of psychology in common currency, both within Western culture as well as across cultures. This suggests that we need a more multidimensional and cross-cultural understanding, not just a Western view, of psychology. We have interpreters of these non-Western systems in the West, but they have been largely devotees mixing science and religion who often come up being fuzzy interpreters of each. The penchant of many of these devotionalists is to take religious experiences out of their indigenous contexts and import them wholesale into the practice of psychotherapy or our understanding of consciousness. Patients now chant Hindu and Buddhist mantras to be healed, or worship Hindu goddesses while doing yoga, or draw mandalas of Tibetan deities, or engage in shamanic drumming to an American Indian song, or sit in a sweat lodge and fast for a vision. At the very least, as scholars such as Vesna Wallace, Michael Maliszewski, and myself have suggested, there is a desperate need for more dialogue between psychologists and scholars in comparative religions before any sophisticated understanding of non-Western systems is to emerge from Western psychologists (Taylor, 1988).

More than just this, we may need a totally new epistemological frame of reference just to understand non-Western thinking. Our present attitude is that we might consider them if they stand up to the scrutiny of our rational models. But this has bred an unprecedented arrogance on our part that prevents us from listening first to what non-Western cultures may have to say in their own right, and at the same time it has fostered an intense hatred of everything Western by some non-Western cultures. I have in several places, however, predicted in the not-too-distant future a cross-cultural exchange of ideas between East and West possibly unprecedented in the history of Western thought (Taylor, 1989, 1995). We have seen the introduction of Asian ideas into American transcendentalism in the 1840s; we saw it again at the end of the nineteenth century with the cele-bration of the World Parliament of Religions in Chicago in 1893, an event which heralded the coming of the Asian teachers to the West. We saw it again in the 1960s when the Communist invasion of Asia again drove Eastern spiritual teach-ers to the West, teachers who were embraced in droves by the psychotherapeutic counterculture. Now, the events of September 11, 2001, involving the terrorist bombing of the World Trade Center in New York by Muslim extremists has opened an entirely new era revealing our urgent need to grasp the meaning of non-Western ways of knowing.

Islam, and particularly Sufism, its mystical wing, is simultaneously an inte-gral part of the prophetic religions of Christianity and Judaism and also the gate-way for the West to enter into a more enlightened and sophisticated understanding of non-Western epistemologies (Taylor, 1995). What this means concretely for psy-chology is that a great dialogue between Buddhism and Western science might soon be in the offing and out of that, it is possible that we shall discover more about the limitations of our own parochial worldview. At the same time, we may also come to better understand the contributions that nontechnological cultures have to make toward a larger and more all encompassing definition of world mental health than we alone are able to conceive.

NOTES

1. Evans-Wentz, W. Y. (Ed.) (1954). *The Tibetan book of the great liberation: Or, the method of realizing Nirvana through knowing the mind*: Preceded by an epitome of Pad-masambhava's biography by Yeshey Tshogyal and followed by Guru Phadampa Sangay's teachings, according to English renderings by Sardar Bahadur, S. W. Laden La, and by the Lamas Karma Sumdhon Paul, Lobzang Mingyur Dorje, and Kazi Dawa-Samdup; with psy-chological commentary by C. G. Jung: Oxford University Press. See also Evans-Wentz W. Y. (Ed.) (1957). [*Bardo thödol.*] *The Tibetan book of the dead: Or, The after-death experi-ences on the Bardo plane*, according to Lama Kazi Dawa-Samdup's English rendering; with a psychological commentary by C. G. Jung; introducing foreword by Lama Anagarika Govinda; and foreword by John Woodroffe. New York: Oxford University Press.

2. The Religion Department had a Ph.D. program, but Psychology offered only the terminal MA. I was determined to stay in psychology, however. In addition to carrying this double major, I also interned as a counselor and therapist at the University's Student Counseling Center, mainly handling cases of drug overdose, and at a local Presbyterian

Social Agency working with runaway teenagers and their families. Simultaneously, I also taught Introductory Psychology, Psychology of Personality, and Advanced Personality Theory to undergraduates.

3. For the four *Vedas*, especially the *Upanishads*, see Muller, 1969; Radhakrishnan, 1953; various translations of the *Gītā* and *Mahābhārata* are recommended. See (Isherwood, 1944; Krishnamacharya, 1983); the *Yoga Sutras* (Woods, 1914); the *Samkhya-karikas* (Krishna, 1887); The *Vedantasara Samgraha* (Krishnamacharya, 1979); Shankara's *Crest Jewel of Discrimination* (Shankara, 1970); the *Sat Cakra Nirupana*, (Woodroffe, 1974); the *Tripitika*, especially the *Dhammapada* (Muller, 1898); *Jataka Tales* (Beswick, 1956); Nāgārjuna's *Madhyamikakarikas* (Streng, 1967); the *Prajnaparamita Sutras* (Conze, 1973); *The Vimalakirtinirdesha Sutra* (Lu, 1972); the *Saddharma-Pundarika Sutra* (Kern, 1963), Ashvagosha's *Awakening of Faith* (Richard, 1961); Śāntideva's *Bodhicaryavatara* (Batchelor, 1987); Tsongkapa's *Six Yogas of Naropa* (Mullin, 1996); *The Five Confucian Classics* (Nylan, 2001); various translations of the *Tao te Ching* (Feng, 1997), *The Sutra of Hui-Neng* (Cleary, 1998); and the *Lankāvatāra Sutra* (Suzuki, 1973).

REFERENCES

Assagioli, R. (1965). *Psychosynthesis: A manual of principles and techniques.* New York, Hobbs, Dorman.

Batchelor, S. (Trans.) (1987). *Santideva's Bodhicaryavatara: A guide to the Bodhisattva's way of life.* Dharamsala: Library of Tibetan Works and Archives.

Benoit, H. (1955). *The supreme doctrine.* Foreword by Aldous Huxley; Brighton, UK: Sussex.

Benson, H. (1982). Body temperature changes during the practice of g *Tum-mo yoga.* (Matters Arising) *Nature, 298,* 402.

Benson, H., Lehmann, J. W., Malhotra, M. S., Goldman, R. F., Hopkins, J., & Epstein, M. D. (1982). Body temperature changes during the practice of g *tum-mo* (heat) yoga. *Nature, 295,* 234–236.

Beswick, E. (1956). *Jataka tales: Birth stories of the Buddha.* London: J. Murray.

Conze, E. (1973). *The perfection of wisdom in eight thousand lines and its verse summary.* Bolinas, Four Seasons Foundation; distributed by Book People, Berkeley.

Cleary, T. (Trans.) (1998). *The Sutra of Hui-neng, grand master of Zen: With Hui-neng's commentary on the Diamond.* Boston, New York: Shambhala Publications. Distributed in the U.S. by Random House.

Coward, H. G. (1985). *Jung and Eastern thought,* with contributions by J. Borelli, J. F. T. Jordens, & J. Henderson. Albany, NY: State University of New York Press.

Evans-Wentz, W. Y. (Ed.) (1954). *The Tibetan book of the great liberation: Or, the method of realizing Nirvana through knowing the mind.* New York: Oxford University Press.

Evans-Wentz, W. Y., (Ed.) (1957). [*Bardo thodol.*] *The Tibetan book of the dead.* New York: Oxford University Press.

Fadiman, J. & Frager, R. (1976). *Personality and Personal Growth.* New York: Harper and Row.

Fadiman, J. & Frager, R. (2002). *Personality and Personal Growth* (5th ed.). Upper Saddle, NJ: Prentice Hall.

Feng, G. F. & English, J. (1997). *Tao te ching* (25th-anniversary ed.). New York: Vintage Books.

Gaskin, S. (1970). *Monday night class.* San Francisco: The Book Pub. Co.

James, W. (1902). *The varieties of religious experience.* New York: Longmans.

Jackson, C. T. (1994). *Vedanta for the West: The Ramakrishna movement in the United States.* Bloomington: Indiana University Press.

Kabat-Zinn, J. (1994). *Wherever you go, there you are: Mindfulness meditation in everyday life.* New York: Hyperion.

Kalupahana, D. J. (1987). *The principles of Buddhist psychology.* Albany, NY: State University of New York Press.

Kern, H. (1963). *Saddharma-Pundarika; or, the lotus of the true law.* New York: Dover Publications.

Krishna, I. (1887). *The Sankhya Karika by Ishwara Krishna. Translated from the Sanskrit by Henry Thomas Colebrook. containing also the Bhashya, or commentary by Gauolapada; translated, and illustrated by an original comment by Horace Hayman Wilson.* Bombay: R. Tookaram, Tatya.

Krishnamacharya, N. V. R. (1983). *The Mahabharata.* (Engl.) Tirupati, India: Tirumala Tirupati Devasthanams.

Krishnamacharya, V. (Ed.) (1979). *Vedantasara of Bhagavad Ramanuja,* with English translation by M. B. Narasimha Ayyangar (2nd ed.). Adyar, India: Adyar Library and Research Centre.

Lu, Y. K. (Trans.) (1972). *The Vimalakirtinirdesa sutra.* Berkeley, Shambala.

Maslow, A. H. (1954). *Motivation and personality.* New York: Harper.

McClelland, D. C. (1955). *Studies in motivation.* New York, Appleton-Century-Crofts.

Muller, F. M. (Ed.) (1998). *Dhammapada: A collection of verses* (2nd ed., rev.). Oxford: Clarendon Press.

Muller, F. M. (Ed.) (1969). *The Vedas.* Varanasi: Indological Book House.

Mullin, G. H. (1996). *Tsongkapa's six yogas of Naropa.* Ithaca, NY: Snow Lion Press.

Murray, H. A. (1943). *Thematic apperception test manual,* with the staff of the Harvard Psychological Clinic. Cambridge, MA, Harvard University Press.

Nylan, M. (2001). *The five Confucian classics.* New Haven: Yale University Press.

Prabhavananda, S. & Isherwood, C. (Trans.) (1944). *Bhagavad-Gita, the song of God,* with an introduction by Aldous Huxley. Hollywood, CA: The Marcel Rodd Co.

Prabhavananda, S. and Manchester, F. (1957). *The Upanishads.* New York: New American Library.

Radhakrishnan, S. (1953). *The principal Upanishads.* New York, Harper.

Richard, T. (Trans.) (1961). *Ashvagosha's awakening of faith,* with an introduction by Alan Hull Walton. Foreword by Aldous Huxley. London: Charles Skelton.

Sankaracarya (S. Prabhavananda and C. Isherwood, Trans.) (1970). *Vivekacudamani: Shankara's Crest-jewel of discrimination, with a garland of questions and answers (Prasnottara malika)* (2nd ed.). Hollywood, CA: Vedanta Press.

Streng, F. J. (1967). *Emptiness: A study in religious meaning.* Nashville: Abingdon Press.

Suzuki, D. T. (1958). *Essays in Zen Buddhism: First series* [edited by Christmas Humphreys]. Rider: London.

Suzuki, D. T. (1963). *Outlines of Mahayana Buddhism.* Prefatory essay by Alan Watts. New York: Schocken Books.

Suzuki, D. T. (1949). *The Zen doctrine of no-mind; The significance of the Sutra Hui-neng (Wei-lang).* London, New York: Rider.

Suzuki, D. T. (Trans.) (1973). *The Lankavatara Sutra:* London: Routledge & K. Paul.

Taylor, E. I. (1973a). *An annotated bibliography in classical Eastern psychology*. Dallas, Texas: The Essene Press.

Taylor, E. I. (1973b). *Psychological Suspended Animation: Heart rate, blood pressure, time estimation, and introspective reports from an anechoic environment*. Master of Arts Thesis, Department of Psychology, Southern Methodist University, Dallas, Texas, Privately Printed by the Essene Press.

Taylor, E. I. (1978a). Asian interpretations: Transcending the stream of consciousness. In K. Pope and J. Singer (eds.), *The stream of consciousness: Scientific investigations into the flow of human experience* (pp. 31–54), New York: Plenum. Reprinted in Pickering, J. & Skinner, M. (Eds.) (1990). *From sentience to symbol: Readings on consciousness*. London: Harvester-Westsheaf, and Toronto: University of Toronto Press.

Taylor, E. I. (1978b). Psychology of religion and Asian studies: The William James legacy, *Journal of Transpersonal Psychology*, 10:1, 66–79.

Taylor, E. I. (1982). Review of Carl Jackson's *Oriental religions in 19th century American thought*, *The Journal of Transpersonal Psychology*, 14:2, 184–186.

Taylor, E. I. (1986). Swami Vivekananda and William James. *Prabuddha Bharata; Journal of the Ramakrishna Society, Calcutta*, 91, 374–385.

Taylor, E. I. (1988). Contemporary interest in classical Eastern psychology. In A. Paranjpe, D. Ho, & R. Rieber (Eds.), *Asian contributions to psychology* (pp. 79–122). New York: Praeger.

Taylor, E. I. (1989). Review of Peter Gay's *Freud, A life for our time*, *Commonweal*, March 21.

Taylor, E. I. (1993). Some epistemological problems inherent in the scientific study of consciousness. In K. Ramakrishna Rao (Ed.), *Cultivating Consciousness: Enhancing human potential, wellness, and healing* (pp. 71–82). Westport, CT: Praeger.

Taylor, E. I. (1995). The transcendent experience. *Prabuddha Bharata, Journal of the Ramakrishna Vedanta Society, Calcutta* (100th anniversary issue), vol. 100, Feb–March, 434–443.

Taylor, E. I. (1996). Sriyogirajmahagurusat Sarvagatananda-ji. In C. Mehta (Ed.), *The Lamplighter: Swami Sarvagatananda in the West. Fortieth Anniversary Tribute to the Ministry of Swami Sarvagatananda* (pp. 141–144). Ramakrishna Vedanta Society of Boston, Mass., Salem, NH: The Frugal Printer.

Taylor, E. I. (Ed.) (1997*). The physical and psychological effects of meditation: A review of contemporary research with a comprehensive bibliography, 1931–1996*, by Michael Murphy and Steven Donovan (2nd ed.). Sausalito, CA: Institute of Noetic Sciences.

Taylor, E. I. (2001). Positive psychology versus Humanistic psychology: A reply to Prof. Seligman. *Journal of Humanistic Psychology: Special Issue*, 41:1, Winter, 2001, 13–29.

van Dusen, W. (1958). Wu wei, no-mind, and the fertile void in psychotherapy. *Psychologia*, 1, 253–256.

Tomkins, S. S. (1992). *Affect, imagery, consciousness*. New York: Springer Pub. Co. Originally published in 1962.

Wallace, R. K., and Benson. H. (1972). The physiology of meditation. *Scientific American*, 226:2, 84–90.

Watts, A. (1961). *Psychotherapy East and West*. New York: Pantheon Books.

Wilhelm, R. (Trans.) (1931). *The secret of the golden flower: A Chinese book of life*. With a European commentary by C. G. Jung; with eleven plates and four text illustrations. London: K. Paul, Trench, Trubner & Co.

Wilhelm, R. (Trans.) (1950). *The I ching; or, Book of changes,* rendered into English by Cary
        F. Baynes. Foreword by C. G. Jung. New York: Pantheon Books.
Woods, J. H. (Trans.) (1914). *The Yoga-system of Patanjali; or, The ancient Hindu doctrine of
        concentration of mind, embracing the mnemonic rules, called Yoga-sutras, of Patanjali,
        and the comment, called Yoga-bhashya, attributed to Veda-Vyasa, and the explanation,
        called Tattva-vaicaradi, of Vachaspati-Micra;* Harvard Oriental Series, 17; Cam-
        bridge, MA: Harvard University Press.
Woodroffe, J. G. (1974). *The serpent power; Being the Sat-cakra-nirupana and Paduka-pancaka:
        Two works on Laya-yoga,* translated from the Sanskrit, with introduction and
        commentary by Arthur Avalon. New York: Dover Publications.

Glossary

PRONUNCIATION GUIDE

ā—"a" as in "father"
ī—"ee" as in "beet"
ö—"eu" as in "déjeuner"
c—"ch" as in "church"
ś—"sh" as in "share"

e—"ei" as in "eight"
ō—"o" as in "open"
ū—"oo" as in "boot"
ñ—"ny" as in "canyon"
th—"th" as in "Thomas"

Abhidhamma (Pāli)   Philosophical and psychological texts that form the third "basket" of the Tipitaka and elucidate and expand on aspects of Buddhist doctrine as it is found in the Nikāyas.

Akusala (Pāli)   Unwholesome or unskillful.

Alagaddūpama Sutta (Pāli)   The Buddha's Discourse, "The Simile of the Snake" (Majjhima Nikāya, Sutta 22), which elaborates on the nature of "right view."

Anattā (Pāli)   Nonself.

Anicca (Pāli)   Impermanence.

Anupada Sutta (Pāli)   The Buddha's discourse, "One by One as They Occurred" (Majjhima Nikāya, Sutta 111), on his disciple Sāriputta's attainment of nibbāna.

Arahant (Pāli)/**Arhat** (Sanskrit)   In Theravāda Buddhism, a person who has achieved liberation.

Ariyapariyesanā Sutta (Pāli)   The Buddha's discourse, "The Noble Search" (Majjhima Nikāya, Sutta 26), on the search for enlightenment.

Ātman (Sanskrit)   Self; Soul. In Vedānta, ātman is Brahman: the individual soul is seen as coextensive with cosmic consciousness.

Attadanda Sutta (Pāli)   A set of verses from the Atthaka-vagga (perhaps the oldest portion of the Pāli Canon) of the Sutta-Nipāta, which is included in the Khuddaka Nikāya.

Awakening of Faith (In Chinese, *Ta-ch'eng ch'i-hsin lun*; in reconstructed Sanskrit, *Mahāyāna-Śraddhotpāda Śāstra*)   Treatise on Mahāyāna doctrine attributed to the 2nd-century C.E. Indian Buddhist philosopher/poet Aśvaghosa. There is no known Sanskrit version of this śāstra; the oldest known copies are in Chinese and it is possible that it actually originated as a Chinese text.

Bahudhātuka Sutta (Pāli)   The Buddha's discourse, "The Many Kinds of Elements"

(Majjhima Nikāya, Sutta 115), on the 18 elements, the sense bases, and dependent origination.

Bhayabherava Sutta (Pāli)   The Buddha's discourse, "Fear and Dread" (Majjhima Nikāya, Sutta 4), which includes the Buddha's description of his own jhāna practice and enlightenment.

Bodhidharma (Sanskrit)   Legendary sixth-century C.E. Indian monk (in Zen, the 28th Indian Patriarch and the 1st Chinese Patriarch) who is alleged to have brought Ch'an Buddhism to China.

Bodhisattva (Sanskrit)/**Bodhisatta** (Pāli)   In Theravāda Buddhism, a future Buddha. In Mahāyāna Buddhism, a person who has resolved to achieve enlightenment for the sake of all beings.

Bön/Bön-po (Tibetan)   Term that is used to refer both to the pre-Buddhist religious practices and beliefs of Tibet, and to a more formalized religion that developed contemporaneously with Buddhism in Tibet. Bön and Buddhism each influenced the other in their respective development, and both continue to be practiced in modern Tibet.

Catuskoti (Sanskrit)   Tetralemma; Set of four alternative propositions: (1) A; (2) not-A; (3) both A and not-A; and (4) neither A nor not-A.

Chachakka Sutta (Pāli)   The Buddha's discourse, "Six Sets of Six" (Majjhima Nikāya, Sutta 148), having to do with sensory perception, consciousness, feeling, and craving.

Ch'an (Chinese)   Chinese school of Buddhism, which emphasizes direct realization through meditation. From the Sanskrit *dhyāna* (meditation, absorption).

Chöten/Chorten (Tibetan)/**Stūpa** (Sanskrit)   An architectural structure symbolizing Buddhist themes and often containing sacred objects, relics, and texts.

Chün-tzu (Chinese)   Confucian virtue of gentlemanliness based on strength of character.

Crest Jewel of Discrimination (In Sanskrit, *Viveka Cudāmani*)   Vedantic text concerning jñāna yoga whose authorship is attributed to Śankara.

Dhammapada (Pāli)   Literally, "Sayings of the Dhamma." An anthology of verses of a primarily ethical character that are attributed to the Buddha and are included in the Khuddaka Nikāya.

Dharma (Sanskrit)/**Dhamma** (Pāli)   A body of spiritual/philosophical teaching; most often used to designate the Buddha's teachings.

Dharmas (Sanskrit)/**Dhammas** (Pāli)   A word with many meanings including "things," "phenomena," and "mental objects."

Dōgen (Japanese)   Dōgen Kigen (also referred to as Eihei Dōgen and Dōgen Zenji), 13th-century C.E. Japanese Zen master who started the Sōtō school of Zen.

Dokusan (Japanese)   A private meeting with a Zen teacher in his or her chambers. In Rinzai Zen, synonymous with *sanzen*.

Dukkha (Pāli)   Unsatisfactoriness; suffering.

Eightfold Noble Path   The Buddha's teaching on the path leading to the cessation of suffering as outlined in the Four Noble Truths. The eightfold nature of that path is (1) right view, (2) right intention, (3) right speech, (4) right action, (5) right livelihood, (6) right effort, (7) right mindfulness, and (8) right concentration.

Ehipassika (Pāli)   The Buddha's invitation to "come and see" for oneself.

Five Precepts   Buddhist lay ethical precepts of (1) not killing living beings, (2) not taking what is not freely given, (3) avoiding harmful speech, (4) not engaging in sexual immorality, and (5) not using intoxicating substances that cloud the mind.

Four Noble Truths   The Buddha's teaching on (1) the existence of suffering, (2) the cause of suffering, (3) the cessation of suffering, and (4) the path leading to the cessation of suffering.

Gelugpa (Tibetan)   A branch of Tibetan Buddhism. The Gelugpa school, headed by the Dalai Lama, emphasizes (1) training in Mādhyamika philosophy; (2) forming the intention to leave cyclic existence; (3) the development of *bodhicitta*, or the intention to become enlightened out of compassion for all beings; and (4) the realization of emptiness.

Gītā (Sanskrit)   The Bhagavad Gītā; the section of the Mahābhārata consisting of an extended conversation between Lord Krishna and Arjuna.

gTum-mo (Tibetan)   Heat Yoga; one of the Six Yogas of Naropa.

Hamsa (Sanskrit) Literally "swan" or "wild goose." One who is liberated outside of a specific spiritual tradition. In Indian mythology the Hamsa was a mythical bird that was flown by Brahma, and was one of the first avatars of Vishnu.

Huang-Po (Chinese)   Tang Dynasty (9th century C.E.) Chinese Ch'an Master.

Jên (Chinese)   Confucian virtue of human-heartedness based on fellow feeling.

Jātaka Tales   Popular tales of the Buddha's early incarnations, which are included in the Khuddaka Nikāya. The Jātaka Tales have moral instructional and inspirational aspects, much like Aesop's Fables.

Jivanmukta (Sanskrit)   In Vedānta, one who is liberated in this present lifetime within the body.

Kagyu (Tibetan)   A branch of Tibetan Buddhism. The Kagyu school traces its lineage to the adepts Nāropa, Marpa, Milarepa, and the monk Gampopa and is the school most often associated with Mahāmudrā meditative practice.

Kaivalyan (Sanskrit)   In Vedānta, one who has separated consciousness from inert matter.

Kakacūpama Sutta (Pāli)   The Buddha's discourse, "Simile of the Saw" (Majjhima Nikāya, Sutta 22). The sutta includes the Buddha's explication of the meaning of right speech. It is called the "Simile of the Saw" due to the Buddha's statement that even if bandits are sawing one's limbs off, one should maintain an attitude of loving-kindess toward them.

Kālāma Sutta (Pāli)   The Buddha's discourse to the Kālāma clan (Anguttara Nikāya, Sutta 3:65) on how to decide on the truth value of conflicting teachings.

Karma (Sanskrit)/**Kamma** (Pāli)   Literally, "action." The doctrine that thoughts and actions are both consequences of past thoughts and actions, and causes of future thoughts and actions.

Karunā (Pāli)   Compassion.

Khandhasamyutta (Pāli)   A group of 159 Suttas on the topic of the aggregates in the Samyutta Nikāya.

Kinhin (Japanese)   The Zen form of walking meditation.

Kōan (Japanese)   In Zen, a conundrum that cannot be solved rationally, which serves as an object of meditation and a vehicle for liberation.

Kusala (Pāli)   Wholesome; skillful

Lankāvatāra Sūtra (Sanskrit)   The "Sūtra on the Descent to Sri Lanka." Fourth-century C.E. Buddhist discourse associated with the teachings of the Yogācarā school of Mahāyāna Buddhism.

Li (Chinese)   Confucian virtue based on reciprocity, rites, customs, and propriety.

Lohan (Chinese)   Chinese term for the Theravāda arahants. Over time, the Chinese iconography of the lohans came to include fantastical elements.

Mahābhārata (Sanskrit)   Ancient Indian epic recounting the struggle between the Pāndavas and the Kauravas.

Mahācattārīsaka Sutta (Pāli)   The Buddha's discourse, "The Great Forty" (Majjhima Nikāya, Sutta 117), concerning 20 wholesome mental factors and 20 unwholesome mental factors.

Mahāhatthipadopama Sutta (Pāli)   The Buddha's "Greater Discourse on the Simile of the Elephant's Foot" (Majjhima Nikāya, Sutta 28), on not clinging to materiality based on an understanding of nonself.

Mahāpunnama Sutta (Pāli)   The Buddha's "Greater Discourse on the Full Moon Night" (Majjhima Nikāya, Sutta 109) on the topic of the aggregates.

Mahāsaccaka Sutta (Pāli)   The Buddha's "Greater Discourse to Saccaka" (Majjhima Nikāya, Sutta 36), in which he responds to a question from Saccaka, described as a "debater and clever speaker," who asks a question about whether the Buddha's teachings stress mental mastery, but not mastery over the body.

Mahāsatipatthāna Sutta (Pāli)   The Buddha's "Greater Discourse on the Foundations of Mindfulness" (Dīgha Nikāya, Sutta 22). This is a slightly longer version of the Satipatthāna Sutta (see below).

Mahāsīlanāda Sutta (Pāli)   The Buddha's "Greater Discourse on the Lion's Roar" (Majjhima Nikāya, Sutta 12) in which the Buddha describes his abilities since his awakening, and also describes his own past austerities.

Mahāyāna (Sanskrit)   Literally, "the Great Vehicle." One of the three main branches of Buddhism. Mahāyāna emphasizes the Bodhisattva vows to liberate all beings out of compassion, the realization of emptiness, and the understanding of the relationship between absolute and relative truth. Mahāyāna Buddhism originated in India, and is practiced today in countries such as China, Tibet, Mongolia, Japan, Korea, and Vietnam.

Mantra (Sanskrit)   A word or phrase that serves as an object of meditation; a word or phrase whose repetition generates merit or otherwise serves as a vehicle for liberation.

Marpa the Translator (Tibetan)   Also known as Chögi Lodrö of Mar, Marpa (1012–1096 C.E.) was a student of Nāropa and the teacher of Milarepa. Marpa was an important figure in the establishment of the Kagyu school of Tibetan Buddhism.

Meiji Restoration (Japanese)   Historical era marking the end of the Tokugowa shogunate and the restoration of the Emperor Meiji (1867–1912 C.E.).

Mettā (Pali)/**Maitrī** (Sanskrit)   Loving-kindness.

Milarepa (Tibetan)   Tibetan adept and poet (1040–1123 C.E.) who obtained enlightenment in one lifetime and who is part of the lineage of the Kagyu school of Tibetan Buddhism.

Mindfulness (Sati in Pāli)   Maintenance of "bare" attention to whatever is occurring in the moment (sensations, affective evaluations, intentions, emotions, ideations, and other mental events and states). This is done with the intention to neither cling to nor avert from these arising and passing mental states, but simply to be with them the way they are without elaboration.

Mūlamadhyamakakārikā(s) (Sanskrit)   Philosophical and poetic work by Nāgārjuna, literally, "Fundamental Verses on the Middle Way."

Nāgārjuna (Sanskrit)   Second-century C.E. Indian adept whose name is associated with the Mādhyamika school of Mahāyāna Buddhism and with the Prajñāpāramitā Sūtras.

Nibbāna (Pāli)/**Nirvāna** (Sanskrit)   Liberation; enlightenment; cessation of desire; freedom from suffering; the Unconditioned.

Nichiren Buddhism (Japanese)   Japanese school of Buddhism, which takes the Lotus Sūtra as its core text; founded by Nichiren Shonen (1222–1282 C.E.), Nichiren Buddhism emphasizes the practice of recitation of the phrase "nam myōhō renge-kyō," "Homage to the Lotus Sūtra."

Nikāya (Pāli)   Collection. Most often used in reference to the five collections of Pāli Suttas (Dīgha Nikāya, the Majjhima Nikāya, the Samyutta Nikāya, the Anguttara Nikāya, and the Khuddaka Nikāya).

Nirguna Brahman (Sanskrit)   In Vedānta, the absolute nature of Brahman that is characterized as formless and without attributes.

Om mani padme hum (Sanskrit)   The mantra of Avalokiteśvara; "om" and "hum" are syllables that have no translation. "Mani" means "jewel," and "padme" means "lotus." Scholars differ on the literal meaning of the mantra, but its meaning lies not in its literal translation, but in its use as mantra.

Pāli (Pāli)   Archaic Prākrit middle Indic language related to Vedic and Sanskrit; the scriptural language of Theravāda Buddhism.

Pañña (Pāli)   Wisdom.

Parinirvāna (Sanskrit)   Complete nirvāna: used to refer to the Buddha's death.

Prajñāpāramitā Sūtras (Sanskrit)   The "Perfection of Wisdom" Sūtras. Buddhist discourses, which serve as foundational texts in Mahāyāna Buddhism. These sūtras, written between 100 B.C.E. and 1000 C.E., emphasize the concept of śūnyatā, the ultimate emptiness of all phenomena.

Pratītya-samutpāda (Sanskrit)/**Pattica-samuppāda** (Pāli)   Buddhist doctrine of dependent origination. This doctrine describes a 12-stage process by which sensory stimulation leads to affective evaluation of sensation, then to emotional attachment and clinging to existence, and finally to eventual rebirth.

Pure Land Buddhism (Chinese: *Ching-t'u-tsung*; Japanese: *Jōdō Shinshū* and *Jōdō Shū*) School of Buddhism founded in China by Hui-yan in the fifth-century C.E., brought to Japan by Hōnen (1133–1212 C.E.), and elaborated on by Shinran (1173–1263 C.E.), with an emphasis on salvation by faith in Amida Buddha and the *nembutsu*, or saying of Amida Buddha's name.

Rāhula (Pāli)   Literally "fetter"; also the name of the Buddha's son.

Rakusu (Japanese)   Patchwork rectangular cloth worn with a cord around the neck symbolizing the patchwork robes of the original Buddhist sangha. The rakusu is conferred on a Zen student when he or she takes his or her vows.

Rinzai (Japanese)/**Lin-chi-tsung** (Chinese)   One of the two principle sects of Japanese Zen. It was originated in China by Ch'an master Lin-chi, and was brought to Japan by Eisai in the twelfth-century C.E. It is particularly known for its use of kōans in meditation practice.

Sabi (Japanese)   Japanese aesthetic term that can be translated as "loneliness," or "solitude," and involves a rustic simplicity.

Saddharma-pundarīka Sūtra (Sanskrit)   The Lotus Sūtra. This sūtra, written between 100 B.C.E. and 100 C.E., emphasizes the concept of *upāya*, or skillful means.

Śākyamuni (Sanskrit)   Appellation for the historical Buddha after his enlightenment; literally "Sage of the Śākyas," the Śākyas being the Buddha's natal clan.

Samādhi (Pāli)   Concentration.

Samaññaphala Sutta (Pāli)   The Buddha's discourse on "The Fruits of the Homeless Life" (Dīgha Nikāya, Sutta 2).

Samatha (Pāli)/**Śamatha** (Sanskrit)   Serenity.

Sambodhi (Pāli)   Enlightenment.

Sammā (Pāli)   Right.

Samskāra (Sanskrit)/**saṅkhāra** (Pāli)   Mental Aggregate; Mental formation. The deposit of experience in mental structures (e.g., cognitive, perceptual, and motor schemas, character traits, dispositions).

Sāmkhya (Sanskrit)   One of six major Indian philosophical traditions, the Sāmkhya school sought the achievement of liberation through understanding the duality of mind and body.

Sāmkhya Kārikā (Sanskrit)   Third-century C.E. text of verses by Īśvara-Krishna elucidating the main points of the Sāmkhya philosophy.

Samsāra (Sanskrit)   The cycle of rebirths.

Sangha (Pāli)   Members of the Buddhist monastic community. More recently in the West, where the monastic tradition is not as well established, the term has evolved to include lay members of the Buddhist community as well.

Śāntideva (Sanskrit)   Eighth-century C.E. Indian monk from Nālandā University and author of the Bodhicaryāvatāra (The Bodhisattva's Way of Life) and the Śiksā Samuccaya.

Sanzen (Japanese)   In Zen, a private meeting with a teacher. In Rinzai, synonymous with *dokusan*.

Sat cakra nirūpana (Sanskrit)   Sixteenth-century C.E. Indian tantric treatise on the cakra system and kundalinī written by Bengali yogi Purnananda Swami.

Sati (Pāli)   Mindfulness.

Satipatthāna Sutta (Pāli)   The Buddha's discourse, "The Foundations of Mindfulness" (Majjhima Nikāya, Sutta 10). The four foundations of mindfulness are mindfulness of: (1) the body (kāya), (2) feeling tones (vedenā), (3) mind (citta), and (4) mental phenomena relevant to the process of awakening (dhammas).

Satori (Japanese)   In Zen, a moment of enlightenment; partially synonymous with *kenshō*.

Sesshin (Japanese)   Zen intensive meditation retreat.

Shibui (Japanese)   Japanese aesthetic term referring to a quiet refined sensibility; severe elegance.

Shōbōgenzō (Japanese)   "The Eye and the Treasury of the True Dharma," a 13th-century collection of *teishō* (Dharma talks) and other writings by Dōgen Kigen.

Siddha (Sanskrit)   A Buddhist adept. A meditation practitioner who has attained special powers (siddhi) and great understanding through meditative practice, often outside the structure of clerical or monastic life.

Sīla (Pāli)   Virtue; ethics.

Six Yogas of Nāropa   Tantric practices of (1) heat (gTum-mo) yoga, (2) illusory body yoga, (3) dream yoga, (4) clear light yoga, (5) intermediate state (bardo) yoga, and (6) transference of consciousness associated with the Indian tantric adept Nāropa, and his teacher, Tilopa.

Skandha (Sanskrit)/**Khanda** (Pāli)   Aggregate.

Sōtō (Japanese)   Japanese school of Zen founded by Dōgen in the thirteenth-century C.E., which emphasizes the practice of zazen.

Śramana (Sanskrit)/**Samana** (Pāli)   During the Buddha's historical era, a wandering ascetic seeking enlightenment.

Stūpa (Sanskrit)   See **Chōten**.

Sutta (Pāli)/**Sūtra** (Sanskrit)   Literally, "thread." A discourse of the Buddha or one of his disciples.

Śūnyatā (Sanskrit)/**Suññata** (Pāli)   Emptiness.

Sūtra of Hui Neng (Chinese)   The "Platform Sūtra," attributed to the Ch'an 6th Chinese Patriarch Hui Neng (638–713 C.E.).

T'ai-i Chin-hua tsung-chih (Chinese)   Literally, "Teachings of the Golden Flower of the Supreme One." A 17th- or 18th-century C.E. Taoist meditation text, often mistakenly attributed to the 8th-century C.E. Taoist adept Lū Yen.

Tantra (Sanskrit)   Among other meanings, a text within the tradition of Tantric Buddhism. Such texts often delineate practices designed to achieve rapid enlightenment emphasizing the use of mandalas, mudras, mantras, rituals, and the practice of deity yoga.

Tao-Tê-Ching (Chinese)   Anthology of Taoist verses attributed to Lao-Tzu.

Tathāgata (Pāli)   The epithet the Buddha used for himself, which translates literally as "thus gone one."

Theravāda (Pāli)   The oldest of the three main branches of Buddhism. Literally, "The School of the Elders." It is sometimes referred to somewhat pejoratively by non-Theravāda schools as "Hīnayāna," meaning "the Lesser Vehicle." Theravāda Buddhism emphasizes the development of sīla, samādhi, and paññā leading to nibbāna and the extinction of desire, aversion, and ignorance. It is primarily practiced in Southeast Asia (e.g., Burma, Thailand, Laos, Cambodia, and Sri Lanka).

Tipitaka (Pāli)/**Tripitaka** (Sanskrit)   The three "baskets" of the Pāli Canon consisting of the Nikāyas (the collections of the Suttas), the Vinaya (the Monastic code), and the Abhidhamma (Buddhist doctrinal writings). The word *baskets* derives from the fact that the original texts were not bound but actually kept together in baskets.

Tsongkapa (Tibetan)   Tsongkhapa (1357–1419 C.E.) was the founder of the Gelugpa school of Tibetan Buddhism. He is known for his book *Lamrim Chenmo*, or the Great Exposition on the Stages of the Path, and for the establishment of the great Gelugpa monasteries of Sera, Ganden, and Drepung.

Upanishads (Sanskrit)   A collection of over 100 ancient texts that form the core of Vedantic teachings. A number of the Upanishads are included as part of the Vedas.

Upekkhā (Pāli)   Equanimity.

Vajrayāna (Sanskrit)   One of the three main branches of Buddhism. Literally, the "Diamond Vehicle," Vajrayāna is another name for the Tantric Buddhism of Tibet. It is associated primarily with Tibetan practices designed to rapidly achieve enlightenment in a single lifetime for the sake of the liberation of all beings from suffering.

Vedānta (Sanskrit)   Literally, "Conclusion of the Vedas." Philosophy derived from the Upanishads.

Vedāntasāra Samgraha (Sanskrit)   Literally, "Compilation of the Essence of Vedānta," attributed to Sri Ramanuja (1017–1137 C.E.).

Vedas (Sanskrit)   Ancient religious and philosophical writings that are the oldest Indian texts.

Vedenā (Pāli)   Feeling tone/precognitive judgment of a stimulus as either pleasant, unpleasant, or neutral

Vigrahavyāvartanī (Sanskrit)   "Averting the Arguments," a second-century C.E. Mahāyāna text by Nāgārjuna providing logical refutations to arguments that had been made against the Mādhyamika (Middle Way) school of Mahāyāna Buddhism.

Vimalakīrtinirdeśa Sūtra (Sanskrit)   An early Mahāyāna Sūtra on the discourse of the lay teacher Vimalakīrti, this sūtra contains teachings that are very similar to those in the Prajñāpāramitā Sūtras.

Vinaya (Pāli)   Buddhist monastic code of behavior.

Vipallāsa (Pāli)   Distortions.

Vipassanā (Pāli)   Insight meditation.

Vitakkasanthāna Sutta (Pāli)   The Buddha's discourse, "Removal of Distracting Thoughts" (Majjhima Nikāya, Sutta 20), on cognitive practices for the removal of unskillful or unwholesome thoughts.

Wabi (Japanese)   Japanese aesthetic term that can be translated as "poverty."

Wu-wei (Chinese)   Taoist idea of nondoing and nonstriving.

Yoga Sūtras (Sanskrit)   Classic Indian text on Raja Yoga attributed to Patañjali.

Zazen (Japanese)   Sitting meditation in Zen Buddhism.

Zen (Japanese)   Japanese form of Buddhism derived from Chinese Ch'an, which emphasizes the direct realization of knowledge by meditation.

Zendo (Japanese)   Hall in which zazen is practiced.

Contributors

Belinda Siew Luan Khong, L.L.B., Ph.D. is a practicing psychologist who teaches at Macquarie University in Sydney, Australia, on Buddhist and Western psychology, meditation and psychotherapy, and exploring spirituality and death. Her interests lie in researching comparative psychology and philosophy, particularly Heidegger's philosophy, Daseinsanalysis, Jungian psychology, Buddhism, Taoism, the phenomena of personal and social responsibility, and coping with change.

Jean L. Kristeller, Ph.D. is a professor of psychology at Indiana State University, where she also directs the Mary Margaret Walther Cancer Research Program. She is a former faculty member at both the University of Massachusetts School of Medicine and the Harvard Medical School, and is a former associate director of the Behavioral Medicine Program at Cambridge Hospital. She is a Fellow of the Society of Behavioral Medicine. Dr. Kristeller coauthored a chapter on "Mindfulness and Meditation" in *Integrating Spirituality into Treatment* (2000) published by the American Psychological Association, and her book, *Meditation and Psychotherapy: Theory, Research, and Practice*, is forthcoming by Guilford Press.

Andrew Olendzki, Ph.D. is executive director of the Barre Center for Buddhist Studies where he leads the Center's Buddhism and Psychology seminar. Dr. Olendzki is also the editor of *Insight*, and is the former executive director of the Insight Meditation Society.

Kaisa Puhakka, Ph.D. is professor of psychology and core clinical faculty at the California Institute of Integral Studies. She holds her doctorate in experimental psychology from the University of Toledo, and a postdoctoral diploma in clinical psychology from Adelphi University. She also has a master of arts degree in Asian and comparative philosophy from the University of Toledo. Her scholarly interests include Hindu and Buddhist thought and practice, object-relations psychoanalysis, and psychotherapy. She has practiced Buddhist meditation for over 30 years, and has been a student of Joshu Sasaki Roshi, a Zen Master of the Rinzai Nyorai lineage, for the past 6 years. Dr. Puhakka is the former editor of the *Journal of Transpersonal Psychology*, and is the coeditor of *Transpersonal Knowing: Exploring the Horizon of Consciousness* (2000) published by SUNY Press.

Robert Rosenbaum, Ph.D. is a staff psychologist and neuropsychologist at Kaiser-Permanente, a clinical faculty member at the Langley Porter Institute, and the former director of the graduate program in psychology at the California School of Professional Psychology. He is the author of *Zen and the Heart of Psychotherapy* (1999) published by Bruner/Mazel.

Jeffrey B. Rubin, Ph.D. practices psychoanalysis and psychoanalytically oriented psychotherapy in New York City and Bedford Hills, New York. He is the author of *Psychotherapy and Buddhism: Toward an Integration* (1996) published by Plenum Press, and *A Psychoanalysis for Our Time: Exploring the Blindness of the Seeing I* (1998) published by NYU Press. He has taught at various psychoanalytic institutes and universities including the Postgraduate Center for Mental Health, The Object Relations Institute, The C. G. Jung Foundation of New York, and Yeshiva University.

Seth Robert Segall, Ph.D. is an assistant clinical professor at the Yale University School of Medicine, director of Psychology and Psychology Training at Waterbury Hospital, vice president of Lotus: The Educational Center for Integrative Healing and Wellness, and a past president of the New England Society for the Treatment of Trauma and Dissociation. Dr. Segall's Buddhist practice has been supported by retreat experiences at the Springwater Center for Meditative Inquiry, the Insight Meditation Society, and the Cambridge Insight Meditation Center, by course work at the Barre Center for Buddhist Studies and Wesleyan University, and by a professional internship at the Center for Mindfulness in Medicine, Health Care, and Society at the University of Massachusetts Medical Center.

Eugene Taylor, Ph.D. holds a master's degree in experimental psychology and Asian studies, and a doctorate in the history and philosophy of psychology. He was a student of the late Frederick Streng, the Indian Mahāyāna Buddhist scholar and protégé of Mircia Eliade, specializing in the Sāmkhya metaphysic of Hinduism, the texts of yoga, and Indian Buddhist conceptions of personality. His background in Asian languages includes training in Hindustani and Sanskrit. He also holds the rank of yondan, fourth-degree black belt, in the Hombu style of Aikido.

Dr. Taylor was recently elected a Fellow in the American Psychological Association for his pioneering work applying the techniques of historical scholarship from comparative religions to archival investigation in the history of American psychology and psychiatry. Currently, he is a lecturer on psychiatry at the Harvard Medical School, a senior psychologist on the Psychiatry Service at the Massachusetts General Hospital, and executive faculty at the Saybrook Graduate School and Research Institute. He is also the founder and director of the Cambridge Institute of Psychology and Religion. Dr. Taylor is the author, among other books, of *Shadow Culture: Psychology and Spirituality in America* (1999) published by Counterpoint, *William James on Consciousness Beyond the Margin* (1996) published by Princeton University Press, and *A Psychology of Spiritual Healing* (1997) published by Chrysalis Press.

Index